THE GREAT BOOK OF
Crosswords

Test yourself with
this fantastic collection
of puzzles

This edition published in 2023 by Arcturus Publishing Limited
26/27 Bickels Yard, 151–153 Bermondsey Street,
London SE1 3HA

AD010813US

Printed in the UK

Contents

1   EASY

Across

1 Combined,
   as numbers
6 Handle the steering
   wheel
7 Acts depressed
8 How checks are
   signed
9 Campers' shelters

Down

1 Grant access to
2 Remote-controlled
   small flying object
3 Use,
   as one's savings
4 Big social gathering
5 Schoolroom
   furnishings

1	2	3	4	5
6				
7				
8				
9				

2   EASY

Across

1 Afternoon social
   drinks
5 New Jersey
   hockey player
6 Wear away
7 Sought permission
   from
8 Desire

Down

1 Without the extra
   words
2 Elicit (response)
3 Was philanthropic
4 Cold-weather
   conveyance
5 Admissions office
   honcho

■	1	2	3	4
5				
6				
7				
8				■

3   EASY

Across

2 Band equipment
   component
5 Sound
7 Suspension of
   hostilities
8 Looks at creepily
9 Amount left after
   expenses

Down

1 Relay racers
   implement
2 Grown-up
3 Computer devices
   to click
4 Balladry
6 Advise someone
   strongly

1	■	2	3	4
5	6			
7				
8				
9			■	

4   EASY

Across

1 Shake happily, like a dog's tail
5 Speak out
7 Olympic athlete's award
8 Enlarge
9 Distant but within sight

Down

1 Girl, eventually
2 Tried to emulate
3 Suffering from vertigo
4 Serious criminal
6 Military alliance involved in many wars, initially

5   EASY

Across

1 Asks on bended knee
5 Lustful looker
7 Address from a lectern
8 Worthiness
9 Perform a bartender's duty

Down

1 Time of prosperity
2 White-plumed wading bird
3 Blinding driving hazard
4 ___ stone (permanent)
6 Gen. Powell's status

6   EASY

Across

1 Chef's protective garment
5 Fall in droplets
6 Far-reaching view
8 Estate owner's document
9 Martial art using bamboo swords

Down

1 Dictionary abbr.
2 Excessive self-esteem
3 On ones feet
4 ___ out of (withdrew from)
7 Word heard after further

EASY

Across

1 Lock
5 Crafts' counterparts
9 Blue-chip tech company, initially
12 At liberty
13 Consider
14 Beach volleyball team, for one
15 ___ in a while
16 Squander
18 Straying
20 Cut with a ray
21 Light knock
23 More easily attainable
25 ___ credit
27 Darjeeling server
31 Cardiac measure
33 Belgrade's republic
34 Woolen cloth
35 Lambaste
38 Any branch of philosophy
39 Succeed, dietwise
42 Become bored by
44 Value
46 Proves helpful
49 Small, in Dundee
50 "___ Land" (2016 musical)
51 Durable timber
52 Hurricane dir.
53 Scurried away
54 Connecting cable letters

Down

1 Corp. board member
2 Pot for some ashes
3 Sense organ
4 Creepy glance
5 Guy who writes slogans
6 Bridle straps
7 Leaving a will
8 Phone text medium, briefly
9 Brainstorming success
10 Cheeks
11 Machine setting
17 Make happy
19 On-tour staffer
21 CSA soldiers
22 Wheel pivot
24 Temporary owner
26 Shoplifter, e.g.
28 Decontaminated
29 Common interest groups, for short
30 Empty out
32 Limited liking
36 Usher's walkway
37 Footprint
39 Park feature
40 Word on a store flip sign
41 Cast forth
43 Inauguration Day promise
45 Alien from Melmac
47 Beaver construction
48 Emulate Lindsey Vonn

Across

1 Inaugurate by oath
7 "NFL Live" airer
11 ___ moment (epiphany)
12 "___ we there yet?"
13 "... baked in ___"
14 Positive reply
15 Piously respectful
17 Fashion or flair
19 Takes, as revenge
20 Stomach-related
22 Passes, as legislation
24 British county
28 Aloha token
29 Made modifications
31 Relating to taste, touch or smell
34 Worthless cloth
35 Cathedral keyboard
36 Created again
39 Became mature
41 Bad luck
44 Licorice-flavoring herb
47 Linked, as a couple
49 Chicken-king link
50 Not having much fat
51 Snooker-player's stick
52 Bit of body art, briefly
53 Without accompaniment
54 Protective head coverings

Down

1 Declares
2 Sharpen, as a knife
3 Very tolerant
4 Most infrequent
5 Extreme irritation
6 "Not in a million years!"
7 Pain in auditory canal
8 Blueprint bit, shortly
9 Pub portion
10 Butterfly-catching devices
16 Live and breathe
18 Race unit
21 Former Russian ruler (var.)
22 ___-ran
23 Elk's cousin
25 Expose to UV waves, e.g.
26 Enjoy a good book
27 Living on the ___
30 Ancient harp
32 Small canned fish
33 Tear-inducing food
37 Dental coating
38 Many adults
40 Simmer, as eggs
41 Large dining room
42 Cookie classic
43 Yemen's neighbor
45 Part of a shutter
46 Enjoys a meal
48 Be regretful about

EASY

Across

1 Mid-February purchase
5 Not failing
11 Killer ___ (cool program)
12 Big night for seniors
14 Beige-like hue
15 Color named for a vegetable
17 ___ player
18 Film role auditions
20 Authorize to
21 Person who searches
23 Hula hoop support
26 Family tree
27 Do something the wrong way
28 Currently leading
30 Draw a match
31 Pack of rewards in a video game
33 Discount word
34 Formally charge
35 Accelerator, so to speak
37 Objectionable
42 Kind of enemy
44 Emergency treatment
45 Items in a table
46 Revert
47 Was first
48 Heart contraction
49 Broke

Down

1 Emulates Eminem
2 Oil-producing gp
3 Argue (with)
4 Impulsive spending frenzy
5 Rhyme creator
6 Forgetfulness
7 Long indoor seat
8 Item of hockey equipment
9 Gun lobby, briefly
10 Eucalyptus varieties
13 Apartment dweller's payment
16 Hair goos
19 Fax or text
22 Sponsorship (var.)
23 Rooftop bases for choppers
24 Clothes-pressing appliance
25 Goods
26 Chicken portion
28 Alphabet openers
29 Loathsome
32 Soldier's helmet, slangy
33 Law school entrance exam, initially
35 Encircle with a belt
36 Common whodunit crime
38 Right triangle ratio
39 Bound hay bundle
40 Fudged the facts
41 Stream swirl
43 Beam of light

Across

1 Multi-vehicle crash
7 Supplementary component
12 Anxiety
13 Cash-and-___
14 Intimidates or frightens
15 Forest growths
16 ___ legs (rear extremities)
17 Preadult
19 Gull-like seabird
21 Puffy swelling
22 Tempting type
24 Ready, in the kitchen
26 Frenetically active
28 Cloudlike mass
29 Facing: abbr.
32 Map collection
34 Fish's breathing apparatus
36 Pearl holders
39 Royal domain
41 "___ we go again..."
42 Accounting write-off
44 Indy 500, e.g.
46 It may be obtuse or acute
47 No longer in bed
49 Transparent, as fabrics
50 Become milder
51 Full of cheeky attitude
52 Applies, as force

Down

1 Urge on
2 Provoke to action
3 Slanted
4 Aural membrane
5 "___ with caution"
6 Annoying insect
7 Performed on stage
8 Mended, as socks
9 Imagine
10 Marjoram kin
11 Wall Street inits
18 How ghost stories are told
20 Univ. sports group
22 Big city pollution problem
23 Place in a crypt
25 Divas have delicate ones
27 Liquid asset
30 Voracious tropical fish
31 Solemn promises
33 Clinically clean
35 Soup scoops
37 Pencil end
38 Relatively new
40 Distrustful
42 Deep male voice
43 Container weight allowance
45 Laryngitis docs
48 T. ___ (dinosaur)

LUXURIOUS CHAMPAGNE

Across
1 Large containers for 15-Across
5 Place of commerce
9 Passing through
12 Eye provocatively
13 Assorted collection
14 Cutoff point
15 French bubbly made exclusively from Chardonnay grapes
18 Literary comparison
19 Moved on ice
20 Grease
22 Process ore in a blast furnace
25 Heading toward one's residence
29 Go nowhere
30 Hoppy beer letters
31 Brew, as tea
33 Sound of reproach
34 Ward (off)
36 Intensify
38 Figure of speech
40 Clear-thinking
41 Livestock's lunch
43 Break down food
47 Term for the top-of-the-range blended sparkling wine
50 ___ Majesty
51 Opposite of contrary
52 Slough
53 Didn't stand
54 Advanced, as cash
55 Love of life

Down
1 Positions
2 Grapefruit-tangerine hybrid
3 Chic, informally
4 Like old politicians who refuse to retire
5 Mild
6 Choice in a pub
7 Barbecue specialty
8 Highway fees
9 Revenge
10 Abbr. in company names
11 TV show interrupters
16 Feline weapons
17 Points (at)
21 Little black ___
23 Following everyone
24 Small boy
25 Bygone stereo set
26 Article with commentary
27 Obvious
28 Quality of any bottle of 47-Across alcohol
32 Hysterical mood
35 Acts
37 Pea or lentil
39 Microwave no-no
42 Flood-control embankment
44 Devilish
45 Liquids in hospital vials
46 Harry Potter, for one
47 Measures of acidity, briefly
48 Fjord relative
49 Tonic's partner

Across

1 One of only five men to achieve the career Grand Slam in tennis
10 Less than a few
11 Llama kin
13 Hide away
15 Hangar contents
16 Knee-to-ankle bone
18 Pesticide banned in 1972: abbr.
19 "And more", shortly
22 Mombasa locale
24 Sounding similar
26 Ready-to-___
29 Formally support, endorse
30 Kids' summer destination
31 Slimy garden creature
32 Of tax revenues
34 "As ___ on TV!"
35 "Told you!"
36 Contribution maker
38 Approximate touchdown hr
39 PC port initials
42 Deepest point
44 Kind of bomb
46 Raccoon resembler
49 Lavishly decorate
50 Demeanor
51 Court legend with 14 major titles who never won a Roland-Garros

Down

1 Crossword solutions
2 "Believe it or ___!"
3 Crime scene letters
4 Enjoy a day off
5 (Of mouth) wide open
6 Ease, as anxieties
7 Fancy resort
8 Beach dust
9 Like some teas
12 Daisylike bloom
14 Walking for pleasure
17 Turn in a road
20 "One of ___ days..."
21 Repetitive process
23 Completely submerged

25 Heap or pile
27 Awards show host
28 No longer linked
30 Type of fruit acid
32 Grocery buy
33 Introductions
34 Baby pigeon
35 Light bites
37 Being chilled, as wine
40 Ballroom basic
41 Foretell
43 One-sided win
45 "Haven't we ___?"
47 It may be hot or fresh
48 Leaves in bags

13   **EASY**

Across

1 Smithy's workplace
6 Row on a monthly calendar
7 Remove, as a tent anchor
8 Big blue bodies
9 Laundromat apparatus

Down

2 Proprietor
3 Settle a debt with
4 Ones flying in formation
5 Heart readout, for short
7 Currency exchange letters

14   **EASY**

Across

1 Forbidden by social custom
5 Where Frankenstein did his research
6 Drop in intensity
8 High-card-wins game
9 Apple holders

Down

1 Starts to melt
2 Sound loudly, as a trumpet
3 ___ milk (nondairy choice)
4 Follows the rules
7 Cave-dwelling flying mammal

15   **EASY**

Across

1 Concerning
5 Daily temperature extreme
6 One-third of a three-piece suit
8 Cartoon shriek
9 Some Washington workers

Down

1 Leader of the pack
2 Feathery neckwear
3 Admitted (to wrongdoing)
4 Chores that are assigned
7 Ball support for a golfer

EASY

Across

1 Wool weight unit
4 Old-style you
8 Hardly next door
12 Madison or Fifth, briefly
13 Carved out
14 Female pony
15 Football officials
17 Air force heroes
18 Gave a talk
19 Inattentive
21 Pain
22 Celebrity athlete
23 Amy Winehouse, vocally
24 Tiny insect
25 Became a particular type of person
30 Froglike fly-catcher
31 Expected behavior
32 Emerging
36 ___ Major (celestial bear)
37 Fantasies
38 Phony
40 Matured, as cheddar
41 Mercenary
43 Without clothes
44 Sneaker problem
45 Comedy ___
46 Medical lab procedure
47 First-rate
48 Gun the motor, for short

Down

1 Starchy tuber
2 Total
3 Actually
4 ___ Blind Mice
5 Listen
6 Be a borrower
7 How some prefer peanuts
8 Accumulate, as a fortune
9 Cut gemstone surface
10 "The Hunger Games" setting
11 Lavatory
16 National spirit
20 Needed a patch
22 Prepare to shoot
23 Plentiful
24 Certain rocket launching
26 Upward part of a plant
27 One way to mark losses
28 Coffee specification
29 Badmouth
33 Verbally disagree
34 Kernels
35 Military Academy student
36 App developers' customers
38 What an actor handles
39 Aired
42 Words during a marriage ceremony

EASY

Across

1 Pt. of speech
4 Longitude line
11 Deceptive tale
12 Verse work
13 Department of Labor agcy.
14 Sterile
16 Horse-hoof sound
17 Claw mark
18 Florida attraction
19 Write in musical symbols
21 Blood donor datum
24 With deep vehicle tracks
28 Identifier for transmitter stations
31 Barn bedding
32 ___-ray player
33 Pirate's stash
35 Day or year header
37 Sputnik launcher, briefly
38 Some playground equipment
41 Sudoku grid feature
44 "Give it a try"
48 Heartbroken
49 Like peace doves
50 Camera or eye part
51 Certain little piggie
52 Noteworthy time span
53 Anonymous
54 Espionage agent

Down

1 "Sad to say..."
2 Spine segment
3 Mock publicly
4 Words often framed
5 King's order
6 Beef up old batteries
7 Courtroom schedule
8 Water-surrounded land
9 Call from a crow's nest
10 Hammock rests
15 Group of experts
20 Sandwich fish
21 Frozen dessert franchise
22 Harvard's historical rival
23 Positive factor
25 Therefore
26 Headphones setting
27 Hair colorer
29 Hearty meat dish
30 Water, as crops
34 Tokyo rolls
36 African bloodsucker
39 They're taboo
40 Airport entryways
41 Dimple locale
42 Ethereal glow
43 Not at all rosy
45 Shorn creatures
46 50-and-up org.
47 Low, heavy cart

EASY

Across

1 Bureaucratic requirements
8 Off-center
13 Covering
14 Doorbell sound, perhaps
15 US railway wagon
16 ___ bear
17 Front yards
18 Cocktail bar
19 Baby food consistency
20 Loud cry of pain
21 Certain nobleman
22 Plunge head first
26 AAA option
27 Entrance hall to a theater
28 Disallow
29 Go-between
31 Plum color
32 British mothers
33 Calibri and Comic Sans Serif
34 Small taste
37 Common sonata movement
38 Influence
39 Outer sail support
41 Striped gemstone
42 Self-disciplined person
43 Restrained
44 While on the other hand

Down

1 Giant bird of myth
2 Assess
3 Prevented entry of
4 Garden implement
5 Dateless, say
6 Decline to participate
7 Cyclone center
8 Outlet output
9 Really ought to
10 Ceramist's appliance
11 Online periodical, briefly
12 Used to be
18 An also-ran
19 Salon curls
20 Round toys on strings
22 Someone else did it
23 Deluge
24 ___ Beckham (David's wife)
25 Couples, after breakups
27 Blamed
30 Attribute
31 Consider deeply
33 "Star Wars" power, with the
34 Healing crust
35 Kelp bit
36 Liquid obstacle around a castle
37 Skin reaction to poison ivy
39 Deviate from the course
40 Hosts at open-mic nights, initially

EASY

Across

1 Deep ravine
6 Assigns fault to
11 Worker who moves
   from job to job
13 Nation's warships
14 Given up
   the enjoyment
15 Strong plow pullers
16 Super cool
17 Comfy cloud
18 Light-headed
20 Baseball stats
24 Rife
27 Easily manipulated
   person
29 Sooner than
   tomorrow
30 Prominent business
   figure
31 Burglars' takes
32 Place in position
34 Cook quickly,
   as a steak
36 Nitwit
38 Film director's unit
41 Not favoring either
   side
45 Ornamental jug
46 Detective's dead
   end
47 Informal turndown
48 Whole number
49 Water park
   attractions
50 Periods with four
   seasons

Down

1 Brief romance
2 Spend carelessly
3 Time past,
   to poets of old
4 Loses firmness
5 Offered one's seat
6 Pleasant wind
7 Incognito
8 Ankle-length dress
9 Get ___
   (take revenge)
10 Effective
   cooperation
12 Hostility
19 Actress Catherine
   ___-Jones
21 "___ reflection..."
22 Pesters persistently
23 Spoke haltingly
25 Kind of talk
26 Exploration org.
28 Cole___ (side dish)
30 Fingerless gloves
31 Immediately after
   this
33 Court game
35 Throne occupiers
37 Windowpane sealer
39 Deserter's status,
   briefly
40 French military cap
42 Arborist's interest
43 Hindu tune
44 Serving whiz

Across

1 Type of fur
6 Romantic songs
12 Pacific, for one
13 Country monogram
14 Like burning candles
15 Hit the hay
16 Less complicated
18 Very beginning
20 Animals that raised Tarzan
21 Barks up the wrong tree
23 Moving at breakneck speed
25 The basics
28 Christmas season
30 Sound from the crib
31 New venture
32 Manipulate
33 Properties owned
35 Black ___
36 Table of book's contents
37 Annual cable sports award
39 Close noisily
41 Dirty cloth at the garage
45 Jumped over
48 Fiddle's kin
49 Call routing no.
50 Suffix for hatch
51 At the pinnacle
52 Remaining part
53 Clinical studies

Down

1 About average
2 Citizens rights org.
3 Plant grown for sugar
4 Memory blanks
5 Drive-through lane marking
6 Coach
7 Big continent
8 Eel-like creature with sucking mouth
9 Pimento or Jamaica pepper
10 Rolling cube
11 Offensively loud
17 Decayed vegetable matter
19 Bold effort
22 Storm hazard
24 Teen fave
25 Successful sort
26 Stroke of luck
27 Sliced assorted meat portions
29 Cowboy's loop
31 Preoccupied
34 Farmer's place, in a rhyme
35 Reporter's name
38 Change direction sharply
40 Brazil's neighbor
42 Spoils
43 Piles and piles
44 Missing links
46 Cut down
47 Coloring substance

Across

1 Great work of literature
7 Bambi, eventually
11 Amass, as a debt
12 Queued up
14 Give reparations
15 Opposite of innocent
16 Common or sixth
17 Confounds
18 Mournful melody
20 Selfishness
24 Just a mistake
27 Make sock holes disappear
28 Put out, as a magazine
30 Of Hispanic heritage
32 Low-power lights
34 About half of us
35 Bully's last words
37 Election day list
39 Summer cottage, perhaps
42 Shooter, before shooting
46 Finding the sum
47 Serious wrongdoing
48 Landlocked African country
49 Unexpressed but understood
50 Sitcom legend Dick Van ___
51 Catch in a net

Down

1 Failed suddenly
2 Guitar's ancestor
3 Mysterious auth.
4 Phoenix netters
5 Drives too fast
6 Roll of tobacco
7 Old calculating device
8 Cash drawer
9 Initial poker chip
10 Yellowstone gusher
13 Prompts
19 "Sure, sign me up!"
21 Black-tie charity event, maybe
22 ___ exam (dental checkup)
23 Lower part of alimentary canal
25 Projection room spool
26 Bookie's concern
29 Chimney filth
31 Atoll unit
33 Place out of sight
34 Go plundering or raiding
36 Responds to stimuli
38 Green growth in a pool
40 Touchy
41 Fargo's st.
43 Teheran locale
44 Shiny mineral
45 Arab dignitary

22   EASY

Across
1 Feline coat
4 Retail revenue
6 Certain chamber ensemble
7 Bright but socially inept
8 Never-never connector

Down
1 Mount Rushmore sights
2 Extreme marathon event
3 Slender
4 Common sitcom character
5 Hardly a neat place

23   EASY

Across
2 Pronoun for a princess
4 Secure, as a job
6 Takes part in an out-of-control riot
8 Canadian province ___ Scotia
9 Sheriff's asst.

Down
1 Start of a promise
2 ___ Doggy Dogg of hip-hop fame
3 Home-theater centerpiece
5 Excellent rating
7 Envelope ready for return, briefly

24   EASY

Across
1 ___ Thai (stir-fry dish)
5 Casual farewell in Italy
7 Remove hair
8 Ceremonial heap
9 Abbr. for seasons played

Down
2 Feeling sore
3 Book that might be locked with a key
4 One opposed to you
6 Declare solemnly as true
7 Letters on tanning lotion

Across

1 Archaic pronoun
5 Turned up
12 Billiard room gadget
13 Horse color
14 Academic e-mail suffix
15 Sunburn reliever
16 Exceptions
17 Shark part
18 Plot
20 Sharp flavor
21 Kitchen item
23 Told
27 Things used by Olympic vaulters
30 Invader
31 Arise
32 Obstructions
33 Arid
34 Becoming
36 Poet, especially Shakespeare
38 Located inward
42 Financial nest egg letters
43 Proceed with difficulty
44 Paul Simon's "___ Rock"
45 Cloudy
46 Small brown singing bird
47 Honoree spot
48 Not heading west
49 Limits

Down

1 Slow-moving vehicles
2 Angelic symbol
3 College major, for short
4 ___ out (barely achieves)
5 Umpire, for one
6 Served the drinks
7 Communion bread holder
8 Alphabetical followers of eMs
9 Made full again
10 Adjust text
11 Sand formation
19 Least polluted
20 Ecosystem
22 Bathroom scrubber
24 Also-___
25 Technical sketches
26 Defeated by a tiny margin
28 Continental prefix
29 Sailor's telescope
31 Struggle (with)
33 Loose-leaf paper container
35 Crown for a princess
36 Endure
37 Operatic lines
39 Amusement park attraction
40 Garlic ___
41 In a crowd
43 Internet address starter

Across

1 Not digital, as a clock
6 Fencing sword
11 Like sad excuses
12 Reach one's goal
14 Sporty trucks, in brief
15 Narrow strips of pasta
16 Breath freshener
17 Bid welcome to
18 Silent acknowledgment
19 Consumes
20 ___ and vinegar dressing
22 Loose ad in magazine
24 Passageway for tears
25 Amusing short tales
28 Vital decision point
31 Widespread
32 Keyless, musically
36 Global lending org.
37 Discount time
39 Antipollution org.
40 Crime locale
42 Exact duplicate
43 Facilities
45 Opposite of up
46 Native to a certain region
47 Tiny parasites
48 Snorkeling spots
49 Go beyond

Down

1 Reunion folks
2 Sovereign state
3 Makes right
4 Kipling's "___ we forget!"
5 Mafia man
6 Cobbler's creations
7 Helping hand
8 Sing loudly
9 Day before a big event
10 Consequences
13 Fruit center
19 Caterer's coffee dispensers
21 Cubes in drinks
23 Lack of trouble
24 Bygone flightless bird
26 Run together
27 Romantic appointment
28 Animal, informally
29 Edge of a cup
30 Soccer call
33 Beginner, slangily
34 For each
35 Arrived on shore
37 Appears to be
38 ___-aging cream
41 Music's pitch indicator
42 Chalky mineral
44 ___ in a million

Across

1 Attractively thin
5 Jumbled mix
12 Arrived
13 Having become aware of
14 Inflation stat.
15 Mail org.
16 ETs pilot them
17 Tiresome routine
18 Thanksgiving dinners, e.g.
20 River mammals
22 Busy night at a popular bar: abbr.
23 Stable groom (var.)
25 Cheese shredder
27 Invitation to eat
30 Face off
31 Musical combo
32 Bollywood land
34 Gradually lessens
37 Consent under pressure
39 Made a pit
41 Kind of therapy
44 Indisposed
46 August zodiac sign
47 Lackluster
49 Absorbed by
50 D-H link
51 The Beatles' "When ___ Home"
52 Disinformation
53 Sewing links
54 Some Scots

Down

1 Shoe mark
2 Sci-fi zapper
3 Weakened
4 Awful state
5 Creamy chocolate dessert
6 Foot soldiers, in brief
7 Three-legged seat at a counter
8 Received in one's home
9 Good-sized suburban plot
10 Cowboy boot accessory
11 Dispatch a message
19 Child in day care
21 Shaman's people

24 Far from fresh
26 Fake name
28 White-flowered fragrant shrub
29 Affronted
30 Golf ball features
33 Like lemon or orange juice
35 Grown folks
36 Ink-filled writing instrument
38 Cold symptom
40 Lip application
42 Importance
43 Cartoon bear
45 Legal inheritance document
48 High-kicking Bruce

Across

1 Study of vision
6 Palindromic river rental
11 "I wasn't ___ yesterday!"
12 New-word creation
14 Still having a shot at winning
15 Looking guilty or dejected
16 Prepare for print
18 ___-to-riches
19 Curative medicine
21 And so on
24 Gp of Republicans
27 Push upward
28 Lying face up
30 Of the North Pole region
32 ___ Peace Prize
33 Nay's opposite
34 Least pleasant
36 Holds the same opinion
37 Linen source
40 Give approval for
44 Without purpose or target
46 Of no value
47 Engage fully
48 Kind of school, briefly
49 Like some interpretations
50 Grooved fastening devices

Down

1 Memorial bio
2 Shetland ___ (small horse)
3 Business ___
4 Loan charge
5 Systematic plan
6 Gene sharers
7 Hot-headed
8 And so on, when tripled
9 Overly eager
10 Gunpowder holders
13 Old cowboy movies
17 Diamond's place
20 Discouraged
21 Online auction website
22 Ripped up
23 Cola lead-in
24 Sarcastic remark
25 Handy bills
26 Hit with snowballs
29 Venom or toxin injector
31 Affectionate gesture
35 Feels intuitively
36 Wheel connectors
37 Prove unsuccessful
38 Prom arrival
39 Bullets, for short
41 ___ of thumb
42 Lots and lots
43 Avenue liners
45 Before, in poetry

Across

1 Good-natured
8 Nightmare feeling
12 Disparage
13 Main purpose
14 Fair
15 An old Germanic character
16 Casino option
18 Mtn. figures
19 Like some football kicks
20 Adding column
22 Boldness
25 Kind of TV screen
28 Rupture in muscle tissue
29 Astronomical time period
30 Inuit hut
31 Pack animal
32 Very clever
34 1980s haircut
36 Brief job
37 Give out in small portions
38 Engine type
40 Say for certain
44 Jut
46 Name of the ___
47 Something brought to the beach
48 USSR successor
49 Put into operation
50 Had creditors
51 Former stars

Down

1 "___-Ca-Dabra" (1974 song)
2 Hefty hammer
3 Lacks existence
4 Bedroom furniture
5 Nobles collectively
6 Safari park beasts
7 Aussie avians that don't fly
8 Garden dispenser for birds
9 On the outside
10 Bright
11 Caviar, before processing
17 Rugby throw-in
21 Issuer
23 Tool with a rotating handle
24 90 degrees, on a compass
25 Shepherd's pie ingredients
26 Missing
27 Cure for poison
28 Lacking a permanent shelter
33 Working together
35 Association of teams for competition
37 Press
39 No-luck link
41 Dining-table centerpiece
42 Can be bad or good
43 Joins in marriage
44 Book page abbr.
45 Column's opposite

Across

1 Handled roughly or clawed
7 Part of a Sherlock costume
12 Pierce with pointed stick
13 Synagogue leader
14 Tree-trunk growth
15 Ring-shaped coral reef
16 ___ trip (vain journey)
17 Toothed gear
19 Acid-tasting
21 Bit of folklore
22 WXYZ phone buttons
24 Sticky substance
26 Receive, as a ball
28 Shout of joy
31 From scratch
33 Major hikes
34 Put to the test
35 State flower of New Mexico
37 Skatepark feature
39 On the highest point
42 Acquire, as an inheritance
46 Up for payment
47 Poppy-based drug
48 Work as a pilot
50 Majestic dwelling
51 Canine quarters
52 What some cuts do
53 Goes inside

Down

1 Marathoner's distance
2 Friend, in Spanish
3 Hinterland
4 Musical syllable
5 Power co. product
6 Signify, mean
7 Move like a toddler
8 Wood-shaping machine
9 Bassoon's little brother
10 Ready and willing
11 Party poopers
18 Reason for stitches
20 Sushi grain
23 Brit med. group
24 Very large dog
25 Mighty tree
26 Underground burial chamber
27 Egypt's cont.
29 Non-Rx, for short
30 Killer whale
32 Song in church
36 Consumption
37 Recycling goal
38 Picked a target
40 Peripheral
41 Orange remnants
43 Australia's national gem
44 Not yours
45 Pizzeria fixture
49 Acct. increase

31   EASY

Across

1 Work well together
4 Common recipe instruction
5 Get in a row
7 Internet connection issue
8 Backyard storage structure

Down

1 Cool amount of money, briefly
2 Banish abroad
3 Put up some paintings
4 Pages of an atlas
6 ___ about (wander around)

32   EASY

Across

1 Filthy accumulation
4 How-___ (handy books)
6 Standard computer font
8 Fam. reunion attendee
9 Far from clumsy

Down

1 Former Russian emperor
2 Serving some purpose
3 ___ good turn (be helpful)
5 Piggy bank feature
7 Color of Mars

33   EASY

Across

1 Halfway, for short
4 Beyond Earth's atmosphere
6 ___ days (time long past)
7 Magnificent meal
8 Hat often with a pompon

Down

1 Lady of the home
2 Does a bakery job
3 Bit of bumper damage
4 Like a comfortable pillow
5 Defendant's declaration

EASY

Across

1 Certain trash receptacle
6 Expelled
11 Letters after an early date
12 Keeled over
14 Bell-shaped fruit
15 Semicircular path
16 Sudden assault
17 ___ fee
18 Outline, as a plan
20 Sign on a bargain
21 Become well again
22 Hurries up
24 Moon shape
27 Sword covering
28 Currency used in several countries
32 Flying velocity
34 Watch attentively
38 Difficult walk
40 Churn
41 Food of the classical gods
44 Chopped
45 In ___ of (as a substitute for)
46 Modern address, for short
47 Contribute
48 GPS displays
49 "Losing My Religion" group
50 ___ drink
51 Points (to)

Down

1 Humiliate
2 Squeal
3 Ten thousand square meters
4 Bushy hairdo
5 Not far from one's location
6 Veterans
7 Bug-squashing sound
8 Make playful fun of (someone)
9 Nosh at home
10 Stage actor's aide
13 Like a gymnast
19 Bloodsucking parasite
23 "Don't say another word!"
25 Amazon.com review symbol
26 Knightly conduct
27 Depository space for goods
29 Toy building block
30 Time available for relaxation
31 Devoted fan
33 Send in a payment
35 Surround completely
36 Utensil with a mesh bottom
37 Adjective for a statesman
39 Oasis trees
42 Octoberfest cold one
43 Trick designed to deceive

Across

1 Person dealing with money
8 Mix together in a bowl
12 TV aerial
13 "This looks bad"
14 Omelet site
15 Hard-to-please female star
16 Two-seated bicycle
17 Exclusive to male lions
18 Joule fraction
19 Spell-checker's prey
21 Creative major
22 Sunny bunch
24 Counsel
26 Spearheaded
29 Living things
32 Of springtime
33 Old senate wrap
37 Gibbon or gorilla
38 Big Apple enforcement org.
41 Stowable bed
42 Minute amount
44 Perform again
46 Greek letter or tiny bit
47 Put pages in correct order
48 Radio response
49 Recites, as a chant
50 Brainy introvert
51 Fully determined

Down

1 Office-chair wheel
2 City southeast of Istanbul
3 Not at all generous
4 Had in one's hands
5 Shoreline nook
6 Hostile party
7 Lab maze solver
8 Any fizzy drink
9 Disappear into ___
10 Contrary in effect
11 Cooked, as some peanuts
17 Broadband device
20 Reviews harshly
23 Extend across, as a bridge
25 Sleeveless garment
27 Totally ridiculous
28 Butterlike
29 Standing ___
30 Scold gently
31 Bigger and better
34 Large expanses of water
35 Pointy beard
36 Say under oath
39 Lying face down
40 Mississippi triangle
43 Gift box attachment, often
45 Move like a tortoise
47 Spanish hero El ___

Across

1 Musical feel
5 Like some art
12 The Beatles' "___ in the Life"
13 Hardly feral
14 Remotely situated
15 Prospector's discovery
16 Kitchen roll
17 Certain NYSE listing
18 Did in the past
20 Band of seven players
22 Bowman
24 Imperfection
28 March 15th
32 Clock setting for your area
35 Sponge-cake ingredients
36 Payback
37 Extra-large drink
40 Say no to
43 Heavenly
47 One of the Eastern elite
48 Env. abbreviation
50 Diminish
51 Pull with difficulty
52 Mountain climber's obstacle
53 Dug out minerals
54 Downwind side of the river
55 Wields a needle

Down

1 Of great worth
2 Bride and groom exchange
3 Expressed, as a welcome
4 Assessed visually
5 Least favorably
6 High jump need
7 Chart-topping hit
8 Cone-shaped dwelling
9 Throw ___
10 Superhero's garb
11 Walk briskly
19 Follower, as in espionage
21 Reward won in competition
23 Cricket's sound
25 Daily record
26 Lines at a hosp.
27 Ship's poles
29 Crime boss
30 Manchester's and London's land: abbr.
31 Having no pips
33 Varied mixture
34 Preceding nights
38 Invasive household insect
39 Emcee's opening
40 Become weary
41 Malaria symptom
42 Profoundly wise
44 Low cards
45 Barely cooked, as a steak
46 Starting freshly
49 Roofing goo

Across

1 Numbers cruncher, briefly
4 Brisk
11 Sharing word
12 Conclusion, in music
13 Bus. honcho
14 Med. diagnostic procedure
15 Desire
16 Battery pack letters
17 Pasta specification
19 Abbr. in many airport names
20 Compensates
22 Dict. tag
25 Backless seat
29 Miami baseballer
31 Kind of call
32 Bagel variety
33 Expression of gratitude
34 Harley attachment
36 ___ and turn
37 Sacred site
39 Boxing weapon
42 Comply with
46 Hosp. drama locale, perhaps
47 Lie next to
48 Apple dessert
49 Endorsing
50 Tall evergreen
51 House wing
52 Thug
53 Bioelectric swimmer

Down

1 Vegetative state
2 Knit alternative
3 Rain-deprived
4 Bloodhound's guide
5 Bridge of boats
6 Arrival
7 Aye's opposite
8 Optimist's credo
9 How the maid leaves things
10 Soccer score
18 Most ancient
19 Solitary
21 Carve in glass
22 Audio equip.
23 Indonesian tourist island
24 Pitt of "Fight Club"
26 Having only one channel
27 Decides to find out
28 Bad or good ending
30 Foot fraction
33 Chicago newspaper
35 Egypt's official language
38 Compound in gunpowder
39 Drum go-with
40 Picture on a desktop
41 Channel-hop
43 Fencing implement
44 Gallbladder fluid
45 Shout
47 Spring mo.

Across

1 Manifests
6 Lofty
12 Airline crew member
14 Taxi ticker
15 Nevada neighbor
16 Nonrecyclables
17 K-O connection
18 Forest foragers
20 1040, for example
21 Completely exhaust
23 Dog's cry
25 Colorful carp
26 Dissents
28 Go to sea
30 Video store categories
32 Individuals
35 Put your hands on
37 Piece for one performer
38 Feeling of astonishment
41 Full of meaning
43 Like a tuned guitar string
45 Many a Twitter thread
47 Amtrak track
49 Confidentiality initials
50 Backup plan lead-in
52 Ignition
54 Prefix for surgeon
55 Least challenging
56 Smiled broadly
57 Puts in sequence

Down

1 Bring close to simmering
2 Insulin, for instance
3 View
4 Expert, for short
5 Liqueur flavor
6 Monies risked on gambles
7 Audi rival, initially
8 Canadian flag emblem
9 Words to soothe a toddler
10 Trains underground
11 Recluse
13 Word on a sale sign
19 ___ shot
22 Maker of foam toy weaponry
24 They're thrown for laughs
27 Part of an apple
29 Pirate's stolen goods
30 Flagrant
31 Nostradamus, e.g.
33 Decorative pot
34 Most noisy
36 Rented
39 Thin cookie
40 Opposite of excitement
42 Pocketed bread
44 Bakery pastries
46 Conflicted
48 Lad's sweetheart
51 Truck scale unit
53 ___ Grande (border river)

EASY

Across

1 Transparently clear
6 Noisy shouting
12 All ___
13 Missing portion of a manuscript
14 Undercover police operation
15 Sums
16 Skin care product
17 Least mean
18 Hold power, as a monarch
20 Light controller
23 One streaming on Twitch, maybe
27 Convention booths
29 Bike ___
30 Contract-signing needs
31 Needlework
33 Voodoo land
35 In good spirits
37 Driver's order
39 Preparing for battle
43 Attach to the end of
46 Old sailor
47 Literature from the internet
48 Regard highly
49 Bunny ___ (place for ski students)
50 Condition of a fire-ready shotgun
51 Grammar class subject

Down

1 On the market, as a house
2 Quaint preposition
3 Money, informally
4 Furthest inside
5 Measure for angles and intensity
6 Metallic sound
7 Dock work activity
8 Band with a lightning bolt in its logo
9 Reflect deeply
10 Burden or duty
11 Euphoria
19 Maddens
21 DIY furniture store
22 Abbreviated version
24 Transferable to another owner
25 Lion's feature
26 MIT grad, probably
28 Religious branch
30 Made of multiple words
32 Like teeth most fit for the photo session
34 Turn a blind eye to
36 Northern soldier in the Civil War
38 Goaded (on)
40 Change over
41 Baby doll's word
42 Short admission
44 Hired muscle
45 "Clumsy me!"

40 EASY

Across
1 ___ a balloon
4 "Pokemon" cartoon genre
7 Like a warm winter jacket
8 Emma of "La La Land"
9 Convent dweller

Down
1 Amigos
2 Handling the problem
3 Attach, as a brooch
5 Computer selection screen
6 Peaceful garden of Adam and Eve

41 EASY

Across
1 Gears with teeth
5 Hand-propelled missile
6 Unflinching
8 Dance done in grass skirts
9 Floored it on the highway

Down
1 Boom box inserts, initially
2 Solemn sworn promises
3 Facebook ___ (community)
4 Fence crossing
7 Dastardly sort

42 EASY

Across
1 Feeling happy appreciation
5 Elongated sandwich
6 Popular date night option
7 Brings charges against
8 High-spiritedness

Down
1 Grave robber of horrors
2 Antiflood structure
3 Come up to the surface
4 Average John
6 Controversial flavoring letters

Across

1 Adhesive
5 Words of one giving way to the other
12 Without a break
14 Potatoland, USA
15 Steal the show from
16 Determined to do
17 Non-mainstream believer
18 Possible cause of mistakes
19 Commercials
21 Certain digits
23 Place for a cabin
24 Flat-bottomed fishing boat
25 Asian waist tie
28 World cultural and educational org.
30 Hospital room object
32 Quite a hgt.
33 Construction sites
35 Dig site
36 Disaster-aid agcy
37 Invoices
38 Shadow cast during eclipse
41 "The home of the ___" (anthem's end)
43 Beauty parlor
44 Permission
47 Powers that be
48 Morally correct
49 Express differently
50 Bottle part

Down

1 Long-tailed antelope
2 Take off
3 ___ rule
4 Extensive land properties
5 Calming exercise
6 Receptive
7 Very wide-angle lens
8 Start-upers have many of them
9 Lab rodents
10 Attempt
11 General quality
13 Clothing labels
19 Run-down area
20 Breathe quickly
22 Balls in the sky
24 Bad thing to expect
25 Great riches
26 Get-out-of-jail cost
27 Taverns
29 Less soiled
31 Outdoor theater
34 They may be reserved
36 Lather
37 Composer Johann Sebastian
38 Computer password creator
39 Father or son
40 Plane, on a radar screen
42 Sacrament, for example
45 Biological pouch
46 Yellowstone bugler

Across

1 Gets away from
7 Offshoot
12 Only just
13 Render blank
14 German city that used to be divided into two parts
15 Enter a correct password, say
16 Extremely good
18 Prickly succulents
21 King, in France
22 Common survey option
23 Disorder
27 "Matrix" main role
28 Old pro
29 Confused
32 Besides
33 Egg dish
34 Pizza order
36 Back-out key
37 Stacked (up)
38 Most important tab in an Excel file
42 Humble living quarters
43 Shiny hard elements which may have magnetic properties
47 Kind of situation you would better avoid
48 Summer cooler
49 Origami birds
50 Web forum grouping

Down

1 Diplomat's bldg.
2 Flight pattern
3 Airport section, briefly
4 13-Across, as computer files
5 Alchemist's bottleful
6 Set to the same time
7 Betrayal
8 One side of a political debate
9 Latest fad
10 Has begun
11 Lady's escort: abbr.
17 Blundered
18 Nation once known as Zaire
19 Best athletes
20 Errand
24 Easily hurt
25 Horseman's spear
26 Wrapped up
28 Climbing plant
30 Assimilate
31 Reduces
34 Lecture
35 Roadside rubbish
38 Provides staff for
39 What the star of the show takes
40 Farm Belt state
41 Radiate, as light
44 Fueled up
45 Pasture
46 Melancholic

Across

1 Keep a low profile
6 Mutant Ninja of cartoons
11 Overly diluted
12 Academic field
14 Call for attention
15 Intellect
16 Living cone bearer
18 Company symbol
20 Eject
21 Evidence-gathering device
23 Poultry product
26 Groan-inducing wordplay
27 Blue ____ Mountains
30 Naps
32 Exhibit explainer
33 Like Chinese, as a language
34 Adding result
35 Dash readout
36 Nuclear trial prohibition
39 Arched recess in a church
42 Inconvenience
46 Middle of the day
48 Pacify
49 Bejeweled item
50 Datebook abbr.
51 Hilarious stand-up performer
52 Appear on the scene
53 Rates of return

Down

1 Web prog. code
2 1803 Union admission
3 Lisa of CNN
4 Fund, as a grant
5 Egyptian paper reed
6 Part of a philosophy
7 Abu Dhabi's nation, for short
8 See-____
9 Spike and Bruce
10 Upper canines
13 Grow mature
17 Thing to discuss
19 Alcoholic liquor
22 Smells
23 Antagonize
24 Glimmer, in brand names
25 ____-X
28 Party person, informally
29 Measure of econ. health
31 Gone, as dinner
32 Uncertainty
34 Deforestation remnant
37 Make nasty comments
38 Pearly shell layer
40 Greeting card text, often
41 A few (of)
43 Achieve perfectly
44 Dolt
45 CPR givers
47 Label on a gift

EASY

Across

1 Meaty drink
7 Stereotypical freight-train hopper
11 Provide space as required
12 Archer's wrist guard
14 Far from clumsy
15 Knocking syllables
16 NBA Hall of Famer Holman
17 Name on a race car, probably
19 Divinity
21 Energy
23 Crowded together
24 Without doubt
25 Annoy
26 Sheriff's group in a western movie
27 Nocturnal fledgling
30 Geographical direction suffix
31 Burn slightly
32 Wash
35 Chain item
36 Facial feature
37 Official who ensures fair play
39 Espionage org.
41 Got back
42 Essentials
44 Adjust to a situation
45 Parts of history tests
46 Nondormant one
47 Skew

Down

1 Coffee tidbit
2 Participate
3 Magazine VIP
4 Opposite of -less
5 Bit of summer attire
6 In a foreign land
7 Conical items at birthday parties
8 Eight-tentacled sea creature
9 Check recipients
10 Food you can barely taste
13 "Atlas Shrugged" author Ayn
18 Sneak ___
20 Not as exciting
22 Really bother
23 Astound
24 Shipwreck finder
26 Fakes it
28 Cabbie's query
29 Baby shower gift, sometimes
30 Besides that
32 Unopened, as wine
33 Pleasant with
34 Mini-burger
36 Lamp gas
38 Quartet count
40 Igor's job, in Dr. Frankenstein's lab
41 Outstanding, in surfspeak
43 Enjoy lunch

EASY

Across

1 Chatter
4 Atlas line
7 Feline predator
11 Discharge by sweating
13 Mideast nation with a cedar on its flag
15 Fatigued
16 Casanova
17 Tel-Aviv's land and southern neighbor of 13-Across
19 Chat filler
20 Kangaroo jump
22 Emulate a professor
24 Practice game
28 An article
29 Ball-shaped part
30 Any NFL player
31 Estate receiver
32 Every last bit
33 Confidence
35 Indentation
37 Chronology segments
38 Earth sci.
40 Throwing event
44 Gondolier
47 Moved sneakily
48 Recording stars
49 Beyond unusual
50 Blade of tall marsh grass
51 Disrespect verbally
52 Incidentally, briefly

Down

1 Fabled snow beast
2 Rotational center
3 Desirable engine sound
4 Make amends for
5 European mountain
6 Ham-slicing store department
7 Beneficiary
8 Yet to lose
9 Cow's call
10 In whichever place
12 Give cards to
14 Pour fat over
18 Nightstand fixtures
21 Break down, as a sentence
23 Modern and sophisticated
24 Blank keyboard button
25 ___ phone
26 Put in a lower division
27 Pumpkin kin
31 Big deal
33 Chemistry 101 models
34 Ups
36 Far from fragrant
39 Back muscles, in gym lingo
41 Parking meter site
42 Indivisible entity
43 Corrupt, as test results
45 Metallic mineral
46 Cryptic org.

Across

1 Pinball player's hangout
6 Furniture store staples
11 Genuine
12 Tummy
14 Nothing more than
15 Student
16 Happily-after connection
17 Personal pronoun
18 Irritates
20 Cook's pinch
23 Belonging to it
24 Nile wading birds
25 Take for granted
29 Fancy hairdo
30 ___ Smurf
31 Pursued, as prey
33 Items that attach corsages
34 Do-it-yourself buy
35 Smithsonian is one, briefly
36 Breakfast menu heading
40 Small power sources
42 Bustles of activity
43 Booth
46 Correctly pitch instrument
47 Constant
48 Pastry finisher
49 Like a thicket
50 Most elegant

Down

1 Landlocked neighbor of Georgia
2 Four-time Superman player
3 It sits on a keyboard above 6 and is a sign of 7-Down
4 Danger signal
5 Connoisseur of beauty
6 Rise high
7 Leaving out
8 Summer cooler
9 Court winner
10 Bed covers
13 Lock up top
19 Green bean
21 Not much at all
22 Very long sentence
26 "Wheel of Fortune" motion
27 ___ - serif font
28 On higher floor
29 Adorable
31 Male reflexive word
32 Feast finale
33 Put (together)
34 Bearlike marsupial
37 Dead language
38 Evoke something latent
39 Sounds
41 Blemish
44 4x4, shortly
45 Big London clock

49

Across

1 Barbecue-grill briquettes
6 Lennox of music
7 Strict belief
8 Arctic Archipelago people
9 Some drink garnishes

Down

1 Southernmost Spanish province
2 Two-___ (court situation)
3 Burger beef
4 Sky, perhaps
5 Accommodates, as an arena

50

MEDIUM

Across

1 Harsh note from a trumpet
5 Like some pasta sauces
6 More seasoned
7 Tiny, hairlike organelles
8 Intense lamentation

Down

1 Suggest otherwise about
2 Gravy pourer
3 Had pizza delivered, maybe
4 Supermodel Banks
5 Simulate unflatteringly

51

MEDIUM

Across

2 Contagious viral infection
5 Froth on the ocean
7 Prevent from escaping
8 Muse of lyrical verse
9 Rotational speed meas.

Down

1 One walking down the aisle
2 Mountain cats or sneakers
3 Don't count
4 Gas used in high-intensity headlights
6 Slangy culprit

INNER BALANCE

Across

1 "Success is where preparation and ___ meet" (Bobby Unser)
11 Flirty toon Betty ___
12 Odd
14 Courtroom fiction writer's first name
15 Bond portrayer before Pierce
16 Lockable chest for documents
18 Unstable particle
19 Yes and no follower
20 Photon, for instance
21 Pre-Tokyo capital
24 Sour buttermilk-like drink
25 Fed a newborn
27 Cathedral nooks
31 Deliberately lose
32 Urge
33 "The Beauty Myth" author Wolf
34 Work ___ lather
35 Extend awkwardly
38 Bit of luggage
40 Entertaining sort
41 Counterweight
44 Opposite the current
46 Earth sci.
47 Revolving
48 Dip ___ in
49 Epicurus: "Only the just man enjoys ___"

Down

1 Dutifully compliant
2 Dermal opening
3 Marie Curie, by birth
4 Pieces expressing views
5 Gave extra help to
6 OS choice
7 ___ Lock (PC key)
8 Organism's double
9 Ballet dresses
10 Swift beast
13 Redgrave of the cinema
17 Cyclists' route
20 Like certain joints
22 Sarcastic retort
23 Bobby of the NHL
26 Light piano piece
28 5-centime coin
29 Organizing soft. for corporations
30 Alarmed
32 Legal stoppage of commerce
35 Clam (up)
36 Emerge surprisingly
37 Peter who played Mr. Moto
39 Shimmer
41 Nota ___ (mark my words)
42 Opener on Broadway
43 After a short time
45 Singer Damone

MEDIUM

Across

1 Like the 1898 war
14 Opening words on an agenda
15 Debt slips
16 Overdo it on the theater stage
17 Be rootless
18 Run with ease
19 Repairer's stock
20 Poor box filler
21 Attack chopper
23 Liposuction target
24 Italian lyric tenor Beniamino
26 Suffers
28 ___ glance
31 Rip open
33 Major California vintner
35 Hockey Hall of Famer Abel
36 Aromatherapy settings
40 Sends abroad
43 Extra list of choices
45 Paste in Japanese soups
46 Exclamation of amazement
48 Classical order of architecture
49 Safe due to shallowness
53 White House advisory gp
54 Coffee bar orders
57 Besmirches
59 Online abbreviation for offline events
60 Dismissal
62 Harness attachment
65 Poultry holders
67 Score just before victory, maybe
68 Legless lizard, e.g.
69 Money in the music business
70 In ___ (properly placed)
71 Independent Rick's head?
72 Internet café staple

Down

1 Plan to gain an advantage
2 Backyard party centerpiece
3 Baldwin or Sandler
4 Food packaging reassuring letters
5 Fodder
6 Fairground throwing game
7 International nannies
8 Tiny bit of time, briefly
9 Doomsayer's sign
10 Min or max trailer
11 Greek tourist destination
12 Damask rose oil
13 Homes in branches
22 Native of India
25 Use ___ lose it
27 Pink cocktail, informally
29 Downtown cruiser
30 Mont Blanc site
32 "___ for Innocent" (Grafton novel)
34 Natural bath sponge
37 Actor Sean
38 Tropical cuckoos
39 Inheritor
41 Bodies of art?
42 Grass patch
44 Jessica of "The Illusionist"
47 Some Jews
50 Printing process
51 Tuna's smaller relative
52 ___ vitae, hard wood
54 Cubed
55 Carve a canyon
56 Doofuses
58 Former SeaWorld attraction
61 Frog-in-the-throat sound
63 ___ on the back (approval)
64 Change one's residence
66 Commercial end for Water

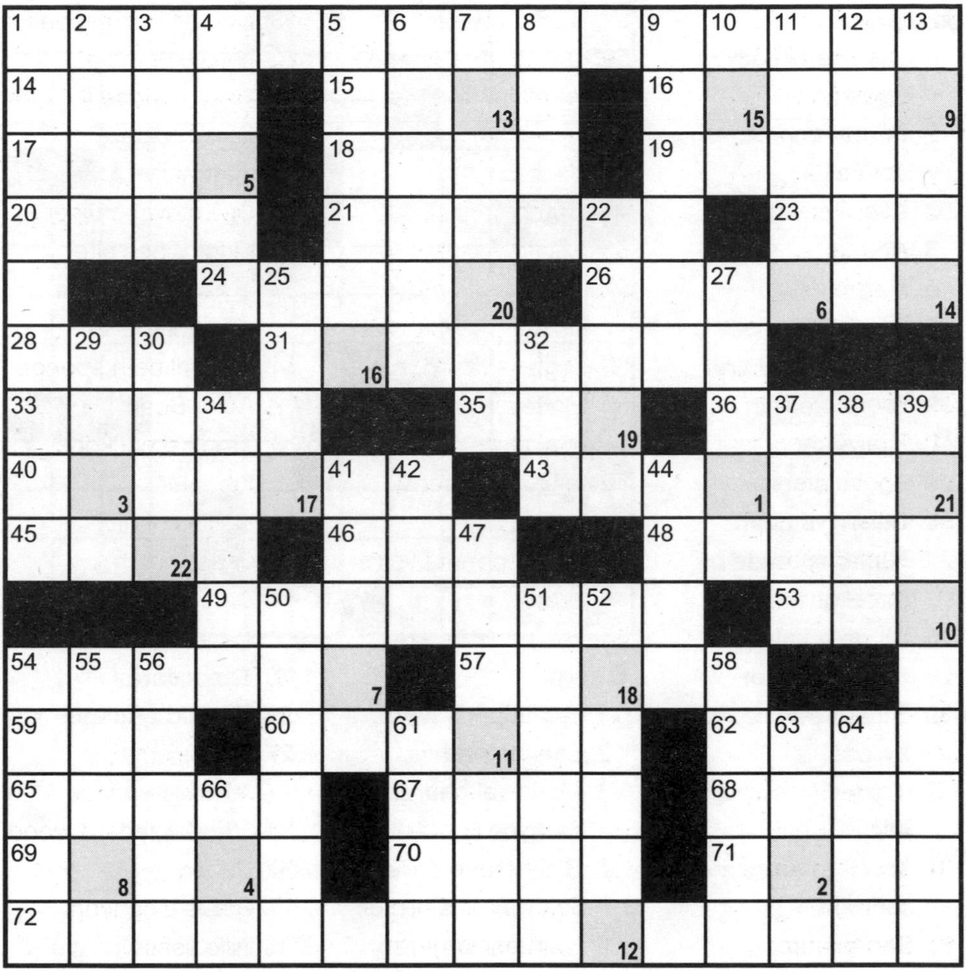

Bonus Clue

Transfer the letters from the corresponding shaded squares above into this grid to form the **Russell Crowe's Oscar role**

1	2	3	4	5	6	7

8	9	10	11	12	13	14

15	16	17	18	19	20	21	22

MEDIUM

Across

1 Chic deep hair waves
7 Fourth in a series of twelve
12 Alias for Cupid
13 Abuse
15 Bug's tail?
16 Some marches
17 Centers of action
19 Separate with a strainer
20 Broad cove
21 Beetle of Egypt
24 Hadrons made of three quarks
28 Bit on a salad
29 Infant follower?
30 Stress-free sound symbol
33 Texter's viewpoint intro
34 To ___ (everyone)
36 More suave
38 Tall slender dog
41 Move like the tide, half the time
42 Sourcing abbr.
43 Member of crocodile family
47 Mythical reptile
50 Arty NYC locale
51 Trammel
52 Pops' partners
53 Professional gps
54 Adventurous journey

Down

1 Hat-tipper's word
2 Lateral lead-in
3 Medieval church hanging
4 Bing who crooned
5 Pretend to sing
6 Camera for a pro
7 Lofty story
8 Easily assembled dwelling
9 Place limits on
10 Am-risk connector
11 Capt.'s underlings
14 Deprivation
18 ___ Ski Valley, New Mexico
22 Top spot
23 Socially inept sort
24 Distorted judgment
25 Coloratura Gluck
26 Practical people
27 Moo ___ (Chinese dish)
31 Vandalized
32 "Mamma Mia" pop group
35 Nile valley native
37 Bottomless places
39 Baking chambers
40 Understood, to a beatnik
44 Dairy noises
45 Words of exasperation
46 Always butting in
47 Lillie or Arthur
48 Reply, in short
49 ___-pitch (softball game)

Across

1 Telecompressor, in photography
12 Midwest oil center
13 Official currency of Haiti
14 Parrot-like
15 Hale
16 Cupid appendages
18 Avoid a pothole, say
19 Hardly any, old-style
22 Tight
24 Time of your life
25 Of lower value
26 Brownish-gray
28 At a higher temperature
32 The Sun City
34 Exorbitant interest rate
35 Kidney related
37 Edgar Allan ___
38 Came out suddenly
41 Inventory
42 Gardener of rhyme
43 Fireball hurlers in fantasy novels
45 Pale one of its species
47 Musical about the Peróns
50 Thinner
51 Artistic puzzle
52 Borrowing with more than a year to maturing

Down

1 Cease motion
2 Little seal
3 Quarter-back Manning
4 Scholarly work
5 "Fantastic Mr. Fox" author
6 Beastly
7 Symbolic hugs
8 Overturns
9 Less feigned
10 50s Ford failure
11 Adjudicate anew
17 Docs grp
20 Bedouin headcord
21 Start another tour
23 Korean metropolis
25 Burdened
27 Evading
29 Amazon valley people
30 God of desire
31 Slice of healthy bread
33 Encore, basically
36 "The Piano" heroine
38 Drink order
39 Kind of diet
40 Densely populated
41 Kept going
44 Bacterium
46 Volleyball barrier
48 Car___ (piranha)
49 Bath mat site

SECRET INGREDIENTS

Across
1 Deceived
4 Near photograph
11 One in the ABA
14 Billy Joel's "___ to Extremes"
15 Attractions for bees
16 Pythagoras' P
17 Flavor enhancer used in many Indian curries, stews and soups
20 Instrument or rhino's appendage
21 Sushi selections
22 Type of interstellar cloud
23 Addiction suffix
25 Causes to yawn, say
26 Juanita's friend
29 National Museum of Iran locale
31 Pass down, as a folk story
33 Make a stink
34 Old IBM display standard letters
37 Of the heart
39 More lustrous
41 With a wink
42 Business group
44 Is afraid to
45 Workaholic's main concern
47 Bouquet holders
48 Electron transfer two-part reaction
51 Polar explorer's jacket
53 Spring, in Hebrew
54 Taste sensation
55 Move imperceptibly
59 Mixture of cinnamon, cloves, fennel, star anise, and Sichuan peppercorns
62 American inventor's monogram
63 Guided a vehicle
64 Sundown, in sonnets
65 Audio file ext.
66 Fearful feelings
67 Atlanta-to-Miami dir.

Down
1 Over the estimate
2 Rural prefix
3 Elevator entryway
4 Atlanta's ___ Center
5 Made the way for
6 Black magic
7 Not as warm
8 Swimmer's woes
9 "Mila 18" novelist
10 Pro bono TV spot, briefly
11 Strong liking
12 Pointer's word
13 Basis of civil lawsuits
18 Like new wine
19 Chime time
24 Capital of Nova Scotia province
25 Honeyed pastry
26 Rainbow shapes
27 Bistro purchase
28 Humble response to praise
30 Common sense philosopher Thomas
32 Den of an animal
34 Struggles (for)
35 Hereditary trait transmitter
36 Martial follower
38 Of richer sauce texture
40 Polish city on the Vistula
43 Threatening person
45 Coastal inlet
46 "The Dark Half" director
48 Bundles of logs, maybe
49 French bottled water brand
50 Plunged
52 Closer to fruition
54 In the hands of
56 Uplifting literature
57 Symbols of sleep
58 Bald eagle's kin
60 Secure online protocol (inits)
61 Some serious hosp. cases

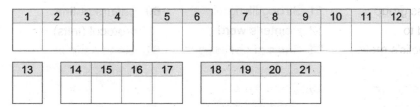

Bonus Clue

Transfer the letters from the corresponding shaded squares above into this grid
to form the **advice from a wise dietitian**

1	2	3	4		5	6		7	8	9	10	11	12

13		14	15	16	17		18	19	20	21

57

MEDIUM

Across

1 Declaration upon a short visit
12 Giant tree, briefly
13 ___ impasse
14 Hungarian-born architect Goldfinger
15 As one
17 Raised metal strip on guitar's neck
18 Couch blotch
19 Medieval fortress city in Italy
21 UPS boxes
24 Employed
27 Finish line in a horse race
30 Afro-Brazilian dancy martial art
32 Cannon's end?
33 Complete a job
34 German 101 word
35 Fuller dome design
37 Aboard a liner, e.g.
38 Like cornstalks
39 Designer initials
41 "Casablanca" lady
43 Patronage
47 Bird similar to an ostrich
49 Softies
52 Boxer Billy aka "The Pittsburgh Kid"
53 Garfield's best friend
54 Persona ___ grata
55 Good deed

Down

1 Nile goddess
2 Piece of copper
3 Blue ocean hue
4 Slight contamination
5 Canonized people, in brief
6 Eastern guiding principle
7 Actress Meara
8 Liberal, slangily
9 Planet motions models
10 About 22.5 degrees
11 Comprehended
16 Opposite of naughty, to Santa
20 Enjoy the mall
22 PX patrons
23 Appetizing
25 Albany's canal
26 "The X-Files" Agent Scully
27 Carry on, as war
28 Brainchild
29 Accustom anew
31 Hockey disc
33 Daily dosages
36 Part of FDR
37 Some responses from sailors
40 Unvarnished
42 Run ___ (go wild)
44 No longer here
45 NYSE newsmakers
46 Certain IDs
47 Early TV brand
48 Ad follower
50 Infamous Amin
51 Sculptor Maya

Across

1 Smashing boxing victory
5 Remove hair by the roots
12 Character in "Young Frankenstein"
13 "A Few Good Men" soldiers
14 Zip
15 Righteous acts
16 One permitting
18 Sermon finisher?
19 All-knowing advisor
20 Chorus from the sidelines
21 Guitarist Ocasek
24 Momma's partner
26 Pollen producer
28 Play terribly
32 Trivial
33 Greek evil spirit
34 Large intestine
36 Historic header
37 Jewish wedding dance
40 Engine stats
42 Former catcher Rodriguez
43 Of the south
46 Deceived others
48 Definitely not polite
49 Do over and over
50 Cab alternative
51 Celestial figures
52 Hardy heroine

Down

1 Seafood menu item
2 Vegan gelatin substitute
3 Luke's mentor
4 Long-armed primate, for short
5 Imperial ruler
6 Get ready for a ring sparring, say
7 Furious feeling
8 Intellectual types
9 "West Side Story" role
10 Sprocket projections
11 Skiers shapes, often
17 Elvis Presley's city of birth
22 ____ spin
23 UPS shipping unit
25 Sacred songs
27 "Carmen" aria
29 Teeny mischief maker
30 Neither follower
31 Church accessories
33 Designates
35 Eerie apparition
37 45 players
38 Like pear tree leaves
39 Fall park alleys attender, maybe
41 Pompous walk
44 Hardly a sophisticate
45 Beverages
47 Big name in caulk

Across

1 They may be first class: abbr.
5 Get rid of this, to proofreaders
9 Past its sell-by date, perhaps
14 Compost ___ (gardener's pile)
15 Jack-in-the-pulpit plant, e.g.
16 Big cat hybrid
17 Constant smoker seen in Sicily
18 Barely noticeable amount
19 Uncoordinated
20 Individuation
23 Ophthalmological ailments
24 Prepare for the judge's entrance
25 Still packaged
29 Pilfers
33 Scattering of a people
37 Invite to enter
38 ___ in gloves catches no mice
39 Angelic, in a way
42 "Sex Education" actor Butterfield
43 New enlistee
45 Radio announcer's blunder
47 Slangy opposite of yeah

48 Approaching from two directions
50 Straw stack
51 Corporate bigwigs, for short
53 Some Protestant followers
55 Lacoste of tennis
56 Snacker
58 Evil glance
60 ___-null (math figure)
65 Certain declaration commemoration
71 Type of pollution
72 Bavaria-based automaker
73 Neuter, as horses
74 ___ blanche
75 Circus site
76 Like many Olym. gold medalists
77 Relatives of emus
78 JFK approximations
79 "Tomb Raider" heroine Croft

Down

1 Peels off
2 Post-joke query
3 Yellow buttonlike flower
4 Sudden inundation

5 Vampire's curfew
6 ___ the Red (Viking explorer)
7 Extreme avidity
8 Royal domain
9 Piggy places
10 Cold metal smiths
11 "A Death in the Family" author James
12 Chops off
13 Balance checkers, briefly
21 Words that end the game?
22 Retired sportscaster Scully
26 Perfectly pitched
27 Make a delivery to the masses
28 Good bud
30 African animals related to the giraffe
31 Cleave
32 Mean comments
33 Sock mender
34 Tool used for scaling
35 City in western Germany
36 Orch. section with violins and cellos
37 Hurry-scurry
40 Voodoo-like practice
41 Run off to wed
44 Letters on Navy vessels' hulls

46 "___ and the Blind Forest" (beautiful video game)
49 NFL ballcarriers
52 Clavichord's kin
54 Table front?
56 Premaritally named
57 Overly embellished

59 Largest fencing weapons
61 Allowed by law
62 Botanical puffiness
63 Having spent less time on the beach
64 Many-headed monster

65 Boost, in brief
66 Wordy Webster
67 Awful
68 Couple's karaoke selection
69 Novelist Ferber
70 Petty criticisms

60

MEDIUM

Across

1 Mottled mount
8 ___/IP (Internet protocol)
11 Start to pass?
12 Able-bodied
13 Exclamation of epiphany
14 Former heavyweight champ Riddick
15 Diner amenity
17 "Hey Brother" Swedish DJ
19 Delights
20 Asian New Year
21 Certain NCO
23 "Ghosts" playwright
24 Title in old India
26 Berry in juices
27 Faction
31 Au ___
32 Main stem
33 Animated Fudd
35 Cry of clarity
36 Bisected fly?
39 "8 Mile" rapper
41 Genre of "World of Warcraft"
43 Computer info destruction
45 Tiniest of margins
46 Comp stub?
47 Pasta ending
48 Building lot
49 Berlin article
50 Soft-top car

Down

1 Hitter's turn
2 Bear out
3 Lapwing
4 Words after just or wait
5 One-kind connector
6 Delta accumulation
7 "Pitfall!" console maker
8 Very spicy pepper sauce
9 French stately home
10 Whitish root vegetable
15 Tourist magnets
16 Leave the ship
18 Ends the part?
22 Have an association with
24 Mermaid for Spaniards
25 19th-century composer of "A German Requiem"
27 Zipped
28 Like hand-shaped leaves
29 Controlling device
30 Grab, in slang
34 Holy artifact
36 Way up a mountain, perhaps
37 Maliciousness
38 Well-plumed bird
40 Homer Simpson's mom
42 Really-really
44 Only child's lack

52

Across

1 "BUtterfield 8" author
6 Type of cat or goat
12 Mass units, briefly
13 Kind of sweater
14 Fernando's farewell
15 Mitch Miller, for one
16 Large pheasant
18 Audio equipment giant
19 Road company
21 Moving day stack
23 Ajar, to bards
25 British composer, Thomas
26 Blinker
28 Signal digitizing devices
31 Chess finale
32 Includes in an email
33 2015 Jason Bateman movie
36 Speaks Dixie-style
38 "The Lion King" uncle
41 Of reason-based religion
44 Noted current
46 Crystal ball alternative
47 Was almost out
48 Construction site machine
49 Cobalt glass pigments
50 Overblown

Down

1 Giraffe relative
2 Surprise party cry
3 Et ___ (and others)
4 Ridgepole
5 Pigeonhole
6 Farthest Moon apsis
7 Small lump
8 Geography-class fixture
9 Miscellaneous assemblage
10 Also-ran Perot
11 Forego
17 Chase romantically
20 Freud subj.
21 Swamp snapper
22 Bridge words
23 "Frozen" snowman
24 Brad of "Ocean's Thirteen"
25 Complainants
27 Diplomat
29 NBA position
30 Follows
34 Wool coat wearer
35 Bug in the system
36 Exercise
37 Made a move
39 Epitome of quiet
40 "Breaking Bad" star Gunn
42 Bear snare
43 Skye of the screen
45 ___ interested

Across
1 Brief holiday
6 App's extras
11 NYPD employee
15 ___ Office
16 Cooking maven Rombauer
18 Form compost
19 Kunis of Hollywood
20 Going rate?
21 Branch of sci.
22 Stupid ending?
23 Book drive orgs.
24 Forensic specialists analyzing marks left by suspect's hands
28 Letters on cleaning and hyg. products
29 Due for harvesting
30 Human tail?
31 Became an issue
32 Greenback
33 Most SAT takers
34 Scanning resolution measure, briefly
35 Copy in fun
38 Red-clad cheese
40 Run down (stocks)
44 Equal in rank
46 Brewed bean
48 Roman goddess of the night
49 Court rival of Bjorn
50 Cuban pronoun
52 Stretch
54 Disposal
56 Investor's buy
57 Easy mark
58 Wide indication
59 Pooh's hand
61 Made with more yolks
63 Nightfall
65 Mini-Vegas
67 Ready to use again
68 Hospital areas, for short
69 Cannes's Palme ___
70 Clutch hitter's stats
72 Car company based in Silicon Valley
75 Button on many remotes
76 To ___ (precise)
77 Aerosol sound
80 Government arm that carries out operations in support of national security
84 Old West defense
85 Affirmative declaration
86 Neurol. readouts
87 ___ admiral
88 Smoky shaft
89 What a retrovirus contains: abbr.
90 Obnoxious kid
91 Garr of "Tootsie"
92 Actor Neill et al.
93 Cling to a surface
94 Himalayan dweller

Down
1 Tips politely
2 Be of value
3 Entertaining tales
4 Soyuz cosmonaut Makarov
5 Root hair
6 Italian opera theme
7 9-Down surrealist
8 Red eye condition
9 Distinguished
10 River of Hades
11 Put at risk
12 Part of TNT
13 Airplane wing extenders
14 No longer in fashion
17 Small wave
25 Vamp played by Susan Lucci
26 Outdoor function
27 Dads
32 Two-footer
33 Lee of cakedom
34 Figure out
35 Patterned fabrics
36 As a substitute
37 Kind of voyage
39 Mailroom gizmo
40 Canadian singer Celine
41 Feelings of boredom
42 Dome covering
43 Paid explainer or interpreter
45 Gains again, as strength

47 Gusted

51 Look over cursorily

53 Boundary lines

55 Away from one's mouth

56 Boxer Max or journalist Bugs

60 Orwellian worker

62 "In the Hall of the Mountain King" composer

64 Expunges

66 Sandinista Daniel

69 Religious teachings, usually

71 Wild ones

72 Mild arguments

73 ___ Gay (famed bomber)

74 Play lightly, as a guitar

75 Article of food

76 Bitter-tasting

77 Cynical response

78 Line of cliffs

79 Damascus' land

81 Ankara cash

82 Cornhusker St.

83 "Harper's Bazaar" illustrator

MEDIUM

Across

1 Congratulations of a sort
5 Made to protrude
12 Gael's tongue
13 Doo starter
14 Chic Chanel
15 Silver screen wannabes
17 Couple's pronoun
18 Carnivorous dinosaur
20 Magazine or website parts, initially
21 Inits in mobile communications
22 70s tennis star
25 Like certain apostrophes
29 Half a dance?
30 Febrero preceder
31 Maker of many bar code scanners
32 Bothering with
34 Dept. heads
35 Secretly email
36 Priv. nonprofit
38 Book launch announcement
45 Clay square
46 California wine
47 Corrida shouts
48 Pewter component
49 1978 disco hit
50 Fix, as a bow
51 Leak through

Down

1 Vermin
2 Creative
3 Bygone Winter Palace resident
4 Shawl
5 Church service
6 ___ cross
7 Chief
8 Boy or Girl follower
9 Reaching suppliers
10 Eggshell color
11 Secret files
16 Highly volatile fuel, for short
19 "I see!" facetiously
22 Mover in a machine
23 NYSE unit
24 Big cylinders on meadows
26 Faced
27 Ventilator of yore
28 DVD forerunner
30 Env. attachment
33 Most treacherous for driving, maybe
34 Wanders about
37 Perceive
39 Seriously unpleasant
40 Italian grape-growing region
41 Country singer Chelsea
42 Lover's ultimatum ending
43 Best way to make a mistake
44 Not springtide

Across

1 Judicial seat
6 Hauling dues
12 Antique jar
14 Leave out in pronunciation
15 Female charmer of myth
16 "Sesame Street" librarian
17 Patricia of movies
18 Corset features
19 Heavy homework amount
22 Hawaiian entertainer
24 Kind of flask
26 Butting bighorn
27 Org. with weighing events
30 Succor
32 Drink of the gods
34 Fabric amts., often
35 "Coffy" star Grier
37 Long time followers?
38 Diet guru Jenny
40 Be inattentive
41 Blue Grotto spot
44 Henning of magic
46 Delon of cinema
47 Heads of a coin
50 Surprising game result
51 More flammable
52 Tons (as things to do)
53 Off. aides

Down

1 Bard's ability
2 Modern rock genre
3 PBS relative
4 Indian city, former Madras
5 Flaw in one's logic
6 One in an alterations business
7 Locals in Cardiff
8 Bush Supreme Court nominee
9 Gershon of "Face/Off"
10 Circular flow
11 Abundances
13 Use a teleprompter
20 Placed the ball
21 Predators on mice
23 Book editor Talese
25 Copied books
27 Was-bad? link
28 Folk legend Joan
29 Ice cream keepers
31 Drone regulator, for short
33 Eccentric oldsters
36 Bowler's neighbor in cricket
38 Wailed
39 Asian desert along the Silk Road
41 Hat lining
42 Brand served on the floor
43 Happens, in Havana
45 Iris holder
48 Bradbury's "___ for Rocket"
49 Unyielding

MEDIUM

Across

1 Spring addressee
5 Appealing to
  nostalgists
7 Strand up north,
  perhaps
8 Final defensive effort
9 Metric weights,
  for short

Down

1 Barley-based
  whiskey
2 Angular opening?
3 Kind of knife or
  sandwich
4 Parts of some
  portfolios
6 Conspiratorial clique

MEDIUM

Across

1 Smokes, briefly
5 ___ a kind (unique)
7 One-named British
  singer
8 Points at the dinner
  table
9 Broken-bone
  protector

Down

1 Jacket
2 Group of languages
  including Sanskrit
3 Davis who played
  Thelma
4 They may hit
  the ground running
6 Suffix with Oktober

MEDIUM

Across

1 Uses a Kindle
5 Villainous Disney
  parrot
6 Appeals to a higher
  power
8 Wedding bouquet
  flower
9 Ed of Hollywood

Down

1 Clothing mishap
2 Spouses of some
  countesses
3 Recurrently
4 Creator of Sherlock
  Holmes
7 Bashar al-Assad's
  country: abbr.

MODERN POULTRY FARM

Across

1 Secure quarters for clucking egg layers
11 Church cry
12 Hand grenade, in slang
14 Nuclear energy science
15 Infamous spy Mata
16 Ocean oasis
17 Shakespearean king
19 ___-walsy (intimate)
21 Infuriation
22 There are 6 in an inning
23 Naysaying
25 Eminem mentor, familiarly
26 Less polluted
27 Oblique cut
28 Degree div.
30 Occurs as if by fate
33 ___ verde (desert tree)
34 Candle shop allure
35 Clam cover
37 Stereotypes
39 Was decisive
41 Future JD's hurdle
42 Literary excerpt
44 Video game giant
45 Skilled craftsman
46 Modern ray catchers lowering the monthly bills

Down

1 Cardamom-infused beverage
2 Rash person
3 Shut off
4 Bedouin bearers
5 Interlocks
6 End-of-letter letters
7 Apollo acronym
8 Type of a man or word
9 Borneo primates
10 Minority member in India
13 ___ Bruno, Italian hermetist
18 Blazer feature
20 Grown forerunners?
22 Weirdos
24 Newspapers
26 Piano part
27 US one-cent coin material
28 Digestive glucose-maker
29 Banned
31 Clears the board
32 Trinidad's twin island
33 Stomach proteins breaker
36 Ornamental plant
38 Train with gloves
40 Black bears' lairs
43 1910s French avant-gardist Jean

Across

1 On ___
(in little space)
5 Jewish period
of mourning
10 Bothers constantly
14 Revolution prefix
15 "City Without Walls"
poet
16 Latin extension
17 Comes before
suggestion?
18 Fuse with heat
19 Long live, in Paris
20 ___ Billy, first film
cowboy star
22 Notch-like
24 Coaxed
26 Variant spelling of
a Hindu honorific
29 Convene
30 Sounded relieved
34 Luke's Jedi mentor
36 Fused, in botany
37 Band's quest
38 Disputed Asian
region
39 ___ Na Na
(retro singers)
40 Annual literary
awards
42 More adroit
44 Basic type of
question
45 Insurance company
bailed out in 2008
47 Craftily

48 Act jointly
51 Shower room sight
54 Remove,
as dead leaves
58 Fried cookie at a fair
59 Debilitated
61 Goddess in some
mandalas
62 New ___
(spiritual type)
63 Ferry stops, at times
64 Boris Johnson's
alma mater
65 Ely and Howard
66 Peril at sea
67 Cotillion figures

Down

1 Resident of Riyadh
2 Stern
3 "Leave ___ me"
4 Colorful lunar arch
5 Olympic skater
Cohen
6 Indulges
7 Fluor finish
8 Dense silky fabric
9 Jittery
10 Citizen of Las Vegas
11 On tenterhooks
12 Contributed
13 Winter glider
21 Place where coats
can be left
23 Passenger car
attachments

25 Teddy's cousin
26 Result of a three-
putt, often
27 Heed
28 "As the World Turns"
actor Jason
31 Impetuous,
like a decision
32 Merman in old
musicals
33 Term of affection
35 "Too Many Rappers"
rapper
36 Red Cross mission
41 Ship parts or news
readers
43 Speckled
45 Most suitable
46 Landscaping
equipment
49 Watery haven in
a desert
50 Yawning gulf
51 Animal that slayed
Adonis
52 2012 Ben Affleck
political thriller
53 Adolescent
55 Potent addon?
56 Messy eater, e.g.
57 One, in Austria
60 "Don't Bring Me
Down" band

Bonus Clue

Transfer the letters from the corresponding shaded squares above into this grid
to form the **name of a Simon & Garfunkel's hit**

1	2	3	4	5	6

7	8	9	10

11	12	13	14	15	16	17	18

19	20	21	22	23

MEDIUM

Across

1 Releases from one's grip
7 Savory Indian appetizer
13 Incarnation
14 Film conventions
15 Thrash
16 Consumers
17 Waiting room
19 Incredulous response
20 Challenge for a translator
22 Veteran
26 One guarded in a soccer game
27 "The Walking Dead" network
28 Four-time Australian Open queen
30 Word after pale or ginger
31 Loaded with calories
33 Industrial processor
35 Some geometric calculations
37 Logical lead-in
38 Software engineers
43 Fuel rating
45 Affectionate nickname
46 Vanderbilt in fashion
47 Join forces?
48 Old-style debt
49 Performs awfully

Down

1 ___ land (dream world)
2 Carell's "Almighty" role
3 Granny Smith descriptor
4 Tosses about
5 South American Cowboys
6 Left alone
7 Flower part
8 Natives of the Middle East
9 Chains built for travelers
10 Collapsible lid
11 Sun. message
12 Task giver
18 Workshop, in Paris
21 Blue shade
22 Revolutionary War battle
23 Turkish title
24 Bill of exchange receiver
25 Reduces in status
29 Section
32 African capital once known as Salisbury
34 Mogadishu native, perhaps
36 Braga of films
39 Bike speed
40 Activist Brockovich
41 Exposure
42 Card collector's quests
44 Calculator letters

Across

1 Domestication material
8 Angel's instrument
12 French white wine
13 Gains maturity
14 Wandering
15 Cerebellum section
16 Watcher
17 Herr's spouse
18 Brief digression
20 Having embarked
22 Type of tenure
23 Zzzzz
24 Help page initialism
25 One of Sherlock's tools
26 Friend of Che
27 Family-show rating
29 Neckties
30 HS lab class
31 How vegetables may be planted
33 Iotas
34 Feels unwell
35 Combusted
37 TV's "___ Team"
38 Capsize
41 Bowling great ___ Anthony
42 Basic substance or feature
43 Give drugs to (a person)
44 Painted screen behind an altar

Down

1 Old channel letters
2 Fish in a tuna roll
3 "Nikita" main actress
4 Wear away by rubbing
5 Inferno
6 Country dance formation
7 Disaffects
8 Humanoid hybrid with tusks
9 Greek marketplaces
10 Concrete support
11 Monikers
18 Connected
19 Madrid Mrs.
21 Fume
23 Carbonated drink
25 "___ & Stitch" (2002 film)
26 On the market, as a house
27 Took without right
28 Hamster healer
29 Haying machines
30 Automotive plating
32 Chinese greeting
33 Windshield attachment
36 Hard drive item
39 Ambient music whiz Brian
40 Shares on Twitter, briefly

72 "PORGY AND BESS" COLLABORATION

Across

1 Sorvino or Nair
5 Mount ___, Utah peak
10 "Diana" songwriter
14 Govt.-regulated business
15 Top-notch
16 Twin of Luke Skywalker
17 Verbalize
18 Largest moon of Saturn
19 Fish oars
20 "(If You Can't Sing It) You'll Have To Swing It" singer with unique, velvety voice
23 Period of sacrifice
24 Pueblo pots
26 Nautical lift
29 ___ the Rabbit (2023 for the Chinese)
33 Stomach remedy
35 Depraved
38 Common gimlet ingredient
39 Caller's need
41 Commercial suffix
42 Put out more of
45 Gone bad, in Britain
48 Decorative hanging tuft
50 Ham ___ (deli order)
51 Of considerable importance
54 Distinctive glow
56 Legendary trumpet player who said: "My whole life, my whole soul, my whole spirit is to blow that horn"
63 Toiling hard
64 Explore deeply
65 1/6th of a drachma
66 It gets a scoop
67 Certain duck
68 Dietary, in ads
69 Cold War country, briefly
70 Unwanted garden plants
71 Supermarket meat label, perhaps

Down

1 Remote button
2 EU lang.
3 Small water source
4 Of potassium-rich igneous rocks
5 Agree to participate
6 Grimly realistic
7 Airheaded sort
8 Kindle download, for short
9 Abstainer's choice
10 Fodder plant
11 "Elysium" director Blomkamp
12 Somewhat, slangily
13 Batteries in some toys
21 Salty Greek cheese
22 Angry people may hit it
25 Calm and dignified
26 Two-letter group
27 Cap-___ (head to foot)
28 Start of an ancient boast
30 Horatian verse form
31 Capital on the Danube
32 Graceful antlered animals
34 Apple cores, briefly?
36 Bleak crime fiction
37 "The Beverly Hillbillies" name
40 "___ So Shy" (Pointer Sisters hit)
43 Comparatively bold
44 Madras wrap
46 Cruise stop
47 Hot
49 Gave birth to a sheep
52 Chorus section
53 Becomes a member
55 Tech-support callers
57 Gush lava
58 Indy winner Luyendyk
59 Teased incessantly
60 NY theater award
61 Bene preceder
62 Crooner Campbell
63 Puncture opening?

Bonus Clue

Transfer the letters from the corresponding shaded squares above into this grid to form the **names of two Jazz legends**

1	2	3	4

5	6	7	8	9	10	11	12	13

14	15	16	17	18	19	20

21	22	23	24	25	26	27

Across

1 Unanimously
5 Mind reader
11 Fraternal T
12 Car sticker letters
14 Dynamic starter?
15 Exchanged
17 Hotel domestic
18 They're needed for passing
19 Ross of flag fame
20 Remiss
24 Hook's helper
25 Bit of Zen dialogue
26 My, in Montreal
29 Noted TV 41-Down
31 Twin city to Minneapolis
33 Some proctors, briefly
34 Left
36 Cacao cousin
37 Female-only refreshing area
39 Tempos
42 Annoying little bug
43 Fed. workplace monitor
44 Fizzy, sugarless beverage
47 European capital bombed in 2022
48 Pakistani tongue
49 Recycling holder
50 Turkish official
51 Pitchfork feature

Down

1 When dusk comes
2 Horror movie with many sequels
3 Choice on a French survey
4 Game-show host
5 Conjurer's command
6 Impetus, for short
7 Animal with three lids on each eye
8 Preliminary round of a race
9 The cornea covers it
10 Buffalo Bill's family name
13 Bound in chains
16 Steven of Aerosmith
19 Minor hit
21 Actress Watson
22 Launch forces
23 Stapled
26 Shortfin or longfin shark
27 Coin from overseas
28 Fast-paced, slangily
30 As-saying link
32 Docking spots
35 Fish and rice only sushi
37 Split, so to speak
38 Paid attention
39 Nose (around)
40 Clueless phrase
41 Master cook
44 Palindromic flop
45 Abbr. after a seller's suggested price
46 Disruptive noise

MEDIUM

Across

1 Wheeze
5 Part of a drum kit
11 "Rigoletto" solo
12 Common linguistic suffix
13 Carte preceder
14 Imagine, as a future event
16 Bad cholesterol
17 Gun ready to shoot
19 Epidemiological adjective
20 Rhythmic pattern in Cuban music
24 Selects by a vote
27 Fairy king of folklore
29 To trailer?
30 "Voice of Israel" author
31 Produce aisle find
33 Observe
35 Oblique-angled, four-sided figure
37 Wrist bones
39 Captivated by to the extreme
45 Expression of amazement
46 Best for bronchos
47 College Web site letters
48 Sort
49 Kudrow of "Friends"
50 Calls for
51 Snooty one

Down

1 Irish language family
2 Cartoon great Peter
3 Hindu deity
4 No longer owed
5 Model Klum
6 Synthetic rubber component
7 Sociable
8 Freeze
9 Fashion magnate Gucci
10 Of greatest height
15 Cut, as ties
18 Toboggan's cousin
21 Mesa howler
22 As blind as ____
23 Watery city
25 Award for an ad
26 Overflow (with)
28 Spoke too highly of
30 Talented
32 Electrical power networks
34 Convert chips into money
36 Running total in a tavern
38 Company cars, perhaps
40 Be a sign of
41 Crawled in water
42 Aromatic bath additions
43 Inner tube?
44 Exxon, formerly

Across

1 Deprives of energy or makes weak
5 Thermometer wielder
9 Feature of some modern stadiums
13 Checked for fit
14 One setting arguments
16 Commitment to the game
17 Particularized
19 Two-wheelers
21 Bygone Chrysler division
22 Bok ___ (Chinese cabbage)
23 Regarding
25 Easy basket
26 Amazon and Orinoco, to natives
27 ___-test (check the software for bugs)
30 Goes around
32 Famed Israeli defense minister
33 Decree or appoint to priesthood
37 Long-standing enemy
39 Cruise fan
41 Draw upon
43 Crisp salted biscuit
45 Big eel
46 Adler who intrigued Holmes
47 Skeletor's 37-Across
49 Part of a purchasing decision
50 Hindu music style
51 Express lane count
55 Flight attendant's workplace
56 Notorious Roman emperor
57 Introductory Greek letters
61 Ukrainian with a huge wealth and political influence
64 Struck wooden bars instruments
66 Prepare in a bread maker
67 Blew one's top and covered the local area in ash
68 Dark low cloud
69 Yields to pressure
70 Expression of approval
71 Alibi problems

Down

1 Use a dagger
2 Tincture for treating bruises
3 Slightly out of tune
4 Casual goodbye
5 Song sung on doorsteps
6 Break, as bad habits
7 Start to bath?
8 Gradually crumbles, as a shoreline
9 Portuguese explorer Bartolomeu
10 Movie director Preminger
11 Come up to
12 Politician, Turkish president
15 Fox or rabbit title
18 Transfer (legal rights)
20 Of a Nicosia's country (var.)
24 Sat for a painter
25 Most August babies
27 Yacht moorage
28 Keeping tabs on
29 Interior designer's strong skill
31 Gospel singer Andrews
32 Testifying in court
34 Not an original, informally
35 Prank starters, sometimes
36 Person acting on behalf of another
38 Flexible mineral sheet
40 Addict's treatment

42 "Dungeons & Dragons" beasts
44 Military unit of ancient Rome
46 Alpinist's winter must-haves
48 Without males
50 Itchy spots

52 Sachet for the pot
53 Printed mistakes
54 Teaching model
55 Skipper, briefly
58 Northern constellation
59 Sink stopper
60 Quick jumps

62 What a colon means, in analogies
63 Global oil and gas company
65 Large guest room in a traditional Albanian house

69

Across

1 Adult states of insects
7 Side of a roof
12 Mechanized, in combinations
13 Half-bull, half-man of myth
15 Gulf of ___, modern pirates realm
16 Wielding
17 Wine buyer's consideration
19 Enjoys the rink
20 Unskillful (as a painter)
23 "The Fountainhead" author Rand
24 Org. dues-payer
25 Bit of traditional medicine
29 Horrible must-do
33 Part of a walk
34 Classic automobile
35 ___-brainer
36 Shrek's territories
40 Observation
43 European capital built on seven hills
44 Manicurist item
46 Money-object bridge
48 Knee-length trousers
49 Email for the spam folder, probably
50 Utopian gardens
51 Deliberately avoids

Down

1 Dinar spenders
2 Reddit admin
3 Temporary disuse
4 No-hoper
5 Abrasive minerals
6 Pack number
7 "The Lower Depths" writer Maxim
8 Embassy diplomat
9 Attractant
10 The moon, in Lyon
11 Pieces of work
14 Parents' home, metaphorically
18 Cash sources
21 No, in Sochi
22 Gushing flattery
26 Quickly fade from memory
27 Camembert coat
28 Flourishes
30 Greek E
31 Keep under control
32 Present-day "carpe diem"
37 Drifts gracefully
38 Reached the ground safely
39 Modern-day horse-and-buggy travelers
40 Suffix with depend or defer
41 Mideastern royal family name
42 Laundry room accumulation
45 Ang or Spike
47 Pass

Across

1 Form of leather
7 Graph start?
11 Scout's mission, briefly
12 Mounded
14 Following behind
15 Cuban ballroom dance (var.)
16 Pledged fidelity
17 1955 "___ Camera"
18 Cheaply lustrous
20 Edible seed
22 Scared shout
23 Barbering obstacles
24 Lusty
28 Drug-yielding plant
29 Tampa Bay NFLers
30 Breakfast cereal
32 Thing above your eyeball
33 Bulge (out)
34 Old NYC subway inits
35 Plea upon bidding soldier goodbye
39 Le menu word
41 Identified
42 Hired escort
44 Late critic Roger
45 Fully-developed animals
46 Burn lightly
47 Dusty little bit
48 Korean name for waters near Japan

Down

1 Backwoods beast
2 French painter Matisse
3 Respond to, as a tip
4 Debates
5 Hell ___ (troublemaker)
6 High-pitched yell
7 Almost round purple fruit
8 Annual reference works
9 1860s gray, in short
10 Changes to fit
13 Words with no idea and no clue
19 Outpaced
21 Continental divide
23 Fair-hiring abbr.
25 Vowel-shaped beam
26 Laugh heartily
27 Berliner's cry
28 Sweet charm
30 Not telling
31 Summer quencher
32 Abstract Shiva representation
33 Full of jokes
35 Gael or Welshman
36 Sister's attire
37 Foreboding signs
38 Join
40 Small rodent
43 Answer to a bailiff

FASHIONABLE TREATMENTS

Across

1 Pressure therapy relieving chronic pain, stiffness and tense muscles
15 As to
16 Take odds
17 Diminish
18 Dishonest types, old-style
20 Meth.
21 Chemical suffix
22 Duke Ellington's "___ It Bad and That Ain't Good"
23 German painter Nolde
24 Type of Japanese syllabary
26 Chief Olympian god
27 Ballerina's costume
28 ___ Giannini, American banker
30 Put away a dagger
32 Pale in complexion
36 Distilled salvia herb
38 Know-it-all
42 Sci. of the galaxies
43 Vegas' st.
46 Swiss particle phys. lab
47 Coral island nation north of Fiji
49 Deadly pathogen
51 Be delirious
52 Like a camera stand
55 10-digit book ID

56 Tees off
57 Transparent gypsum
58 Baccarat device
59 Personal records
61 Enter furtively
62 Goes to the left
63 Summer hours on the Atl. coast
64 Bit of theatrics
67 Numerical prefixes
69 Hazard in frozen waters
71 Musical show without mikes
72 Was a glutton
75 Epoch in the Cenozoic Era
79 California-based oil company
80 Deal preceder
82 Electron acceptors
87 Talking penguin or rabbit, say
88 Sunroof cousin
89 Fireball in the sky
90 Capital east of Riyadh
91 Recital selections
92 "Looking for Mr. Goodbar" actor Richard
93 Crowd, in Turin
94 Illustrated
95 Cosmetic procedure used to refresh skin tone and texture

Down

1 Saucer, e.g.
2 New Age music superstar
3 Start for while
4 Acting Wilson
5 Flanged structural support
6 Racing legend Ayrton
7 Position
8 Body surface parasites
9 Learned one of yore
10 Stimulates
11 Jumper's opposite
12 Perfume compound
13 Scale
14 Piaf of song
19 Twist around (var.)
25 Immanuel ___, philosopher
29 Evaded
31 Leprechaun's land
32 Credit (to)
33 Tried to tarnish
34 Crop
35 Hemingway or Borgnine
37 More flamboyant
39 The Practice VIPs
40 Act the siren
41 Look that inflicts harm
43 Quality of an open desert area
44 Crowd jostler

45 Actress and activist Redgrave

48 In times gone by

50 Piece in a chess box

53 Force ___ (draw)

54 Jazzy Horne

60 Org. concerned with toy safety

65 Stop obsessing

66 Assisted (a felon)

68 Dorm denizen

69 Perversely amusing

70 Grim figure?

72 Muesli bits

73 Sound of a revving engine

74 Food-spoiling bacteria

76 Spanish seashore

77 Community outside the city

78 NFLer of San Fran

81 Aggravated

83 Tosses in

84 Maki seaweed

85 James of the "Divergent" films

86 Cut

Across

1 Contemplation or rest days
8 Car with a bar
12 One way to get to the top
13 Copied
15 Addendum conjunction
16 Tedium
17 Settle snugly
19 Redress
20 More cretaceous
22 Inferior of a brig. general
24 Terminal-to-hotel transport
25 Galleria display
28 John Smith's wage
32 Diamond holder
33 Hesitation sounds
34 Again, in the music notes
35 1984 Oscar winner Shirley
39 Hardly refined
42 Spanish rice dish
45 Adjustable work schedule
47 It may be capital
48 Translucent gemstone
49 Fault of an earthquake
50 Click to e-mail
51 Salon staffers

Down

1 Comic book publisher Lee
2 Amply skilled
3 Baritone part starter, in musical notation
4 Gravy ingredient
5 Streaming delay
6 Med. setup
7 Egyptian peninsula
8 Gridiron maneuver
9 Words between lay and the line
10 Convalesce
11 Wide-ranging adventures
14 Strong-spined volume
18 Rock that flows
21 Bend the knee, say
22 Throwaways
23 Eggs in labs
26 16th-century French satirist
27 Half of hexa-
29 Like a new version of a song
30 Finely formed
31 Largest continent
36 Regarding, in legalese
37 Poker stacks
38 Pola of early Hollywood
40 Living ___
41 Spore maker
43 Hitchhiker's request
44 Crumb carriers
46 Bath accessory

Across

1 Neeson in movies
5 Rounded like eggs
11 Jessica of "Sin City"
12 Marvelous, slangily
13 Bossy Stooge
14 Anchorage area
15 Blubber-stripped
17 Viking weapon
19 Knitting stuff
20 Famous exile site
23 Not connected
26 Autumn drink
28 Ticket info
29 Average Joe
32 Identify, in a way
34 Longtime Elton John label
35 Writer Sir Walter
36 Celtic, for example
38 Try, as something new
39 Artist Sedgwick
41 ___ Wars, series of 20th century Asian military conflicts
45 Large guns
48 Stands fronts?
49 British Empire decoration letters
50 Issa of "The Lovebirds"
51 Wind current catcher
52 Parades
53 1999 "___ Wide Shut"

Down

1 Small bed desk
2 Kulik on the ice
3 Assist in shady business
4 One dying for belief
5 Proposal
6 Window treatments
7 Goat of the Alps
8 Mantric syllables
9 Type of deer
10 News people, collectively
16 Extremely poor
18 Unrealized
21 Intermediate proof
22 Uncomfortable neckwear
24 Dignity
25 US surveillance plane
27 Peaceful
30 Balloted against
31 Talks through a film
33 Was accepted
37 Show good manners
38 Tostada relatives
40 Needle amounts
42 "A Doll's House" heroine
43 Dr. Watson outburst
44 Baseball team minimum
46 Litigator's org.
47 8-bit system, briefly

81 MEDIUM

Across

1 Grand Canyon pack animal
6 Strategic Mideast port
7 Looks after
8 Bobbing harbor marker
9 Sleep clinic issue

Down

2 Consume the last of
3 Like some long sentences
4 Make even brighter, say
5 Abbr. in a birth announcement
7 TV schedule inits

82 MEDIUM

Across

1 Destructive bacterio- suffix
5 One way to cook
6 Long range shooter aim improver
8 General on some menus
9 Be crazy about

Down

1 Grade schooler's adhesive
2 Happening now, as the game
3 Org.
4 Gaze at
7 Civil War side, for short

83 MEDIUM

Across

1 Garment below the waist
5 Man, objectively
6 Slogan creators
8 Causing skidding, maybe
9 Mercedes-Benz competitor

Down

1 Legalese future tense
2 Elementary school student
3 Combine well
4 Broadway theater awards
7 Euro forerunner

EARLY STARDOM ACHIEVERS

Across

1 Dashing
7 Chinese carvings
12 First name in whodunits
13 In the open
14 Small fishing boats
15 Temporary skin decorator
16 Measure of herring
17 Not as thick
19 Long. crosser
20 Things in eyeglass frames
21 Rattled weapons
24 Company shares, for short
26 Wicked
27 Use as a chair
29 Leg part
32 Suffix of shapes
33 Outside, in combinations
34 Fleming of filmdom
37 Addressed a deity
39 Somewhat
41 Nervous
42 Champagne designation
43 FDR's affliction
44 Of historic importance
46 Roofing installer
47 Tuesday preceder
48 Elegant flair
49 Writer Sheldon

Down

1 Portrayer of noted Hogwarts student
2 Ancient Athens hub
3 Gold standards
4 Pack ___ (give up)
5 Common pronoun
6 Gave a hard time to
7 Screen superstar that made her debut at the age of nine
8 Professes to be true
9 Most mindless
10 Carmaker Maserati
11 Any of this puzzle's theme persons
18 Allocation word
22 Cartoon monkey
23 Girl who achieved fame with the role in "E.T." movie
25 Actress given an own agent being only three years old
28 Polit. label
30 Misuse
31 In a righteous way
32 Divine female
35 Giggling syllable
36 Cooler, in brief
38 Disney's mermaid
40 Socially skilled
41 Real est. units
42 Frequent flyer
45 Fraternity letter

Across

1 Metrical foot of two syllables
5 Sami people
13 Go high
15 Norse trickster god
16 End of abyss?
17 Famous collie
18 Sun's path graph
20 At the wheel
22 Iconic 1990s computer game
24 Folk singer Axton
25 Big name in Old West justice
28 They precede self-defense
31 Recording of a sort
36 Supply that exceeds demand
37 Freedom Marcher's monogram
38 Coats of paint
39 Hollywood filming locale
40 Canoeist
42 Co-founder of Air Greenland (inits)
43 Avoids restaurants
45 Barrett of "Pink Floyd"
46 Teensy amount
47 Underwater breath-holder
49 Listless
50 Vidi, in English
51 Apple e-book reader
53 "Return of the Jedi" actor Guinness
56 With grassy undertones
60 Large, noisy parrot
63 Church hymn
65 ___-Magnon (early human)
66 Become less appealing
67 Engage in brainstorming
68 Rookies
69 Hit hard, as a baseball

Down

1 Different ending?
2 DuVernay et al.
3 Spray-bottle product
4 Batter's success
5 Not at all trusting
6 Sketch out
7 Ached
8 Nicknamed
9 Common cricket score
10 Oscar's cousin
11 Lambs' dads
12 Wooden strip
14 Attach, as a lure
19 Bottle to recycle
21 Florence's country
23 2018 Super Bowl champs
26 Needed to skip work, perhaps
27 Sound of approval
29 Dagger's partner
30 Everyone in 21-Down
32 Czar's edict
33 Legendary fabler
34 Talk idly
35 Disquisitions
37 Hot fad
40 Disney Channel target audience
41 Irving of the NBA
44 Slight incision
46 Certain halogen compounds
48 German classic on the road
49 Hairy, in a way
52 Of lesser importance, in law
53 Abbr. on a bank statement
54 Handed-down knowledge
55 Nobel Prize category, for short
57 Impersonation
58 One of a Navy elite
59 African tribe
61 "Tarzan" critter
62 Asphalt kin
64 "Family Guy" family member

Bonus Clue

Transfer the letters from the corresponding shaded squares above into this grid
to form the **awake-the-greatness motto**

1	2	3	4

5	6	7	8

9	10	11	12	13

14	15

16	17	18	19

20	21	22	23

MEDIUM

Across

1 Word of action
5 Carnival game
12 Chat room initialism
13 Determined cry
14 Vowel-sequence start
15 Taken to court
16 Star with attitude
17 Abbr. after Brooklyn or Cleveland
18 Like some TV
21 Mag. printing
22 One of a gene pair
23 Morse code snippet
24 Observes
25 Bambi's kin
28 It may have a twist
30 Boomers' kids: abbr.
31 Fictitious story
32 Starch from palms
35 iPhone purchase
37 2001 French romantic comedy
39 Marseille sight
40 2013 woman Wimbledon champ
44 Deg. for a yuppie
45 Has office hours
46 Author/poet Bates
47 Mr. Onassis, in headlines
48 Applaud
49 Equal in society
50 Portable lights
51 Mark of "Game of Thrones"

Down

1 Gluey
2 Mix mayo ingredients, say
3 Dimming gadget
4 Beach displays, informally
5 Brainteaser or coarse sieve
6 Melting spike
7 Groups of warships
8 Bump on a log
9 Diamond Head island
10 UFO-tracking org.
11 Maid of honor, sometimes
19 Hassle-free state
20 Surrender, as a legal right
26 In love
27 Cast out
29 Asian cuisine choice
30 Ending meaning attendee
31 Warm-blooded vertebrate
32 Burglar alarm part
33 Ancient name for Great Britain
34 Towering fantasy creatures
36 Monastery
38 Fabric pattern
41 Cadabra starter?
42 Favorable forecast, to farmers
43 Palm genre

Across

1 Took it easy
8 "Superman" journalist Lane
12 Making a scene, say
13 Facts, briefly
14 Wrinkles-removing toxin
15 Eric of "Hulk"
16 Backside
18 Spot specialist
21 Emporiums
22 Malay wavy dagger
23 "My Life" author Golda
25 Sicken
26 Green area next to the house entrance
30 Ancient Spain peoples
32 Goat's sound
33 Renders moist
34 Marshlike
35 Former European gold coin
38 Courtroom demand
39 Sunset prayers
42 Rip dramatically
43 Sand puppy (rodent)
46 When doubled, a freshwater South American turtle
47 DNA component
48 Gp with common goals
49 Fits back into place

Down

1 Sequel to a classic teen martial arts series
2 Hawaiian food fish
3 Halifax hrs
4 Mound-like shrines
5 Avian grabber
6 Shield used by Athena
7 Mark of knock
8 Volume setting?
9 TV studio sign
10 Otherwise
11 Takes off
17 Eastern potentates
19 Minute amount
20 Big victory margin
23 Castle fortification
24 Almost eternity
26 Cuts the carbs
27 Encompassed by
28 Steak preference
29 Payment types
31 Like Tutsi
34 Leblanc's burglar Lupin
35 Body layer
36 Parts of eyes
37 Coppers
38 Looks lustfully
40 Epps of "House"
41 Botanical joint
44 Fjord kin
45 Social critter

MARYLIN MONROE

Across

1 Nickname of the 50s and early 60s world sex symbol
14 More, as the saying goes
15 Toon explorer
16 Saigon's former foe
17 DOJ employee
18 Flabbergast
19 Nervous feeling
20 Director Joel or Ethan
21 Expiator
23 Road no
24 Bad-mouth
26 Brewpub staples
28 Give consent
32 Turner of rock
35 Fishing tool
38 Late-night talk pioneer Jack
39 Femoral
41 First words of the legendary serenade performed on 05/19/1962 at a Kennedy's meeting
44 Jeans length measurement
45 Te Kanawa of opera fame
46 Fast plane, for short
48 Unconventional one
49 Iranian oil port
51 Head of technology?
53 Avoid cleverly
57 Nutrition letters
60 Aggravation
64 Western Union co-founder Cornell
65 Scarcely detectable amounts
67 Skating site
68 Notice of demise, briefly
69 Love madly
70 Dog-trainer's shout
71 Glacial snow
72 This puzzle theme person's name before she became a pop culture icon

Down

1 More pitch-dark
2 Reveal, as feelings
3 Path start?
4 "It's Gonna Be Me" boy band
5 Ancient literary work
6 Captain's charge
7 Pasta that looks like rice
8 Frenzied woman
9 Instagram action
10 Sci-fi's Solo
11 Dept. in many universities
12 In need of directions
13 Not figurative
22 Actress Carmen
25 Certain sorority member
27 Texas Holdem alternative
29 Caribbean UK territory
30 Taxi
31 Eleniak or Slezak
33 Investments for old age: abbr.
34 Side in a vote
36 Expression of dread
37 Hyphen-like punctuation
40 Kind of German white wine
42 Unskilled laborer
43 Disburden
44 Spanish or Portuguese
47 Tab grabber
50 Foreign stock exchange
52 On the ocean blue
54 "Glassheart" singer Lewis
55 Turkic tongue
56 Determination
58 Dummy
59 Valid conclusion?
61 Oscar-winner Moreno
62 ___ awful way
63 Terrier breed
66 Activate, as a bomb

Bonus Clue

Transfer the letters from the corresponding shaded squares above into this grid
to form the **titles of two movies starring this puzzle's theme thespian**

1	2	3	4		5	6	7	8		9	10		11	12	13

14	15	16	17	18	19		20	21	22	23	24	25	26	27

MEDIUM

Across

1 Cold-water craft
6 Funds hold in trusts
12 Market section
13 "Green Book" Oscar winner Mahershala
14 Charge that might be hidden
15 Hank of yarn
16 Problem drinker
17 Bass appendage
18 Put out feelers before acting
21 Powers of spydom
22 Amassed
27 Major river of Pakistan
29 Commission
30 Some premium seating
31 Encipherer
32 Not particular or specific
34 One looking at a funny picture
36 Glow-up materials
42 Chairman of China
43 Cartridge contents
44 Food thickeners
45 Drink, informally
46 Mil. abbreviation
47 Performance space
48 Vehicles without wheels
49 Sudden sharp sensations

Down

1 Remove a cork
2 Karaoke necessity
3 Finishes a cake?
4 Take ___ (lose one)
5 Clark of the Daily Planet
6 Relent a bit
7 Applies the brakes
8 Commendation for bravery
9 Criminal
10 Low dam built across a stream
11 You can come to yours
19 Transport proceeds of robbery
20 Touch part of heating element
23 Debut discussed in the WSJ
24 Southern wormwood
25 Antagonist
26 Ridiculing
28 Dream Team jersey letters
30 Big scallion
31 Cookie bits
32 Wall climbing lizards
33 Red-ink entries
35 Midday ritual
37 Scottish Highlander
38 Washrooms, briefly
39 Marvin Gaye's "Can ___ a Witness"
40 Junior spoiler, perhaps
41 Oater fare

MEDIUM

Across

1 At the end of the event's duration
11 African master
12 Around the corner
13 Hagiography subjects
14 Name in fine stationery
16 Affront, in street slang
17 Wrestling venue
18 Abbreviation for the rest
21 Chef
23 Dishonor
25 Allergic reaction
29 No duality theories
31 Embarrassing loss
32 Like the WTO
33 Desdemona's husband
35 Take in gradually again
37 Golf's ___ Cup
38 Cable sports network award
40 Fed. benefit
41 Unaffectedly trusting
45 Drips in an ICU
47 Strong fiber
48 Chaplet
51 Low land between hills
52 Explosive stuff
53 Fast aquatic railway

Down

2 Bouncers org.
3 Light lead-in
4 Palm's place
5 Emulates the sirens
6 Rope used by Wonder Woman
7 Quarterback options
8 Rupture
9 Night out
10 Cal's twin brother in "East of Eden"
13 Wrinkle fighters
15 Indoor pool
19 Something to gnaw on
20 Slopes
22 Farm drier
24 Tower for grain storage
26 Deuce taker
27 Clings (to)
28 Hybrid pack animals
30 Crowds
34 Ukraine's coin
36 One in a whirl
39 Large musical instrument
42 1871 Verdi debut
43 Peace-hand link
44 View from a mount
46 Certain admission exams
49 Police dept. rank
50 Ahead of, in verse

Across

1 Withdraws
10 Shut dramatically
14 African plant used in many lotions
15 Fictional lover from Verona
16 Type of equestrian contest
17 Occupying first place on a leaderboard
18 Ephron and Charles
19 Standard monetary unit of China
20 Gold coins of ancient Rome
22 On duty, as a politician
24 Table of contents page, often
26 Parlous
27 Gripping parts of gecko footpads
31 Fairy tale boy who outsmarts a witch
33 Member of the herring family
35 Pulpy refuse
39 In this location
40 Sheriff is one
43 Hoodwink
44 Madison and Lexington in NYC
45 Relating to sight and the eyes
46 Electrical impedance units
47 Republican, on an election map
48 Stick plus pocket
49 In-of linkup
50 Loss of words condition
52 Textual analyst
54 More repellent for the observer
57 Pacific starch sources
58 Italian restaurant serving
61 Involving only main features
63 FR, DE and PL economy
65 Finishes awarded with bronze medals
70 Mine egress
71 Two-color treats
73 Darer's cry
74 Give as a source
75 President Grant's given name
76 Certain MP3 player
77 Did groundwork?
78 Non-ordained preachers

Down

1 Lea sounds
2 Lead-in to cumulus or stratus
3 Like a cucumber, in a saying
4 Hat for De Gaulle
5 Hudson of "Ghostbusters"
6 Scooby-___ (toon canine)
7 Hindu drink of immortality
8 Use a support
9 Just fine
10 Secret agent movie genre
11 Fashion maven Vuitton
12 Shakespearean lament
13 Mint product
21 Three, in Bonn
23 Strictly controlled refrigerant
25 For next to nothing, in slang
27 Much of Libya
28 Soccer team count
29 Marine mollusk that damages ships
30 Causes massive wonderment
32 Private-sector rocket launcher
34 Of blossoms
36 Increasingly uncomfortable
37 Arrive back to consciousness
38 Eventuates
41 Oz. and others
42 Stingy hoarders

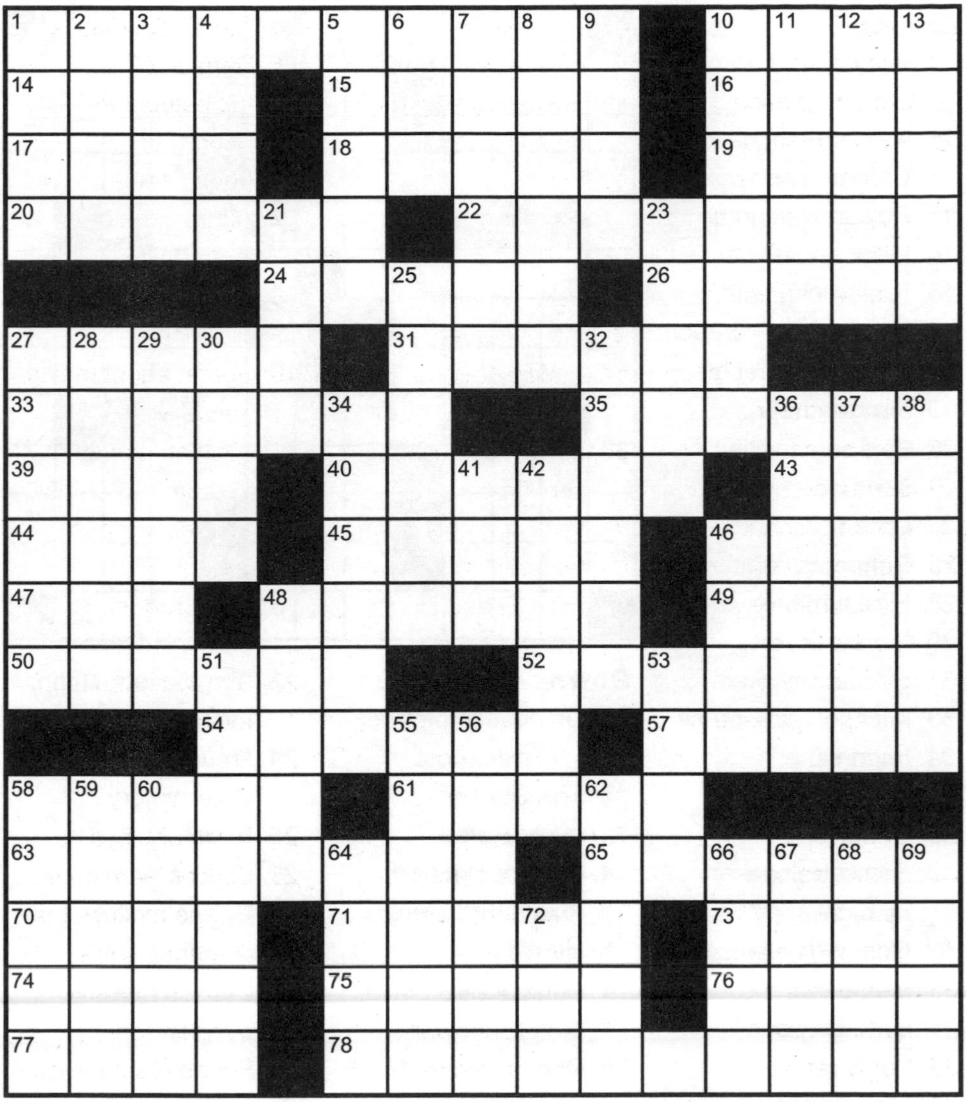

46 Gymnast Korbut or actress Kurylenko
48 Havana item
51 Underwent change
53 Imprint vividly
55 Region north of Morocco
56 Casual diner
58 Pinkish yellow
59 Sound component of a broadcast
60 Afflict
62 Utterance at a front door
64 One-time German chancellor
66 Brief admission
67 Part of a boxing ring barrier
68 Designer Christian
69 Govt. guidelines
72 Competitive rower's equipment

92

MEDIUM

Across
1 Alleys away from the main road
10 Calgary's prov.
11 Colorful pond carp
12 Pull an all-nighter
14 Litter's smallest
15 Really long time
16 Bye-bye, in Florence
17 Humming deeply
19 Tennis shots
20 Like some repair services
22 Lace tips
26 Bahamas capital
29 Fine furniture wood
30 Florida resort
31 Siouan speakers
33 Michael Jackson hit
34 Imprints, as in memory
36 Unbarred
39 Schwarzenegger, by birth
43 Coat with a precious metal
44 B. A. Baracus portrayer
45 May Sarton's "___ Are Now"
46 Lockmaker of note
47 End-of-page abbreviation
48 Blood flow blockage
49 Amusement park attraction

Down
1 Unfocused picture
2 ___ extra cost
3 The Censor of old Rome
4 Items for knitters
5 Pixar characters
6 Herald
7 Ancient Athens public meeting
8 Dumas' musketeers, for example
9 Defunct Swedish automaker
10 Scientific study of excavations
13 Anti-insect curtain
18 Procrastinator's words
21 Most meek
23 "Pygmalion" author's monogram
24 Mauna ___ Observatory
25 Beget
27 Used a rocker
28 Self-reflective question
32 Sautéed shrimp serving
33 Present
35 Inflicts pain
37 Edith, the Little Sparrow
38 Fashion periodical
40 Census form info
41 Buried treasure location, often
42 Badly off base: abbr.

88

MEDIUM

Across

1 Groupings of eight
6 Bulging
11 Meson that is a nuclear binder
12 Florida beach
14 HCl, for one
15 Shrinking Asian lake
16 Suffer illusions
18 Thicken, as a mystery
19 Shows assent
21 Possessed, old-style
22 Curious thing
24 Counting from
26 Head of a crime syndicate
27 Georgia Tech's sports org.
30 Noisy dove
32 Pursues with bloodhounds
34 Reflected in silence
37 Very big wind
38 Capital of ancient Egypt
40 Goes against
43 Involving public disorder
44 Pacific Coast salmon
45 Quaint street lighter
46 Units
47 Need a bandage
48 First name of the first woman on the Supreme Court

Down

1 Silvery fish
2 Summer droner
3 Slogged away
4 Interminable
5 Blank
6 Certain Fed
7 Plateau
8 Prominent bone behind the ear
9 Phrase upon duty calling
10 ___ favor
13 Venezuela divider
17 Mood rise
20 Church council
21 Owner of Regency hotels
23 Considered
25 Questionable remedy
28 Extremely important
29 Locomotive trailer
31 Caesar's point of no return
33 Portion
35 Dueler's attendant
36 Swimming actress Williams
39 Gate closers
41 Frog relative
42 McGwire's onetime home-run rival
43 Old specification of PC monitor

FEEL-GOOD MOVIES OF THE 2000s

Across

1 Cinematic story of a British single lady in pursuit of Mr. Right
14 Bananas
15 Whale-killing back of a harp?
16 Thing given as a concession
17 Average fellow
18 Clarifying phrase
19 Asian part of Turkey historically known as Asia Minor
21 Julio's home
22 Well, in France
23 Kuwaiti money
24 Point maker
26 Winged celestial being
28 Evening dress?
31 Scattered
34 Re-chewed food of a ruminant
35 Poet Shelley
38 2006 Disney movie with the "Breaking Free" song
44 Al's nemesis
45 In a loop
46 Punch
48 Pro camera choices, in brief
49 Indochinese republic
50 Ancient Italy dweller
52 Enshroud
54 Auto dial

57 Makeup of some cabins
58 Rocks, in a Bonn bar
59 Schubert religious masterpiece
63 Very, to Vivaldi
64 Coppola's romantic comedy-drama about two people who met in Tokyo
67 Set apart, as funds
68 Big inits in Dutch banking
69 Marsh duck or bluish shade
70 Prepares the way for
73 Neutralize
78 The ___, annual noted telecast
81 Sculptor James ___ Fraser
84 Kazan of filmdom
85 Nuclear physicist Niels
86 Recipe measure
89 Irish ancestor
90 "Old MacDonald" repeating fragment
91 No longer in active serv.
92 DUI's excess
93 Exclamation of disbelief
94 2009 hit which won eight 78-Across and four Golden Globes

Down

1 Tells
2 "Riveting" poster girl
3 More wintry
4 Designer Karan
5 Cager Kukoc
6 Actress Crawford
7 Ready to serve
8 YMCA grammar class
9 ___-disant (so-called)
10 Painful muscle twinge
11 Open a tad
12 Bouquet beauty
13 Every twelve months
19 Special-purpose
20 Augur
21 Trig ratio, briefly
25 Income stat word
27 Head-turning summons
29 Checkers move
30 Score words for a pair
32 Horse halter
33 Action to avoid
36 Filled type of pasta
37 Grip
38 "Siddhartha" author
39 Venom
40 Opal glowing in bright light
41 Innkeeper, e.g.
42 Choice conjunctions
43 Frame band

47 Quark/antiquark particle
49 Actor Zachary
51 Rorschach test component
53 Mad ___
54 Chorus line syllable
55 Fails to be, casually
56 Beer purchase
60 Blyton of kid-lit
61 High-elev. spots

62 Bickers
63 French Sudan, now
65 From the sun
66 Burdened
67 Brick buildings
71 Aerospace starter
72 Of the Vatican
74 Tone of old photos
75 Defense of a sort
76 Cooking implement
77 Dullish

79 Pot contents
80 800-year Chinese dynasty
82 Restaurant freebie, perhaps
83 Particular places
87 Brain wave record, initially
88 Popular machine

91

Across

1 Tilt somewhat
6 Damnable
12 Serology ratio
13 Craggy hilltop
14 Cycle opening
15 Violet head?
16 Annals excerpt
17 Lust ending
18 Illinoisan supermodel and television personality with a characteristic mole
21 Unnatural whiteness
22 Get more attendees
27 Large Japanese wrestlers
29 Traditional wisdoms
30 Entertained
31 Like some superheroes
32 Cylindrical arbor
34 Mooring line
36 Catwalk icon and the first Black woman on the covers of French and British "Vogue"
42 Convivial
43 ___ King Cole
44 Befitting a monarch
45 Skating champion Midori
46 Shaggy beast
47 Well beyond plump
48 Fencing moves
49 Ruminated (over)

Down

1 Plaster product
2 1953 Leslie Caron role
3 Abbr. on a letter
4 Geeky person
5 Highchair feature
6 Devoured without cooking
7 Pink marine substance
8 Slides to, as snake
9 Calvinist, for one
10 Cowboy-boot attachment
11 Spanish language features
19 Financial report preparers, in brief
20 Came upon
23 Spat ending?
24 Grand prize
25 Vision
26 Detroit team
28 Praiseful piece
30 Close, in a search
31 Duck dish
32 Internal entry passage
33 Vegged out
35 Hardly enough
37 Bibliographical info, for short
38 Gun on stage, e.g.
39 1930s-'40s pitcher Newsom
40 Admirer from afar, maybe
41 Emit amplified light

Across

1 High points
6 TV host Conan
11 Arizona city on the Colorado
12 Dipl. official
14 Ecto- opposite
15 Strike callers
16 Small, in dialect
17 Alteration canceler
18 Snap judgements
21 Unconscious prototypes of personas (in Carl Jung's works)
22 Refines, in a way
26 Small dining chairs
30 Hampers
32 Nocturnal noisemaker
33 Parts of the lungs
35 Cruel Athenian lawgiver
36 Types of steaks
38 Urban preacher
44 Dispense drinks
45 Cistern
46 Bank seizure, briefly
47 Altar alcove
48 "The X-Files" subjects, for short
49 Command to a helmsman
50 Lacked something essential
51 Minty seasonings

Down

1 Hindu medicine with doshas
2 Predator of ungulates
3 Some "World of Warcraft" minions
4 Green in hand
5 "The Crucible" setting
6 Binds legally
7 Electrical circuit part
8 Absorbed by, as a hobby
9 Big name in organic foods
10 Forget-me-___
13 Aluminum silicates
19 Prepare for the jacuzzi
20 Disliked person
23 CTRL-ALT-___
24 Digital distribution of entert. content
25 Swayed back and forth
27 Gershwin of note
28 Tokyo-based IT co.
29 Spelunking sites
31 Placed in a schedule
34 Data entered
37 ___ and Young
38 Plane measure
39 Be a sot
40 Stratagem
41 Get on one's knees, perhaps
42 Captain's spot
43 Blunt-tipped weapon

97 MEDIUM

Across

1 Dandy
4 Attention-getting sound
6 One-on-one academic helper
7 Picture postcard features
8 Old broadband type

Down

1 Unconstrained in movement
2 Hall's partner
3 Move in a predatory manner
4 Off-road buggy, for short
5 Miss after marriage

98 MEDIUM

Across

2 Title that means wealth
4 Disgusting
6 Aggravation, so to speak
8 Lhasa ___, breed of dog
9 Stinging remarks?

Down

1 Costume party headwear
2 Omits
3 Tavern offerings
5 Sticking point, of a sort
7 ___ Fighters, rock band

99 MEDIUM

Across

1 Drug in Shatner stories
5 Impose, as a ticket charge
7 Of element no. 76
8 Calif. wine valley
9 "Waterfalls" girl group

Down

2 Actress Pataky
3 Meticulously maintained
4 Times Sq. locale
6 Blood sample container
7 Prov. bordering Hudson Bay

FOUND IN THE OLD OFFICE

Across

1 Classic database for storing contacts
9 Indigenous people of Manitoba
10 Quality or character of sound
12 Asimov or Newton
14 Needs scratching
16 Swindler's victim
18 Citizenship Day mo.
19 Internet address numbers, briefly
22 Bulb holders
24 Vancouver pro
26 Cow of milk commercials
29 Scalawag
30 Battle injury
31 Bikini, e.g.
32 Winged singers
33 Golfer Ko
34 Disney head, once
36 Leg extender
38 Suffix with social
39 Deep Blue corp.
42 Less common
44 Anterior wings in beetles
46 Irritated
49 Electronics giant
50 Donate
51 Vintage product used to create one or more copies simultaneously

Down

1 Caustic
2 Some ER staffers
3 "Narcos" org.
4 Realize, as a profit
5 Quake
6 Alternative to Rx
7 Amazed outcries
8 All fours part
11 Glimpsed
13 Handy device that performs arithmetic operations
15 Machine for penners and reporters made by Christopher Sholes in 1868
17 Heist haul
20 Birthday celebration
21 Headband
23 Thorny shrubs
25 Sweet tangelos
27 ___ Islam
28 Alaska, often
31 Friends in a cause
32 Fuse, in a way
35 Process footage
37 Sun Valley site
40 Bipartisan coalition
41 Certain starling
43 Latvia's capital
45 Norse sky god
47 Gloss destination
48 "Rich Girl" rapper

Across

1 Message including photos, in brief
4 Dolphin's limb
10 New Orleans clock setting, initially
13 Of a vowel sound
15 Dianion in spinach
17 Generate
18 Articulated
19 ___ course
20 Lineup on a computer screen
22 Hawk, as food
23 Gate-breaking small bomb
25 In la-la land
26 Tends to, as an icy sidewalk
29 Jigsaw puzzle components
31 Whereness (archaic)
33 Be rude at the dinner table
34 "Counter-Strike" genre, briefly
37 European short-horned animal
39 Writing rooms
41 VCR button
42 Was a pilot
44 Captivated
45 Pampered pet
47 Toys requiring wind
48 Driver's invitation
51 Fruit blemish
53 Graph lines
54 Country between Togo and Nigeria
55 Toned-down expletive
59 Less glowing
61 In the form of a pipe
63 Legendary city of Perseus
64 Oklahoma Native American
65 Lead-in to haw
66 Certain derivative contract
67 Compass dir.

Down

1 Annual sports award recipients
2 Something extra
3 Gentleman in a kilt
4 Global pandemic of 1918-19
5 According to law
6 Polar formation
7 Ones battering
8 Nos on the office switchboard
9 Tattler
10 Insertion mark
11 Old British carbines
12 Kid's bear
14 Made fit
16 ___ Stadium, home of the 49ers
21 Reproduction's opp.
24 Singer Gloria
25 Refutes
26 Browse the Web
27 Take ___ (react to applause)
28 Told falsehoods
30 Blanchett who won an Oscar for "The Aviator"
32 Puppy's plaint
34 Binding order
35 Texas pop star Aguilar
36 Transatlantic fliers, once (inits)
38 Military police cap in many countries
40 Withered
43 Like secondhand clothing
45 Fine glove material
46 Stringed instrument
48 Over-the-top, as acting
49 Yellow-and-white flower
50 Concord
52 Habituate
54 Gallant
56 ___ unto itself
57 Nope's kin
58 Become taller
60 Data: abbr.
62 Relief preceder

Bonus Clue

Transfer the letters from the corresponding shaded squares above into this grid to form the **sentiment shared by Oscar Wilde**

1	2	3	4	5

6	7

8	9

10	11	12

13	14	15	16	17	18

19	20	21	22	23	24	25	26	27

Across

1 Venezuela's Chavez
5 Thu. preceder
8 Batting figs
12 Mighty-oak link
13 Vote in favor
14 When doubled, a Pacific island
15 God's head?
16 Like certain wines
17 Served a winner, in tennis
18 George Orwell's alma mater
21 Recording area
22 Change to suit the conditions
26 Author's alias
30 Racket
32 Land, as a fish
33 Menu section
35 ___ Martin, wheels for the 007
36 Babbler
38 Grayish layered thick cloud
43 Pastures
44 Oil-drilling machinery
45 Corner PC key
47 Confront boldly
48 Ancient hail
49 Lingerie edging
50 Commodious boats
51 "___ So Bad" (Tom Petty song)
52 FBI workers

Down

1 Ate a romantic dinner, perhaps
2 It may be extended
3 Competitive activity with rules
4 Attending to the matter
5 Had no being
6 Binocular part
7 Unscrambling device
8 Edible mollusks
9 Viva ___ (by word of mouth)
10 Olympic champ Louganis
11 Grammy winner born in Nigeria
19 Grooms at old taverns
20 Outline drawing
23 Request payment
24 Qty
25 Intentions
27 Aviation stat
28 "O ___ babbino caro" (Puccini aria)
29 Assigns high status
31 Drinks platter
34 Contend
37 Showing keen interest
38 Popular Italian car, informally
39 Drama king?
40 Bulletin board sticker
41 West-coast sch.
42 Dateless party
46 Store slip, for short

Across

1 Global time standard
4 Gossip papers for older kids
11 Female carnivore
13 Teen facial affliction
14 Least desirably
15 Avoid on purpose
16 Certain audition
18 Trojan War warrior
19 Urban settlement
22 Length measures, for short
23 Smart remark
26 Far from calm
28 Dexterous
30 Stocking fiber
31 Cocktail garnishes
32 Business phone no. add-on
33 Steelers conference letters
35 Call in a waiting room
36 Makes minor revisions to
38 Heavy woven hangings
42 Se-al or se-er linkup
43 Less resonant
45 Dundee damsel
46 Competitive final stage
47 Mormon tea ingredients
48 Among, in poetry

Down

1 19th century British statesman
2 Sch. in Cambridge
3 Pulls, as a barge
4 Foreign land
5 Main idea
6 High self-___
7 A schooner has two
8 Need an ice pack, perhaps
9 Serengeti herd
10 Email condition, sometimes
12 Out of the question
17 Twangy in speech
20 Blackish form of quartz
21 Fight reminder
23 Lively dance
24 Writer Haley
25 Started moving
27 Acts the rodent
29 Root for herbalists
31 Small cousin of the flute
34 Shackle
36 Emotionally strained
37 Bub
38 Part of an anthology
39 Initialism of urgency
40 Upper-crust
41 Thailand's former name
44 Defunct UK label

Across

1 Recognized flower and tree of Virginia
12 Cave dweller's diet
13 Camera named for a goddess
14 DOD intel arm
15 Forgets to include
16 Trendy vegetable
17 ___ moss (type of fertilizer)
18 Spanish step
19 Written reminder
20 Equally
21 River of Pittsburgh
23 Throat danglers
24 Beautiful symbol of two union members
29 Execute, archaically
30 Tableware
34 Flying whiz
35 Commander in chief, for short
37 Pai ___ ("Kill Bill" tutor)
38 Three-eyed, say
41 Dogpatch resident
43 Georgia's floral emblem which name derives from one of the native tribes
46 Of Cambridge
49 Home of Taj Mahal
50 Mountain nymph
51 Glacier breakaway
53 Cosmonaut's insignia, once
57 Indecent
58 Lugosi of "Dracula" fame
59 Instrument in the violin family
60 Slick surface in winter
61 Grp that helps stranded drivers
62 Hunter in the sky
63 Bright orange plant commonly seen at the Golden State roadsides

Down

1 Per unit, informally
2 First word, often
3 Ivy Leaguers
4 Modernizes, as a factory
5 Platform for Siri
6 Cleverly effective
7 Allot
8 Ending of sugars
9 Baseball pioneer Buck
10 Tennis star Naomi
11 Appointments
16 Musical gang leader?
17 Jam fruits
19 Part of a fountain pen
20 Bell-ringer of commercials
22 Agitated (with up)
23 Applications
24 Comedian Sandler
25 Just a little, in music
26 Hammer's end
27 Best
28 R-V connection
31 Dido "___ Angel"
32 Cask sediment
33 Regal term of address
35 Proletarian
36 Contraction in old hymns
39 Eight united
40 Paper-ballot bit
41 Fizzy prefix
42 Mexican laborer in agriculture
44 ___ Zor-El aka Supergirl
45 Bird-to-be
46 Baby's ailment
47 Tropical palm
48 Flight support
51 Bull's counterpart
52 Flair
54 Staple alternative
55 Hoof sound
56 Small liqueur glass
58 Chinese steamed bun
59 Badge wearer

Bonus Clue

Transfer the letters from the corresponding shaded squares above into this grid
to form the names of Pennsylvania and Ohio symbolic plants

1	2	3	4	5	6	7	8		9	10	11	12	13	14

15	16	17	18	19	20	21		22	23	24	25	26	27	28	29	30

Across

1 Some coding projects
5 Underwater quake aftermaths
12 Ancient Semitic idol
13 Type widths
14 Deeply engaged
15 New shares recipient
17 Words before many words?
18 Not spiritual
19 Modern camera feature
20 Italian polymath Vilfredo
22 Cruises the Net
26 Muscle cords
29 Authoritarian regime
31 To be neatened, as beds
32 Absinthe flavor
34 Connective tissue
37 ___ above (better)
40 Short passes-filled soccer way of play
44 Hoops Hall-of-Famer Thurmond
45 Uncommon thing
46 Luau instruments
47 Collections of sayings
48 Pigeon shed
49 Blood out-heart contractions
50 Had liabilities

Down

1 Puts an end to
2 Opposite of flushed
3 Tree common in Miami
4 Sty food
5 Neon fish
6 Defame
7 Of no value
8 Late senator John McCain, for one
9 Hand-held grinding stone
10 ___ facto (therefore)
11 Treads loudly
16 Upper part
21 Shakespeare's fairy queen
23 Network absorbed by The CW
24 Data storage acronym
25 Least hilly
27 Sentient beings not from Earth, initially
28 NBA's Unseld
30 Fundamental
31 Zeus grandfather
33 Rubbed off the page
35 Actress Keaton
36 Sticky green pods
38 Encrusted
39 Beehive State natives
41 South-of-the-border order
42 Openly declare
43 High flyer

Across

1 Druid, for one
6 Saturation
11 Greek salad sprinkle
12 Young Obi-Wan portrayer
13 "The Lost City" co-star Channing
14 Suffix
16 Barcelona beach
17 Really little
18 Huckster's line
20 Awake far past midnight
24 Academy trainee
28 Lifters
30 Nerve part
31 Looting spree
32 Font-related letterspacing
34 Not shared with anyone else
36 Lane boundary, in bowling
37 Invisible household hazard
39 Marriage
42 Pizza cookers
46 Northern cruise destination
47 Infective particle
48 Policy wiz
49 Small fishing boat concern
50 Muscle twinges
51 Yard tools

Down

1 Medley
2 Drying-up Asian sea
3 Job opening?
4 Alison Moyet "___ Like You"
5 Indian salutation
6 Certain raccoon
7 Obnoxious (var.)
8 Wister who wrote westerns
9 Pontiac Le ___
10 "Toy Story" youngster
15 Bit of fowl language
19 Employment benefit
21 Unpleasant sensation
22 Common symbol in heraldry
23 Footnote indicators
25 Step out
26 Fried-chicken leftover
27 Immerses
29 Utah state flower
33 Spill
35 Pool-room triangle
38 Barters
39 Axioms
40 Raindrop sound
41 Turner on screen
43 Roman life
44 Viking history VIP
45 Art class figure

Across

1 Dark enchanted timberland of "Harry Potter" book series
14 High-pitched instrument
15 Former Houston athlete
16 War god of Greek mythology
17 Strap for stopping a horse
18 Must, jocularly
19 Backup, in titles
20 Actor MacLachlan of "Twin Peaks"
21 Winged archer
22 Musical silence
23 Shirt spoiler
25 Perfectos, e.g.
26 Insulating material, for short
29 Aesthetic pursuit
30 Lord's land
31 Do something in response
33 Really excite
35 Flood
37 Says over
42 Tesla invention
43 Deafening
45 Assist, as a theater patron
46 Adorn brilliantly
48 Untroubled
50 Drop in standard

52 Like some wine casks
53 Study of events
57 Education basics, briefly
59 ___-Blo (fuse type)
60 Conveniently available
61 Determined person
63 Major tributary of the Missouri
64 College admissions bigwig
65 Grounded Australians
69 Winter weather accumulation
70 Mints in a roll
71 Angle ratio
72 ___ opportune moment
73 Inducing goose bumps
74 Noble Italian family of Ferrara
75 Tree-covered area inhabited by Winnie-the-Pooh and his friends

Down

1 Setting piece
2 Faithfully follow commands
3 Get in an agitated state

4 "Seinfeld" character Elaine
5 Folded corner
6 Crystalline intrusive rock
7 Singer and pianist Sir ___ John
8 Midcourt sights at tennis tournaments
9 Term of address in a monastery
10 Bring ruin on
11 Author Jong and others
12 Distinguish
13 African fly that carries a threat
22 Track official with a stop watch
24 Body designs, informally
25 Et ___
26 Listed cost
27 Defense mechanism in animal kingdom
28 Native Trinidadian, perhaps
30 Factual info
32 Destroy selectively
34 Detroit's pro football team
36 Expose to danger
38 Not on shore
39 Shipbuilder's woods
40 Item in an atelier
41 Courtroom shorthander

44 Of poor quality (informal)
47 How most writers work
49 Made a rip in
51 Variable
53 Triumphant shout
54 As found
55 Tribal healer
56 Remnant
58 Kitchen helper
61 ___ incognita (unexplored area)
62 Fix, as a lining
64 Evidence of ownership
66 Seasoning in Japanese cuisine
67 Golden rule word
68 Favorable position in a tournament
70 Bee chaser?

MEDIUM

Across

1 Relating to coats of arms
8 Veni, vidi, ___
12 Palatal hangers
13 Primitive fellow
15 Fruit high in potassium
16 Send packing
17 Not as meaty
18 Any dogwood family tree
19 Shade providers
20 Lock type
21 Amateurs no more
22 Roll up tightly
23 "Superman" villain Luthor
25 Cutie pie
26 Migraine precursors
27 Taxonomic suffix
28 Director Lee
29 Ball stands
30 Campaign expense
31 Cause of a rush
32 Residue
33 Powerful Greek deities
36 Semi-sheer fabrics
38 Acknowledge
39 Whole
40 Teacher in dojo
41 Inadequately small in number
42 Voice mails: abbr.
43 Impoverishment

Down

1 Meccas
2 Noted Madonna role
3 Get going
4 They signal danger
5 Places for strikes and spares
6 Beloved one
7 Coffee cherry teas
8 Turns off
9 Bruce Springsteen "___ Fire"
10 Eatery with sidewalk tables, often
11 Bent inward
14 Magazine that names the "Sexiest Man Alive"
20 Found a remedy for
21 Apparition
22 Bunkering vessel
23 Amorous experiences
24 Pieces of furniture to display curios
26 Without delay or immediately
30 Neptunian moon
31 Eponymous German physicist
32 Blood drive contributor
34 "A Holly Jolly Christmas" singer
35 Grab, as at a smorgasbord
36 President's rejection
37 Works in the fashion business

Across

1 Hair color gradations
6 Get into hot water, perhaps
11 Word heard on a golf course
12 Reprimand
14 Hotfoot it
15 Framing candidate
16 Of gray-barked hardwood tree
18 Gossipy tidbit
19 "Ars Poetica" poet
21 Beyond budding
24 Letters in replies to the hosts
27 Mowry of "Sister, Sister"
28 Partly paid back
30 Made a pained sound
32 Part of a trio
34 Peculiarly
35 Like glazed-over eyes
37 Released
39 Street monitoring system (inits)
42 Surviving spouse
45 Incoming plane
47 Exasperate
48 End a split
49 Grand verses
50 Classic suit fabric
51 Odysseus temptresses

Down

1 Wacky
2 Intelligence agency worry
3 Fonda's role in "Klute"
4 Reverberate repeatedly
5 Great male heroes
6 "Monty Python" network
7 Most bohemian
8 Stretched to the limit
9 Fill an opening
10 Some moisture overloads
13 Colada fruit
17 Stadium cheers
20 Held protectively
22 Dallas, familiarly
23 Ingredient in a flaky crust
25 Certain clinicians
26 Once-popular organizers, initially
29 Hoodwinks
31 Greenish silicate
33 Evergreen conifer
34 Prairie schooner
36 Fond person
38 Hit smartly
40 Rowing team, e.g.
41 Not false
43 Clear the screen
44 SpaceX CEO Musk
46 Quick clip

MEDIUM

Across

1 Low-carbohydrate eating regime
9 Court competition for partners
15 Arc sound
16 Ear-relevant prefix
17 Microwave
19 Pacific republic
20 SALT subj.
21 And, in Germany
22 Cheater's device
23 Citizen of Tehran
24 WWI pistol
26 Research
28 Count on
29 Join a rebellion
31 Explosive letters
33 Having no kinetic energy
36 Most valuable shots in basketball
38 Chooser's word
41 Chocolate coffee
42 Bridges who sang "Coming Home"
43 Deadly Asian rock snake
45 By ___ of (owing to)
46 Billboard list
48 Absence of germs
50 Snow transportation
51 Talking tree of Middle-earth
53 Painter's plaster
54 Crime syndicate
58 PO arrival
60 Electric fish
62 Of earth vibrations
64 Flip over
66 Dirty Harry's org.
69 Architectural projection
70 ___ state of affairs
71 Old enough to buy booze
73 Without ___ (unprotected)
74 Jewish calendar starter
76 Distant radiation source
78 Clickable text
79 Chronological records
81 Commerce pact since 1994
85 Hazy with pollution
87 Barely registering
90 Perjurer's admission
91 ___ avail (futile)
92 "Red Letter Year" singer DiFranco
94 Federal performance funder, for short
95 Leadership group
96 Mass utterance
97 Funny shorthand?
98 Beat regularly, in sports
99 Awaiting delivery
100 Ones attacking

Down

1 Showy flowering shrub
2 Forbidden perfume?
3 Accounting giant, initially
4 Strengthen
5 CNR facility
6 Avoid by sudden move
7 Create a cryptogram
8 Become
9 Prepare filets
10 Components
11 Mystery novelist Nevada
12 Big Island banquet
13 Taloned predators
14 High-end hotel offerings
18 Persian baby
25 Put together
27 Endure beyond
30 Factory vent pipe
32 Sounds of admonishment
34 Response to oversharing, briefly
35 Pal of Harry and Hermione
37 Parrot fashion
38 Alternative to glue
39 Cobra's warning
40 Pathologist's suffix
44 Govt. agency rules
45 DC contingent
47 Raised landform

48 It's ___ (high praise)
49 Betrayed for money
50 Corresponding
52 Wanting
55 Many millennia
56 Cannoneer's command
57 Start of a guess
59 ___ hour
61 Rx for Parkinson's
63 Choir voices

65 Role models
66 Chip topper
67 NFL scoring stat
68 Salad tidbit
70 Words from indifferent dad
72 Satisfy (as terms)
73 Magnet alloy
75 Insect's life stage between molts
77 Sunbathes again

78 Weighed down
80 Striped antelope
82 Codebreaker Turing
83 Classic canine name
84 Oreg., once
86 Fit to be called up
88 Briefed about
89 Small amphibian
93 Some prefix?

Across

1 Ordering party
8 Celestial bear
12 LAX tower service
13 Excavate
14 Brushoffs
15 Fish-eating predator
17 Pledges
18 Food plan which fills body with energy, nutrients and antioxidants
20 Tackle
21 Scoffs
23 Agents' cuts, in brief
26 Ones fidgeting
29 Sixth note
30 Baseballer Stengel
31 Dijon season
32 Ideal gas law scientist Amedeo
34 Raised, as horses
35 Diamond size measure
36 Symbol of resistivity
38 One of the most deeply researched Ayurvedic herbs
44 Baroque titan
46 Baddie
47 Comic strip dog
48 Radio knob
49 Vitamin and supplement retailer
50 Bladders
51 Rationality

Down

1 Moonshine mix
2 Suitable standard?
3 College Football Playoff gp
4 Violinmaker Nicolo
5 Miser
6 Scarcely unique
7 Bagpipe, e.g.
8 Introduce
9 Fizzy quaff
10 Stitch together
11 Imposed, as a payment
16 Lodge members
19 Pop's Pop
22 "Flower Petal Gown" sculptor
23 Inert medications
24 Vena ____ (main vein)
25 Of the chest
27 Neighbor of Syr.
28 Relating to the Tbilisi's country
30 Certain mass, briefly
33 Cuts
34 Fictional spy or certificate of debt
37 Berry of "Monster's Ball"
39 Terminates the engagement, say
40 Puma competitor
41 Bygone magistrate
42 Feathered females
43 Parabolic paths
45 Abbreviation on a toothpaste tube

MEDIUM

Across

1 Manicurist's cutter
12 Fallen ___
13 Beltway region, briefly
14 Archipelago known as the Friendly Islands
15 Caused by the wind
16 Regional phrase
17 Arctic divers
18 Winery vessel
19 Fountain order, sometimes
21 Tolkien meanie
23 Football squads
25 Ladies court gp
26 Hatch back?
27 Assume as a fact
28 Flowerless office plants
31 Pro in the sticks
32 Tax-ers linkup
33 Ballpark staples
37 Org. for a start-up, maybe
38 Rubik's creation
39 Blather
40 Did pool laps
42 River of Lyon
44 Favorable aspect
46 Housecleaning, in politics
47 Aimless traveler
48 Chipped in chips
49 Bastet and Anubis

Down

1 Concerning birth
2 Like one battery terminal
3 Set aflame
4 Minifigure toymaker
5 Hoosegows
6 Core values
7 Talent finder
8 Polio immunologist Jonas
9 Sacred petitions
10 "The Crying Game" star
11 Small wild desert kitten
20 Not specific
22 Hitter's no.
24 Stop holding it in
25 Archaism, e.g.
27 J.M. Barrie boy
28 Long crack
29 Diplomat's res.
30 Examine again
31 Shipping abbr.
33 Arm bones
34 Wine city north of Lisbon (var.)
35 Attacked as a group
36 Ticket numbers
38 Officer of the future
41 Coward
43 Suspended
45 Disk in a 1990s fad game

113   MEDIUM

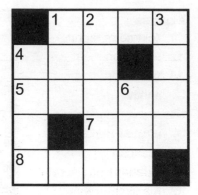

Across

1 Pale grayish
4 Sound of
  a hearty laugh
5 Fundamental
  proposition
7 Pre-album albums,
  briefly
8 Beer, slangily

Down

1 One of the stereo
  syst. rear jacks
2 Went downhill
3 Holiday veggies
4 Deviates from
  a course
6 Photo ____
  (PR events)

114   MEDIUM

Across

1 Sitcom actress
  Swenson
4 Doc's orders
6 In the slightest
  degree
8 Recognition for
  some stars
9 Sea-going vessel

Down

1 Certain religious
  leader
2 Annual report chart
3 Guns N' Roses' old
  front man Rose
5 Blunder
7 Hospital room
  staples

115   MEDIUM

Across

1 Monopoly buys,
  in brief
4 WWII attacker
6 Yellowish-brown
  lion color
7 Terse observation
8 Member of Attila's
  horde

Down

1 Atkinson of British
  comedy
2 Emulated the Avon
  lady
3 Eye ailment (var.)
4 Great Salt Lake's
  state
5 Soul singer Erykah

MEDIUM

Across

1 Volume of reprints
8 Letters on meat packaging
12 Nation
13 Brood
14 International east-west conflict of old
15 Japanese ring sport
16 In a slothful way
17 Figure
19 Stop talking immediately
20 Region bordering Tuscany
24 Dance makeup
27 Serving bowl
28 Chess org.
29 Sap or weak add-on
30 Goes on a spree
32 "Science of Logic" author Georg
33 Footwear design
34 Bottle denizen
36 Clothing
39 Dench of the screen
42 Union of two
43 Corrals
45 Quaint store sign word
46 Small intestines elements
47 Admit everything, with up
48 One proceeding confidently

Down

1 Back of the skull
2 Emotional condition
3 Without value
4 Annual 500 race
5 Cousin of FYI
6 Of the first Greek sky god
7 Cough remedy
8 Distressing
9 Kind of cream
10 Lower chamber of Russia's parliament
11 Coral Sea features
18 Fizzle
19 1963 Chemistry Nobel winner Karl
21 Drug smuggler
22 Naval guardhouse
23 Traitorous group
25 Avant-garde
26 Spa treatment
30 Financial rescue
31 Informative session
32 ___ steam (driving force)
35 Geeky guys
37 Be a whiner
38 Bruise preventers
39 Heroic "Star Wars" warrior
40 Like some eBay goods
41 Have supper
44 Favor lead-in

Across

1 Fairy tales romantic hero who resembles Guy Smiley
13 "Time" founder
14 Part of speech
15 Goodbye, in Spain
17 Others, to Ovid
18 Groceries carrier
19 French impressionist painter Claude
20 Bit of change
21 Shaft for wheels
22 Nonchalantly unconcerned
23 Criminal slangs
25 Lead-in to cone
27 Backside
30 Guru's retreat
34 Prepare wings, perhaps
38 Mark Zuckerberg's creation of 2021
40 Harbor fleet
41 Blue muncher with a sweet tooth known for his voracious appetite
44 Unit of time
45 Math offshoot
46 English town noted for its salts
48 Region on the Rhine
50 Half of Hamlet's dilemma
52 Commit a misstep
54 Jungian souls
58 Fodder for sports analysts
62 1946 song "___ in Calico"
65 Bathroom rugs
66 Truth benders
67 Unmannerly sort
68 Ballet's beginning
69 Hawke of Hollywood
70 Come ___ surprise
71 Mother of Titans
72 Singer of "I love trash, anything dirty or dingy or dusty, anything ragged or rotten or rusty" lyrics

Down

1 Slogan-bearing panel
2 Geometry class tool
3 Cake topper
4 Quaint cool
5 Preserve, in a way
6 Goad gently
7 Utter angrily, as insults
8 Starts the pot
9 Latin dances
10 "White Wedding" vocalist Billy
11 "Four Women" chanteuse Simone
12 Sets off
16 Vaporizes
24 Long, arduous journey
26 Flatbread baked in a tandoor
28 From New York, say
29 Invoice directive
31 WWW intro
32 Certainly won't repeat
33 Farming prefix
35 Env. science
36 Some signed notes
37 "Iron Chef America" celebrity Cat
39 Like a take-out order
42 Roman road of yore
43 Viewed
44 Big headache
47 Expected deliverer of the Jews
49 Small plane name
51 Durin's Bane in "Lord of the Rings"
53 Moroccan capital
55 Final stage of insect
56 Asian gambling destination
57 Place for a ghost
59 Former Yugoslav dictator
60 Oohs and ___
61 King's head?
63 Comment of amazement
64 Highest-quality rating

Bonus Clue

Transfer the letters from the corresponding shaded squares above into this grid
to form the **names of two famous stars who visited the Big Bird & co.**

1	2	3	4		5	6	7	8	9

10	11	12	13	14		15	16	17	18	19	20	21	22

MEDIUM

Across

1 Jack-o-lantern feature, perhaps
5 Baseball's Williams and others
9 Java holder
12 Make keener
13 Bleach, as a plant
15 Ones prone to clumsiness
16 Argues against
17 Transparent tape or type of whiskey
19 President Lincoln's beard
20 Online comment groupings
22 Loose soil
23 Matured
26 Green expanse
27 Theater personnel
31 Machine rotator
32 Incursion
33 Egg without a shell
35 English church honorific
39 Pickled condiment
42 Greek amber spirit
43 First performance
45 Ever so slightly
46 Vital
47 Succeed on a diet
48 CIA's predecessor
49 Shade of blue or a military branch
50 Youngsters

Down

1 Basic Halloween costume
2 Household scurrier
3 Soon to experience
4 Money put aside for future expenses
5 Nerds' festival, say
6 1940s command, briefly
7 Microwave signal, sometimes
8 ___ speak
9 Historical region of Spain
10 Pronouncer
11 Former Andorra currency
14 Old stained-glass windows element
18 Isn't apathetic
21 Congregate
24 Not expected
25 "Age of Reason" writer
27 Zodiac 40-Down
28 Alehouses
29 Talismans
30 Kind of psychology
34 Performer with no speaking part
36 Prohibition
37 Be among the real
38 Local taxes on commercial property
40 Agree formally
41 Mount Olympus queen
44 Toyota's ___4

MEDIUM

Across

1 Performed slow Cuban dance
8 Crack from cold weather
12 Functional
13 Itinerant person
14 Auto extra
15 Gosling of "The Notebook"
16 Allegro and adagio
17 House surrounder
18 Grand Central, e.g.
20 Deep red veggies
22 Burger and fries complement
24 Awaited with horror
28 Look for
30 Whistle wetter
31 Fast food choice
33 Money saver to the extreme
34 Celestial
36 Not at all lethargic
37 Santa's helpers
39 Olive ___ (Popeye's love)
40 Classroom stand-ins
43 Squashed Os
45 End of a peg?
46 Train again
49 More than irk
50 Knickknacks
51 Be ___ in the ointment
52 High hat

Down

1 Neighbor of Fin.
2 As a rule, briefly
3 Cerebral maturity level
4 Expose, as skin
5 WWII weapon
6 Lammed for love
7 Opposers
8 Cocoon resident
9 Big East hoopster
10 Cinn___ (pigment)
11 Body in a garden, perhaps
18 Signs of healing
19 Namely, in legalese
21 Word often cried after go
23 In a random way (as wandering)
25 Removals
26 Each one
27 Hall of music
29 Lanky
32 Gambols
35 Backslide
38 Composer Erik
40 Long heroic story
41 Fighter letters
42 Certain optimist
44 Abandoned port
47 Organization chart topper
48 TV channel for consumers

MEDIUM

Across

1 Satisfy (a desire)
7 Race on the water
13 Circuit
14 Mandolin's relative
16 About 1% of
the atmosphere
17 Rest between
active times
18 Score ___
19 Assignment
20 Prolongs a date,
perhaps
22 Org. for paid tennis
players
24 In which case
25 Negative vote in
the Senate
26 "Taxi Driver" director
29 Paper-thin French
pancake
30 Hang in the breeze
33 Wrap maker
36 Stone ___
(cavemen)
38 Ending for many
elements
39 "1984" author
41 Pass to a scorer
43 State touching Can.
44 Compilations
46 Sailing vessel
48 Vertigo
50 Pine exudation
52 Advocates
54 Subj. that may
include a lab

56 Tori of pop/rock
59 Excel command
60 Angle symbols
62 Galley drudge
64 Cooks in
a microwave
66 Book designer's
selection
67 Bluefin, for one
68 Leading
69 Exclamation with
a drum roll
70 Octet followers,
in Italian sonnets
71 Jennifer of "Friends"

Down

1 City hosting
the 1996 Olympics
2 March master
3 Harness racing
carriage
4 Clickable addresses
5 Bounce (off)
6 Home to Benelux
7 Allows to use
temporarily
8 Burner fuel
9 More flamboyant
10 Weekend whoop
11 Great weights
12 Opposite word
15 Saharan nomad
21 Six-Day War
participants

23 Some still-life
subjects
27 Gems mined
mostly in Australia
28 Quite unmanly
29 Female elephant
31 Half of CD
32 Barbie doll creator
Handler
34 Prospector's
bonanza
35 Mountain peak
37 Lessens a load
40 Uneven gaits
42 "At Seventeen"
singer Janis
43 Reveals
45 Novelist Capote
47 Lover of Isolde
49 React indignantly to
51 Urge to attack
53 Peloponnesian
potables
54 Mink cousin
55 Got your back
57 Sullen look
58 Has bought
61 Immature
salamanders
63 Alternative to
whole wheat
65 Holder of school
meetings, briefly

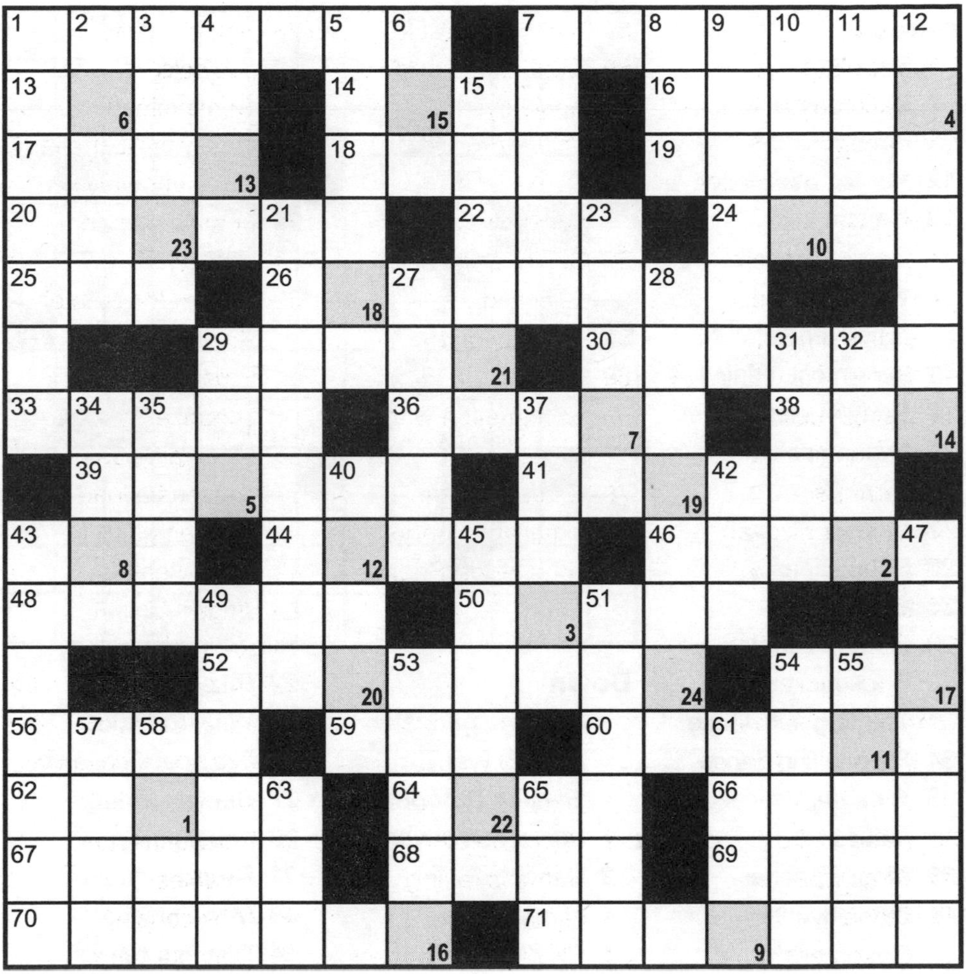

Bonus Clue

Transfer the letters from the corresponding shaded squares above into this grid to form the quote attributed to Ludwig van Beethoven

1	2	3	4

5	6	7	8	9

10	11	12	13

14	15	16	17	18

19	20	21	22	23	24

MEDIUM

Across

1 Sand hill
5 Body's volume determination
12 Alma mater visitor
13 Caricatured
14 Carrier puller
15 Winslet of "The Reader"
16 Innermost meninx
18 Early stages
20 Noted healer
21 Fidel Castro's brother
23 Stipulations
25 6-pt. plays
28 Hummingbirds do it
30 Book jacket items
31 Tainting substance
34 Storytelling dance
35 Citta del Vaticano setting
36 Mobile phone network inits
38 Heroic works
40 Tastes gingerly
42 One to hang with
44 Sell, as a business
47 High monastery office and rank
50 Half a Chinese circle
51 Exec. level
52 San ____ Obispo, CA
53 Walk in the wild
54 Composition writer
55 Charming scene

Down

1 Robbing gangster in India (var.)
2 Eastern European horseman of yore
3 Loony
4 Mideast title
5 Pill-shaped
6 Longtime name in the news
7 Drummer's responsibility
8 Allow entry to
9 Stating
10 Have regrets
11 Theater exit
17 Variant spelling of a micro organism
19 President before Woodrow Wilson
22 Ritzy wheels
24 Witty remarks
26 Bra specification
27 Seeks formally
29 Least bold
32 Crunchy dipper
33 Mane location
34 Distress call
37 Cattle's beety snack
39 Irritably unfriendly
41 Introduce oneself
43 American snorkeling mecca
45 Put down, as track
46 Covered in black liquid
48 Some NFL blockers
49 Apostrophized affirmative

Across

1 Corned-beef dishes
7 Aids in evil
12 Infamous New York prison
13 Ended a blackout
14 Cocoa solids and butter + sugar
16 Alpine parrot
17 Brownish Asian larvae silk (var.)
18 Completely
21 Buddhist monastery
22 Treacherous one
23 Source of red food coloring
24 DJ's stack, once
25 Informal address
26 Scottish bodies of water
29 Small child
30 Phil of the poker table
31 Sour condiment
35 Foot finisher
36 Form a chain
37 Relating to the UK
39 Comfy slip-on, briefly
40 Period given to finish the task
43 De Gaulle's birthplace
44 Keep from getting out of control
45 Medieval drinks
46 Choose

Down

1 Shown to be insecure
2 Armored Greek goddess
3 Short-tailed weasels
4 Sot's sound
5 Writer Umberto ____
6 Some shakers
7 Pretentious
8 Honey makers
9 Entrenched
10 Adorned with a diadem
11 Fugal overlapping
15 "____ Lang Syne"
19 Anxious
20 X-ray dosage units
23 The 46th President
25 LPGA tour player Lorie
26 Stick in a purse, maybe
27 Cover
28 Sign to soften C
29 Tenth-part-of-income donors
31 Boundless
32 Street girl
33 Kind of clock
34 Contemporary
36 Quotes as authority
38 Related, as a story
41 Unsatisfactory grade
42 As late as, for short

Across

1 "King of Pop" who is the 3rd best-selling artist ever after The Beatles and Elvis Presley
13 Texas-based computer company
14 Folder's declaration
15 Cajun ingredient
16 Doing nothing in particular
17 Mop target
18 Give an impression of being
19 Rum-infused confection
20 Survivor's head?
21 Mineral layer involved in fracking
22 Thin or narrow
24 Altar plates
26 Without a warranty
28 Maledictions
30 Geometry calculations
34 Slugger Hank
36 Somewhere in the crowd
38 Jocund
42 Less then minimal
43 Reaction to an idol, possibly
45 Liqueur similar to Sambuca
46 Roads connector
48 Rice paper screens
50 ___ pants (baggy garment)
52 Immaturely imitative
53 Garner
57 "James and the Giant Peach" author Roald
59 Music theorist Jean-Philippe
61 Butler's underling
66 Large constellation also known as the Whale
67 Bias
69 Not displaying proper manners
70 Respond well to medical care
71 Main reason for traffic jams
72 Added stipulations
73 Highest stage of development
74 Discarded material
75 Colored eye part
76 "The Voice" behind the most successful soundtrack album of all time

Down

1 Olympian's goal
2 Post-revelation exclamation
3 Concealing no weapons
4 Passages for worshipers
5 Big retail stores
6 Cut of pork that can be tender
7 Medicated drink
8 Madeira Isl. surroundings
9 Like some delis
10 Leaf-shaped Irish daggers
11 They precede the consequences
12 Rank and serial number go-with
13 Childish claim
21 Dangerous trick
23 Honored guests' platform
25 Fall cache
27 Siberian sled dog
29 Stomp in a puddle
30 Southwestern farm
31 Subject for a mariachi band
32 Nat. history museum exhibit
33 "Beware the ___ of March"
35 2011 animated film about a blue macaw
37 Southern African Bantu speaker
39 Earring variety
40 Extinct volcano on the 58-Across
41 Israeli burp guns

44 Simple card game for kids
47 Turns (away from)
49 Circle overhead?
51 Italian gangster
54 Rifle's rear section
55 Dojo surface
56 Repeller of evil
58 Largest of the Japanese islands
60 Lending at criminal interest
62 Distinguishing attribute
63 2013 Nobel-winning writer Alice
64 Recipe direction
65 Crimefighter of early 60s TV
66 Tobacco quid
68 Chief god of ancient Memphis
71 Took the cookie, say

124 MEDIUM

Across

1 Two-color buzzers
12 ___-deucy (dice roll of three)
13 Tranquil discipline
14 Sweet gat frontside?
15 Add cargo
16 Court hearing
17 Otto ___ Bismarck
18 Type of support
20 Dinosaur remnants
22 Big inits in payroll
23 Ottoman
25 Phony (with up)
26 "Cosmos" author Sagan
27 Lemon, for one
28 Preparing for war
31 Hosts entertain them
32 Equity transactions
33 Hunt for
34 Authority figure
35 Future woman
36 Summer time in St. Louis
39 Refuses to retire
41 Rub to clean
43 Healthy sun-burned color
44 Highway havens
46 Alternative to orchestra
47 DEA employee
48 Had dealings with
49 Of the same sort
50 Be at an impasse

Down

1 Black Sea resort town
2 Greeting not needing a stamp
3 Was a prelude (to)
4 Caustic substances
5 The Equality State, briefly
6 Very happy
7 ___ reason
8 Budget rentals
9 Jealous of others' success
10 Collection for a handyman
11 Days ends
19 Stretches across
21 Swamp toon of filmdom
24 Web address ending
26 Brady Bunch female
27 Provides energy for
28 Best of the best
29 Underground tree system
30 Arrowroot source
31 Lang. of Austria
33 Fell from grace
35 "___ Fly Now" ("Rocky" theme)
36 Singer Sam
37 Started to dine
38 Election night development
40 Member of Hindu religion
42 Dressed (in)
45 Scand. land

124

Across

1 Urban pollutions
5 Mister Khrushchev
10 Model Hurley, to friends
11 "The Medallion" star
13 Paperback publishing giant
14 Gold, in Peru
15 Mild exclamation
16 State-run ID issuer
17 Got there first
18 Central California county
20 Apparent
22 Orchard pests
24 Backs, anatomically
28 Grow rapidly
30 Go soft
31 Pass idly, as time
32 Matador's assistant
34 Chilly fall
36 Mirth
37 Warner Bros.' subsidiary
39 Skin flecks
42 Office VIP
45 Body-blow grunt
46 Web site visits
47 ___ de Cologne
48 Bubble source
49 Tired heads?
50 "Final Fantasy" genre, initially
51 Volume measures
52 They run in winter

Down

1 Hoping for more customers
2 Abstract artist Joan
3 Atmospheric layer depletion
4 2001-2011 Google CEO Eric
5 Inlay option
6 Reciprocally
7 ___- European languages
8 Woolen caps
9 Edison's middle name
12 Advisory notice
19 Type of toxin in rotten food (var.)
21 Like some bad weather
22 Poses questions
23 Collins of Genesis
25 Ones to the rescue
26 Casino machine
27 Worth ___
29 Litter in a sty
33 Artillery wagon
35 Computer pro
38 Impulses
39 Swamps or fens
40 Awkward brute
41 John Legend hit "All ___"
43 Stare in shock
44 Cheap toupees

126

MEDIUM

Across
1 Tailor's junction
5 Country singer McCann
9 Get into a yellow car, say
16 Larger forearm bone
17 Stasis
18 Spaghetti sauce brand
19 Piano student's time keeper
20 Draft org.
21 Hardly any
22 Shrub providing indigo
23 Exclamation of dismay
24 Sleeper's support
26 Manioc (var.)
28 Puerto ___
30 Actors Holm and McKellen
31 Person against government
33 North American hawk
36 One with ambitions
40 Minute plant structure
42 Doubly
43 Like some bridges
46 Cuba, to Cubans
49 Folksy accounts
50 Furniture assembly piece
51 Bar stock
53 Islands west of Lisbon
55 Industry magnate
57 ___ Valley (California)
58 Drill inserts
59 Politician Clinton
61 Lauder of scents
62 Court tool
63 Birds, e.g.
65 Fabric measure
69 Gas components
72 Outhouse door symbol
73 A case for sewers
74 Arboreal snakes
79 Old Western Union delivery
82 Bit of friction
84 "Sesame Street" giggler
85 Pandora's boxful
86 "Woe ___" (grammar book)
87 Ethereal
88 Payment guarantee
89 Traditional beliefs
90 ___ Ferrari, auto designer
91 The hypocrite in Molire's comedy
92 In ___ (actually existing)
93 Submachine gun in the Suez Crisis

Down
1 Rash cause, maybe
2 Author Ferrante
3 Cons
4 Maples on 90s tabloid pages
5 Insecticidal neurotoxin
6 M-less youngster?
7 Hollywood's Hedy
8 Containing vinegar
9 Gadget (var.)
10 Sub ___ (secretly)
11 Biol. branch
12 Dormant Turkish volcano
13 Connected series
14 Former Djokovic's coach
15 Blooms-to-be
25 Oceanic flux
27 French "Arcana" composer Edgar
29 Contaminated water disease
32 Yankees great, familiarly
33 Streak
34 Mtn. road info
35 Dogfight preventers
36 Encouraging cry
37 Language of Southern Africa
38 Steer
39 Frosting tools
41 Fortitude
44 Aristocratic

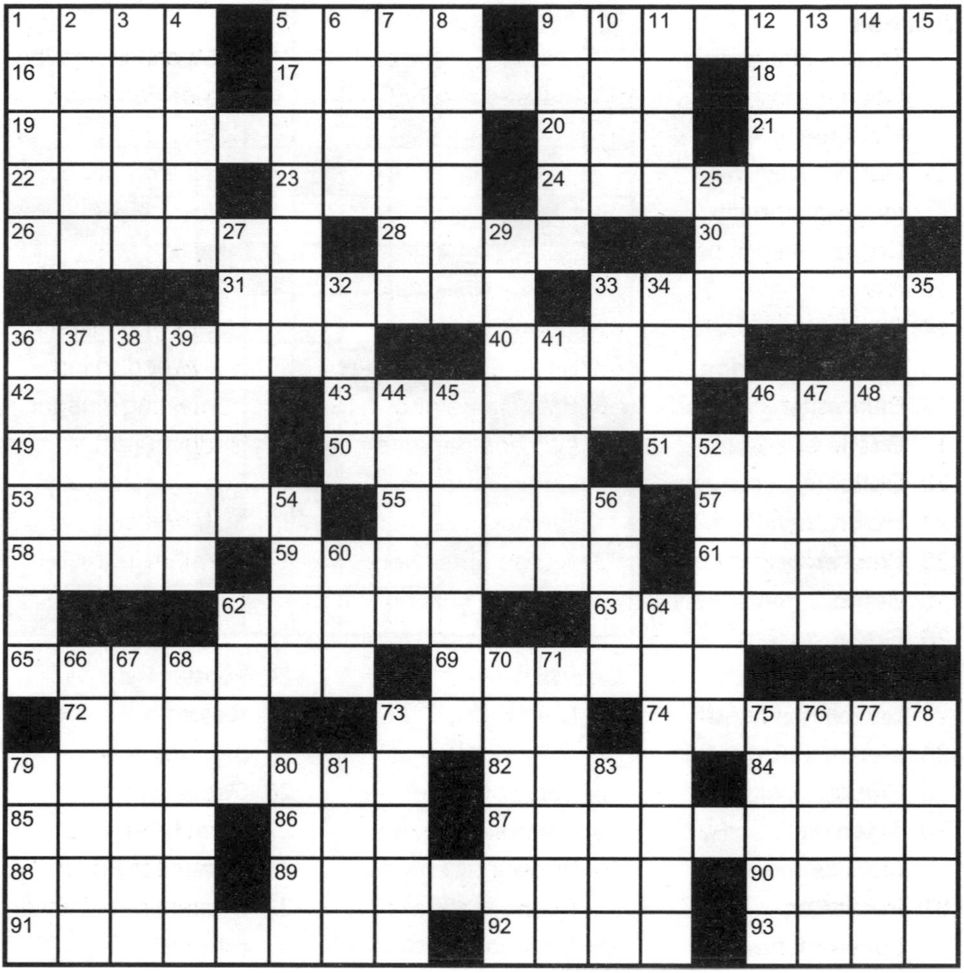

45 Online purse
46 Latin clarifier
47 Stingray cousin
48 Not just yet
52 City in the Ukraine or Texas
54 Rug type
56 Part of a Wall St. address
60 Express end?
62 Group of hoodlums
64 Stately source of shade
66 2009 biopic starring Hilary Swank
67 Brush alternative
68 Janet Jackson "___ Really Matter"
70 Scuffle
71 Huge herbivores
73 Monsieur Zola
75 Parcels (out)
76 Lacking sharpness
77 Leave completely floored
78 Wise Athenian lawgiver
79 Pinball stopper
80 Guitar solo
81 Starting from
83 Artificiality

THREE TRIANGLES

Across

1 Portion of a classic fast food to enjoy in Florence or Rome
11 Corner office denizens, briefly
12 Cry to a fly
13 Alley-___
14 Sunday garb
15 Puzo family name
17 Backwater
19 Brings to a stop
20 Optometrist's exam
22 Monk's condition?
25 West in old movies
26 Between the sheets
30 Green protector of Yuletide gifts that sometimes faints
34 Decisive boxing win
35 Election night fig.
36 Traveling together c-ool innards?
37 Indifferent
41 Leave off (from)
44 Hold in debt
47 Exorbitant demand
49 Home to Iowa State University
50 Do-over, in tennis
51 La Roux singer Jackson
52 Grandmotherly nicknames
53 Crunchy wafer filled with gelato

Down

1 Dump
2 Gray wolf
3 Topic of dispute
4 Reversion of the heirless property (to the state)
5 Discoverer's call
6 Impel
7 Flag bearers
8 Safari parks
9 Shipping charge factor, often
10 Great swingers
11 Chorister's robe
16 Trouble greatly
18 Locker sites
21 Try to seduce
23 Ballroom dance syllable
24 Type of wit
27 Victoria's Secret product
28 Poet's always
29 Push down
31 Column style
32 Initialism
33 Informal guess
38 Poly ending in plastics and fibers
39 Having some benefit
40 Argentine plain
41 Hero seller
42 Biz bigwig
43 Fill
45 Single-named supermodel
46 Basic unit of inheritance
48 Rio greeting

Across

1 Goal of some political party donors
6 Flexible response
11 Indent key
12 In need of a massage, maybe
13 Emerged from slumber
14 Go too far
16 Groups enjoying superior status
18 Take close aim
19 Six-pack units
20 Make stronger
22 Gen.'s assistant
25 Gooey lump
28 High-class diner
30 Of ancient Greek final period
33 In the mood
34 Forms of moisture
35 AWOL chasers
36 Prompt
39 Birthday food
41 Amount added to price
45 "In Search of Lost Time" writer Marcel
47 Poisonous gas that smells like garlic
48 Indulge in mockery
49 Big name in antacids
50 Comedian's asset
51 Slope gently
52 Forgive

Down

1 The gamut
2 Spelunker's milieu
3 Trucker with a transmitter
4 Maugham's Miss Thompson
5 Quick bread
6 Cameraman's vision shields
7 Hotel choice
8 Spicy condiment
9 Scratch out a living
10 Matter in law
15 Heist figure
17 Blue rock, briefly
21 Lavish dinner
23 Score the same
24 Animation frames
25 Toy gun noise
26 Aladdin's find
27 Ear examination instrument
29 Fall drinks
31 Does chef's work
32 Half-moon-shaped window
37 Muslim worship leaders
38 Gator territory
40 Teller of Ice-Age tales
42 Ostrich's smaller kin
43 Distributor of degs
44 Astronaut Conrad
45 Outfit rarely worn out, for short
46 Expression of support

129   MEDIUM

Across

1 First X or O
4 Hairdos at Woodstock
7 Wartime maneuver
8 Button word, sometimes
9 Expression of disinterest

Down

1 News agency based in Moscow
2 Words before matters?
3 Eclair filling
5 Barbarous one
6 MacFarlane of "Family Guy"

130   MEDIUM

Across

1 Light contact in billiards
5 Insect attracted to a flame
6 Made a solemn declaration
8 Wonderstruck
9 Hot tip

Down

1 Canadian highway distances, briefly
2 Hawkeye
3 Ski mecca near Mount Mansfield
4 Small mouselike mammal
7 Asner et al.

131   MEDIUM

Across

1 Legendary advice giver
5 Native of southeast Africa
6 Macaroni wheat
7 Rifles and such
8 Exclamation of agreement

Down

1 Hue of a clear sky
2 Myanmar, by another name
3 Look embarrassed, maybe
4 Response to a tasty treat
6 Certain trader

Across

1 Bar measure
5 Accidents
11 City in Kansas
13 Soothe
14 Tarzan wannabes
15 Source of milk
16 Himalayan mammal
18 Music genre of Jamaican origin
19 Not heads
21 Sets with LCD screens
25 Sheepskin made to resemble seal or beaver fur
28 What olden days were of
29 Brandenburg Gate setting
30 Panoramic views
32 Bitter dispute
34 Downward distances
35 Bones of the foot
36 Begin a volleyball game
38 Gambling letters
41 Metal fences
45 Gabbana's partner in fashion
47 Make muddy
48 Quark sites
49 Like some dancers or pets
50 Summer period
51 Didn't ditch

Down

1 Stiff
2 Expectation
3 Daily essay
4 Seasonal staffer
5 Heaven-sent food
6 Very dirty state
7 Cabinet dept.
8 Supports
9 Do a little cheating
10 Bloodline
12 English odist John
17 Coins
20 Infection-fighting drug
22 Avian symbol of peace
23 Power ___
24 Bodices, e.g.
26 Arena level
27 Daunting duty
29 Economic capital of Iraq
31 British Ex-PM May
33 Cut open
34 Thingumbob
35 Fax's ancestor
37 Aura, informally
39 Movie terrier
40 Internet diary
42 Statement of reassurance
43 Dark time, in ads
44 Hold tightly
46 Mil. headquarters

Across

1 Ancient bug trapper
6 Free stuff
10 Attend
14 Dig out
15 Attire for Antonius
16 Forever and ___
17 Cook's cover
18 Chamber
19 Standard measurement
20 Some pseudonyms
22 Hijacked group of computers
24 Traveler's aid
25 Cote sounds
26 Shows feeling onstage
30 Fragrant healing ointment
31 Datebook letters
33 Contented sigh
34 Fuel ___
36 Reproduction of a picture
38 Tormented
40 British restroom
41 Moorland shrub
42 Allotrope of oxygen
43 Creates a fantasy
45 Floating gate front?
46 Greensward
47 Oktoberfest quaff
49 Allowed to enter a country
52 Helsinki native
53 Gal at a ball
54 Little hooters
57 Taverner
61 Recommend
62 Flapjack restaurant chain
64 Fiji neighbor
65 Engine conduit
66 Capable of standing trial
67 Make a correction
68 Condition treated with Ritalin, in brief
69 Norse hammer-wielding god
70 Salacious selfies

Down

1 Highest forms of love (var.)
2 Sulk aimlessly
3 Effective insult
4 Harold Ramis' Ghostbuster
5 Change the title
6 Throat trouble
7 Pays court to
8 Gone by, as time
9 Frisk
10 Throws, as a baited hook
11 Boss at Valhalla
12 Challenge for a rat
13 Incisor neighbors
21 Pron. category
23 Personal charm
25 Give birth, as a whale
27 Sweetcorn
28 Shout of excitement
29 In those days
30 "The ___ Witch Project" (1999)
31 Diamond-studded accessory
32 Liberate from restraints
35 Barkin of film
37 Field judges
38 Calvary
39 Accountancy term
44 Dutch speed-skater Kramer
48 Be stubborn
50 Storklike wading birds
51 Is anxious about
52 Entertained lavishly
53 Habitual user
55 Club option
56 Fancily furnished
57 U2's lead vocalist
58 Antonym of anonymity
59 Financial page heading
60 Eur. or Australia
63 Exclamation of triumph

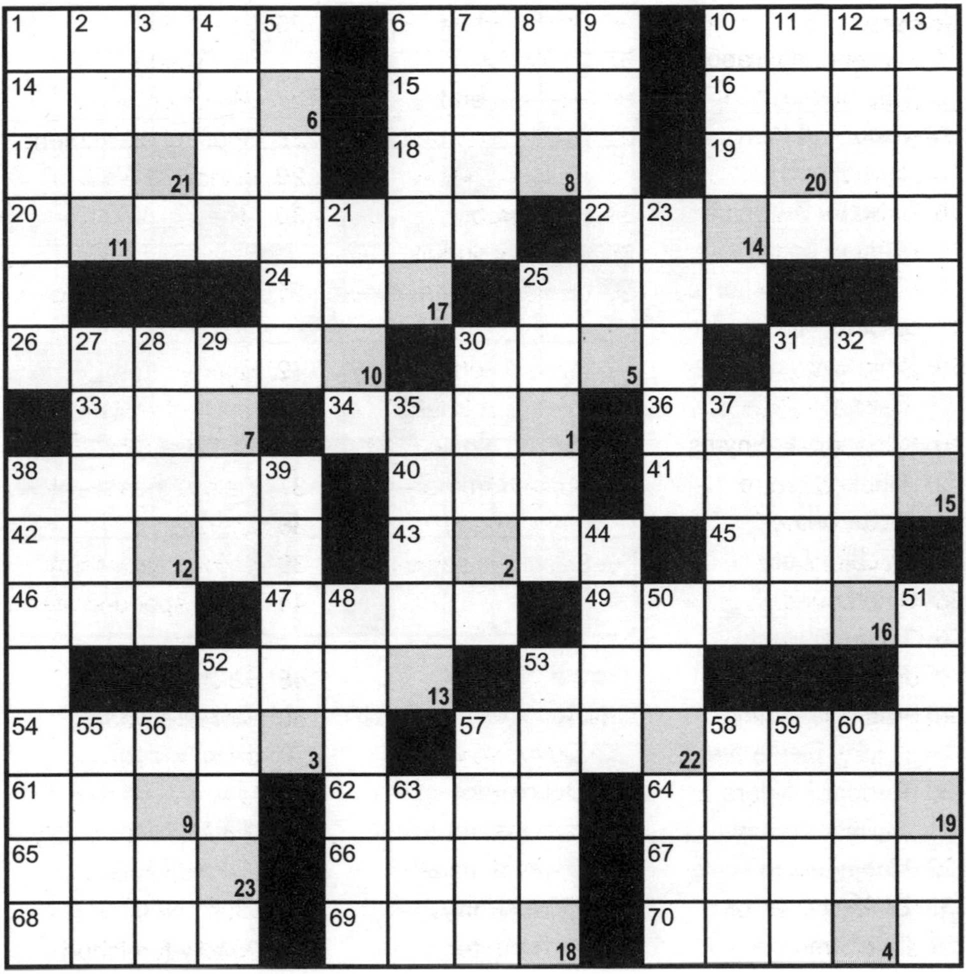

Bonus Clue

Transfer the letters from the corresponding shaded squares above into this grid to form the **title of a successful series of children's novels**

1	2	3	4	5	6

7	8	9	10	11

12	13

14	15	16

17	18	19	20	21	22	23

Across

1 Three-syllable feet
7 Late name in rap
12 Returned from dreamland
13 Coastal East African country
15 Home of a fictional falcon
16 Thin overlays
17 Expert
18 Cleaned by brushing
20 Oom-___ (tuba sound)
21 Hill hundred
23 Way in
24 Find enjoyable
25 Feathered flier
26 Walks leisurely
29 Prickly plants (var.)
30 Redder inside
31 Stylist's creation
32 Unhinged, in slang
33 Difficulty, with a
37 Tyler who played Arwen
38 Dutch painter, Jan
39 Slip behind
40 Head wreaths, once
42 NBA great Patrick
44 ___ oblongata (brain part)
45 Metal-forging tool
46 It can be found in the pudding
47 Kept quarters

Down

1 Reduces in intensity
2 On top of things
3 Double-dot punctuation
4 B'way purchase
5 More smelly, as fermenting beer
6 Draconian
7 Feature of some car windows
8 Off-road vehicle, informally
9 Put together
10 Faucet attachment
11 Tropical nuts
14 Contract negotiators, for short
19 Quick-cooking pans
22 Narrow street
23 Dirty money
25 Desert attribute
26 Electric light
27 Tar
28 Fanfaronade
29 Evoke yawns
31 Rubicon crosser
33 Web pg. language
34 Epic relating the siege of Troy
35 Skin disease of cats and dogs
36 Urged (on)
38 Subject of introspection
41 Pair
43 International conflict that began in 1914, briefly

MEDIUM

Across

1 Source of quality mutton
7 Didn't walk
11 2017 sequel to "The Wolverine"
12 Antique refrigerator
14 Coolish
15 Bricks-and-mortar workers
16 Etching tools
17 Personal property recipient, in law
18 Skin ailments
20 Dubai or Qatar
24 Slander, legally
27 Bagel or doughnut shop quantities
28 Actress Rogers
29 Artist's workplace, often
30 Stately Renaissance dance
32 Alan of "M*A*S*H"
33 Forwards, say
34 Extremely tired
36 Engraved deeply
39 Any Presley's song, now
43 Cleansing solution
44 Soak
45 Old TV component
46 Certain razor namesake
47 Nameless auth.
48 Long-tailed primates

Down

1 Fastened
2 Lester of the news
3 Rich in yolks
4 Colorado skiing hotspot
5 Ratio or hint
6 Distinctive tone
7 Like touchscreen
8 Ancient Greek weight or coin
9 Completed
10 Remove surgically
13 "Thief" star James
19 NFL game extensions
21 Gangster's gal
22 Polo brand
23 Alter
25 Arabian Peninsula country
26 Melon part
28 Extinct elephant ancestor
30 Parker or Waterman
31 Values greatly
32 Zoroastrian scripture
33 Get out of hock
35 Await judgment
37 Glacial lake
38 Commercial prize
40 Piece of hair
41 Mussolini's moniker
42 British expression of surprise

Across

1 Long bath
5 Contagious viral disease
10 Maori war dance
14 Not at all vivid
15 Corner
16 Noted Ancient Roman poet
17 Concerning, in other words
18 New parent, e.g.
19 Devious stratagem
20 Tried to lose
22 Luggage danglers
24 ___ Center (Chicago skyscraper)
25 Scombroid fish
27 Mortise's partner
29 Certain Mideast habitant
31 Abruptly, on a score
34 Partial radioactive decay periods
39 Diagonal face of a chisel
40 Super-food fruit
41 Very dry region of Israel
43 Banks do it
44 Crotchety
46 Indigenous ones favorers
48 Deployed, as troops
50 Actress Spelling
51 Easy on the wallet
53 Children's nurses
58 Dissatisfied cry
60 Christmas tree varieties
62 Bush or Foreman
63 Gas co., for one
65 Game of chance
67 Wizard, old-style
68 Pre-stereo sound
69 Bring to mind
70 Nuclear energy source
71 Guitar parts
72 Some towed vehicles, briefly
73 Man caves, often

Down

1 Arboretum feature
2 Desert mirage, in cartoons
3 Former Mexican empire
4 Where Nintendo is headquartered
5 Chinese dialect
6 ___ corda (music marking)
7 Bus. runners
8 Skirt fold
9 Worsted wools
10 What students want to know
11 Alters by culturing in a chick embryo
12 Narcs seizure
13 Red Sea port
21 Lander at Ben Gurion
23 Social rebuff
26 Bird seen on totem poles
28 Marks on old manuscripts
30 Brought forth
32 Something to pitch
33 Automobile pioneer Ransom
34 Fairy tale crones
35 Development unit, perhaps
36 Introducing (as a product)
37 Liquor bottle size
38 Serious about
42 Termagants
45 Vassal's holding
47 Napa Valley sight
49 Carpenter's gadget
52 Leave no doubt
54 Person always on the move
55 Ready to explode
56 Encourage
57 Looks as if
58 Car slower
59 Stub ___
61 Terminate
64 Word in several city names in California
66 Boxing ref's ruling

Bonus Clue

Transfer the letters from the corresponding shaded squares above into this grid
to form the **"Halloweentown"** quote by Debbie Reynolds

1	2	3	4	5		6	7	8	9	10	11		12	13

14	15	16	17	18	19		20	21	22	23	24	25	26	27	28

Across

1 Important parts of a ketogenic diet
5 In the attic, maybe
12 Angler's attraction
13 Slammer
14 Turn inedible
15 In ___ (sequential)
16 Toss a coin
17 1949 "Sands of ___ Jima"
18 Old currency studier, often
21 TV aliens home
22 Navajo dwelling
23 Sty squeal
24 Image Awards org.
26 Ethiopian kings
28 Yank enemy
30 Walker's charge
31 Proved logical
35 Seeker's question
39 "Star Wars" royal
40 Forest newcomer
42 Flier to Seoul, for short
43 No deference
46 NYC subway of yore
47 Fuzzy textile
48 Ono from Tokyo
49 Zoo bird
50 Act indolent
51 Remorseful one
52 Lands attached to manors
53 Comics bulldog

Down

1 Capped fragrant bottle
2 Natural light phenomenon
3 Russian three-horse coach
4 Stitched
5 Psyched about
6 Springtime concern for allergy sufferers
7 Quite proficient at
8 Casting director's category
9 It might cause photophobia
10 Best seats at a concert
11 Baby deliverers, symbolically
19 Dealt with adversity
20 Respiratory infection
25 Squeaky sound
27 Prom staples
29 Goofball
31 In a partnership
32 Diary entry starter, perhaps
33 Authoritative declaration
34 Jailbird's wish
36 Scrape together
37 Noise
38 Corrida performer
41 "The Invisible Man" author
44 Mail carriers at Hogwarts
45 Fire fan

MEDIUM

Across

1 Dish choosing list
12 Seated yoga position
13 Celtic language of France
14 Pilfers
15 Really riles
16 Currency exchange table letters
17 Hoist into the air
19 Humanitarian organization
21 Sagebrush st.
23 Took place as a result
24 Medieval Scottish clan chief
26 Enthusiastic vigor
28 Road map abbr.
29 Legal start?
32 Gloria Estefan "Love on ___-Way Street"
34 Troubling signs
36 Obstruct
40 Lib. arts major
41 Top-bottom teeth misalignment
43 Security request, briefly
45 Tavern
46 Minor aspect
48 Sidestep, as a question
50 La Scala offerings
51 Actor Bruce
52 Inattention

Down

1 Enticement
2 Give some slack to
3 Conflicting
4 Profit share
5 Confidence builder
6 Ski resort fixtures
7 Nobelist Hemingway
8 Colossal
9 Godlike
10 Certain correlative
11 Not backed up
18 Daises
20 From Havana, say
22 PO box item
25 Nuclear weapon
27 Word with worldly or woman
29 Aspiring prof, maybe
30 Selfishly start to rally?
31 Speaker
33 Prison officials
35 Relating to human groups
37 Long metal tubes system
38 Piano school lessons
39 Insurgency troops
42 French formal dance
44 Have the guts
47 Air-quality agcy
49 "Fast and Furious" Diesel

Across

1 Scientist who digs up dinosaurs' bones, artifacts, old coins and mummies
12 Be cruising
13 Hoofed beast of the tropics
14 Fuel that saves the day when there is no wind and no sun
16 Zilch, south of the border
17 Ocean, poetically
18 Idris of "The Harder They Fall"
19 Pt. of YWCA
20 Incorporate, as new territory
21 Wormhole ships
22 Yellowstone Park attraction
24 Abstract style of the 60s
25 Mr. Castro
28 Important numbers for the IRS
30 Got by somehow
33 Ostracized
38 ___ out
39 Peripatetic group
42 Hardly a revealing skirt
43 Haute couture or prêt-à-porter pro craftsman
46 Passage for Santa
47 Enter completely
48 Five-star initials
49 Bit of a Roman army footwear
51 News reporting pioneer Paul
53 Mexican newborn
56 Bubbly pops
58 Femur neighbor
62 Addressed the nation, say
65 43-Across Cassini
66 Site of many organs
67 Empty room phenomenon
70 Grain grinder
71 In memoriam items
72 Baldwin known for impersonation
73 Salad crunchy
74 Quinine-flavored drink
75 Citizen of Istanbul, probably
76 Professional creator of dance routines for performances and big shows

Down

1 Some batteries
2 Unburdens (of)
3 Rattled
4 Prevented from attacking
5 Receives in return for effort
6 Throws in one's two cents
7 Accommodating vessels
8 Long-horned antelope
9 Freeze, as a windshield
10 Act of singing the scales
11 Fife-and-drum corps instrument
12 Chow (down)
15 Be usable for a long time
23 1985 Malkovich movie
24 Modern Mac interface
26 1958 Chevrolet debut
27 Nissan, formerly
29 Legendary loch monster
31 Absent-minded drawing
32 1980s Dodge
34 JPEG or BMP
35 Came back to Earth
36 Open niche
37 Desperate, as a warning
38 Puts away for good
40 Thesaurus abbr.
41 Woodland forager

44 John Denver "I Guess ___ Rather Be in Colorado"
45 Operating right now
50 Sleeveless Arab garment
52 Extremely
54 Yogi Bear's pal
55 Messing up
57 Jolt
58 Crypt, for one
59 Pertaining to a pelvic bone
60 Impolite expression
61 Arctic dome home
63 Not lifeless
64 Popular Puccini opera
66 Conference freebie, sometimes
68 Piece of evidence
69 Munich term of address

Across

1 Incited
8 Banner
12 Sch. founded by Jefferson
13 "Coffee, Tea ___?" (1960s best seller)
14 Bart's brainy sister
15 Flanders of TV
16 Fussy dressers
17 With a fighting chance
18 ___ horse
20 False front?
22 Second-guessing phrase
23 More vulgar
24 Manure
25 Memory item
26 (Of production) limited in number
32 Amigos
33 Tel follower in the air
34 Church bells maker Henry
38 Whodunit focus
39 Songlike
40 Wisconsin athlete
41 Traipses
42 Enforcer
44 Kilt wearer's refusal
45 Jackson of jazz
46 Leave-me bridge
47 Cases for EMTs
48 Lifetimes
49 LAN system

Down

1 Pleasant activity description
2 Infest
3 "Borderline" singer
4 Really lean
5 Sci-fi flick of 82
6 Japanese or Chin. ruler of old
7 Marauds
8 Frequent type of traveler
9 Double Nobelist Pauling
10 Offhand remark
11 Croc's cousin
19 Runs for health
21 Easy targets
23 Agnew, one of the Celtic Woman stars
25 Scottish-born US steel magnate
27 Wall St. hirees
28 Deck member
29 French city on the Rhone
30 Ingredient in some margaritas
31 Major hurdle, metaphorically
34 Molten igneous rock
35 Ferguson of shows
36 Edge along slowly
37 Parasites living quarters
38 Creek transport
40 Inclusive choice
43 Baseball great Mel

Across

1 Branch of Islam
5 Guard stats
11 Rooster's feature
12 Closed pen's head?
13 Company quota
14 Far out of
16 Deadeye's skill
17 Charmin layer
18 Small private area on a train
20 Sable relative
21 Diagrams
24 First mate's superior, slangily
27 Traveler's stopover
28 "Chicago" showgirl Hart
29 Crude dudes
30 Yields via treaty
31 Old newspaper section
32 Shoulder-related
34 Marine crustacean
36 One who is owed
39 Tails of a fly?
41 Mo. with no major holidays
42 Star clusters
44 Day, in Madrid
45 Farrow of moviedom
46 Jared of "American Psycho"
47 Inspires admiration
48 Eminem alter ego Shady

Down

1 Vistas
2 Wolf's sound
3 Noncommittal reply
4 Jumping back of a wall?
5 Of colorful sky lights
6 Honkers
7 French battlefield
8 Emergency room imperative
9 Razz
10 Unnamed source
15 Physiques
19 Like some spy messages
20 Nintendo space shooter
22 Jimmy of shoes
23 Hilarious sort
25 Pink-slip giver
26 Famous tower city
28 Shark attachment
29 Kimono material
30 Dome toppers
32 Balloon type
33 Agile
35 Standard deviation letter
37 Destroy financially
38 Dated expletive
39 Actress Jessica
40 Mountain giant
43 Large sizes, briefly

142 MEDIUM

Across

1 Knocked, slangily
7 Spa mixtures
11 Penne and the like
17 Areas between two concentric circles
18 ___ fail (fiasco)
19 Fine or decorative garments
20 Singer Twain
21 Carly Simon "___ Want Is You"
22 Say hi, say
23 Solidify
24 "Damn Yankees" temptress
25 Obsess over
26 2019 Grammy winner ___ Mai
27 "The Thin Man" canine role
29 Screeners at JFK
31 Arizona city named for a landform
32 Visit twice
34 Morsel
36 Early PC go-with
37 Caught in ___
39 Extremely sharp or intense
41 Welsh Corgi dog breed
45 Forced work colony
50 Am-early connector
51 Knightly exploits
53 Of the soft palate's end

54 German WWII 45-Across cousin
56 Rowdy of "Rawhide"
59 Whiten
60 Certain welcoming gesture
63 Makes less pleasing
65 "Chicago" actress Zellweger
66 Boating hazard
67 Pod-bearing tropical tree
71 Tycoons
73 Footballer Michael
78 It can be raised by a desperate one
79 Shocked yelp
80 Extends outward
82 Fictional tea-party attendee
83 Meadowlark relative
85 Edible part of a litchi
87 Long-armed institution
89 Indian chief
90 Boudoir wear
91 Live (at)
92 Flammable gas
93 Pillow filler
94 Keeps occupied
95 Liam who voiced Aslan
96 Bridgelike game
97 Most sage and knowledgeable

Down

1 No slowpoke
2 Sniff and then some
3 Hairbrush targets
4 Hot fudge creation
5 "Night" memoirist Wiesel
6 Goddess of the hunt
7 Eating hours
8 Transfer, as data
9 Pickle flavorer
10 Neuralgia
11 High Ottoman official
12 Congratulatory contraction
13 Forecast warnings
14 Rewarded the server
15 Musical passage or direction
16 Purgative herbs
28 Ante
30 Ballgame souvenir
33 Pencil parking place
35 Light wood
36 ___ Griffin Enterprises
38 Wobble
40 Dishevel
41 Dismissive remark
42 "Jump Into My Fire" vocalist James
43 Muffled cry
44 Audacious
46 Fashion fold
47 Jai ___ (Basque sport)
48 Synthetic

49 Corp. officer
52 Mellow personality
55 Prefix meaning height
57 Violently disturbed
58 Discharge, as lava
61 Word on a memorial
62 Away from the Great Britain's shore
64 Willie Nelson "___ Had My Way"
67 Picked out
68 Let in fresh air
69 Trite
70 Island farewells
72 Native people of Canada
74 Type of small monkey
75 Travel bag
76 Sultan's decrees
77 State-of-the-art
79 Nation south of Saudi Arabia
81 Camel's proverbial backbreaker
84 Carson's successor
86 Tower-shaped chess piece
88 Sphere opening?

Across

1 Extremely dense object in space from which even light cannot escape
8 Periodical
11 Spanish district
12 Khaki fabric
14 Ancient Greek harpists
16 Tennis coach Ivan
17 Office PC nexus
18 Earning regularly
20 Revels (in)
22 B-movie heater
23 Freelancers encl.
24 Cosmetic fine paintbrush
26 Brook's singing partner
27 100 centesimos
28 Small quantity
30 Certain contraction
32 Expansive view
34 1980s gaming inits
35 Cool, to surfers
36 Pore in a leaf
39 German guidebook
42 Dunno preceders
43 Go off, as a volcano
44 Match wrongly
47 Skylit spaces
48 Made aerodynamic
49 Equation part, briefly
50 First step toward US Citizenship

Down

1 Crude amt
2 1971 Clapton classic
3 Elegant tapestry
4 Like a shirt with wrinkles
5 It stops the waters and enables lake surface travel?
6 Red ___ (candies)
7 Flair
8 Little underwater vessel
9 Of Peruvian peaks
10 Period of great prosperity, joy and achievement
13 "In ___ shoes" (2005 movie)
15 Man of wisdom
19 Enriches, as a roast
20 Hibernating gigantic beast that can run fast and climb trees
21 Bro's counterpart
25 Serving Djokovic
26 Having two elements
27 Fakers
29 ACLU interests
31 Fireside setting
33 As previously said
35 Label again
37 Cinematic Scarlett
38 Corner joint
40 Image res. stat
41 In abundance
45 Title of respect in Tokyo
46 Byrnes or Hall

Across

1 Polar North
12 Canada's largest city
13 Tree of holly genus
14 Tying up a ship
15 Coldplay's
"Viva la ___"
16 Action film fodder
17 Caesarian attire
18 Computer brains,
briefly
19 Like some approvals
20 Annoying kitchen
sound
21 Senate aide
22 Anatomical tip
23 Air toy's flowy end
27 Dash specialist
29 Certain ratio for
dieters, initially
30 Ostrich relatives
31 Deposit of minerals
32 Evolves, perhaps
35 Musician nicknamed
Sugar Lips
36 Subjects for biopics
37 Joseph who wrote
"Heart of Darkness"
39 Tablet compatible
with Apple Pencil
40 Guttural
41 Woodshop tool
42 Roll of paper money
43 Up-point link
44 Gamer-turned-
businessman

Down

1 Withdrawal
machines, for short
2 Carrots, e.g.
3 Casino dealer
4 Ripped to shreds
5 Personal ltrs
6 Cig. boxes
7 Gearwheel tooth
8 A small stream
9 Country singer Patsy
10 Did ushering
11 Obtain,
as vengeance
17 Woods on the links
19 Fills fully
20 Shakes at rehab
21 Tabbouleh holders

23 Yacht speed units
24 Stray from the norm,
in London
25 Copycat
26 Chinese writer
___ Yutang
28 One hampering
31 Ristorante
intoxicator
32 Not out of
the tournament yet
33 Plunge
34 Stop, in pirate-speak
35 Rowdy crowd
37 Barbecue badly
38 Half a tetrad
40 Municipal div.

HARD

Across

1 Road trip stop
10 Government div.
14 A flowing
15 Congress hallway persuader
17 Ornamental shell source
18 Insectivorous plant
19 "The Hallucinogenic Toreador" painter
20 Weatherspoon of the WNBA
22 Wharton, the first woman to win a Pulitzer
24 Sap of strength
28 Hidden lair of an animal
29 German composer Carl
32 Catnaps
33 Ostentatiously rich
36 Short but not sweet, as a response
37 Part of the British military forces
41 Her follower?
42 Marine 10-legger
43 MacDowell on the screen
45 Word on a blue ribbon
46 Holder of a Grand Slam event (inits)
49 Paper marketing device
52 Marks left by surgical procedures
54 Moistens overnight, perhaps
57 Gershwin's title song words before the rhythm
58 Breeding colony of penguins
62 Think well of
64 Put on the line
65 One that watches by way of caution
66 Antiquing apparatus
67 Things needed

Down

1 Prodded
2 Poem greeting the dawn
3 Russian dictator
4 Trouble for a bowler
5 A number's homophone
6 Volunteer babysitter, maybe
7 Depiction of lineage, frequently
8 Long-gone
9 Language that gave us reindeer
10 Canadian 90s punkers
11 Feature of a needle or cyclone
12 For every
13 Burlesque
16 Committee
21 Having a relation
23 Kachina doll carvers
25 SAT fare
26 Bleu shade
27 Kind of life insurance
30 Always-the-same routines
31 Resting place for a polar bear
33 Gold or silver lace
34 Leading resort on the French Riviera
35 Spreads pitch on
37 Type of rum liqueur
38 Apennine erupter
39 Angler's tools
40 Long. crossers
44 Campfire glower
46 Chinese temple
47 Fawn
48 Butterfly-attracting flowers
50 Cliff hanger?
51 Pastoral poems
53 Fleecy clouds
55 Undertake
56 Like a cocoon
59 Wow, when texting
60 Shakespearean verb
61 Plunk lead-in
63 Boston footballer, in brief

Bonus Clue

Transfer the letters from the corresponding shaded squares above into this grid
to form the **two best spots for art enthusiasts in London**

1	2	3	4

5	6	7	8	9	10

11	12	13	14	15	16

17	18	19	20	21	22	23	24

146   AZTECS' TREASURE

Across

1 Chocolate is regarded as such
10 "Love Story" composer
11 Ladder step
12 Made mention
13 Sprout canines
14 Covers up
16 Have no destination in mind
18 Oregon license-plate depiction
19 Pelvis bones
20 Morning beverages
23 Bad pun response
24 Papeete's location
26 Soviet leader
29 Sunburned
30 Surgeon's stitch
31 Smoking, to many
32 Research outpost co-developed by NASA
33 Iranian faith
36 Leaves in the bag
38 Do exactly right
39 Avian ailment?
42 Easily attachable
44 Fearsome fate
45 Powerful disinfectant
46 Historical time unit
47 Certain stress reducer found for example in cocoa beans

Down

2 Not just live in the present
3 Samson's strength
4 Without anymore
5 Gripes of wrath
6 Be litigious
7 Private electronic network
8 As needed
9 Forecast word
12 Neurotransmitter of happiness
13 Gibbs of country
15 Large group of professionals
17 Dark dessert bar is rich in this element
19 Private, at times
21 Cal. opener
22 Alternative to HBO
25 Medicinal vapor
27 Ge-ne center?
28 Apr. 15th addressee
30 One form of civil disobedience
34 Popular English doll
35 Closet contents
37 Stirred in
39 Single-edged knife
40 Discussion spots
41 Shark offering
43 Pasty food served in Honolulu

Across

1 Listing on a business sched.
4 Made happier
12 Dwarf in "The Hobbit"
13 Dressed for choir
14 Cute beginning?
15 Requiring much effort
17 Bear's extremity
18 Aware of the latest
19 Bull or ram
20 Rounded ear projection
21 Certain verdict
23 "Mr. Blue Sky" band, for short
24 Emergency room system
27 Part of a music score sheet
32 Pulls
33 Kingly name
34 Fixes deeply
37 Bus. bosses
38 Without
39 Renter's document, maybe
43 "Entourage" role
44 Illegal arms dealer
45 Fictionalize?
46 Northern vessel
47 Alarm ending
48 Revolutionary War French general
49 Dol. change

Down

1 Detachable sections
2 Capital of Libya
3 Container with presents
4 Framework of crossing lines
5 Table start?
6 Border
7 Entrust, as authority
8 Harmful pesticide, initially
9 Mountainous republic
10 More than praise
11 Loser to Roosevelt in 1944
16 Challenger, to a champion
19 Aura
22 Expressions of repugnance
24 Elevated for driving
25 Adopt again
26 Accts. payable receipt
28 Unspecified folks
29 Like some produce
30 Most to the point
31 Thrusts out
34 Including everything
35 Tennis champ Sharapova
36 Concise instructions
37 Gents
40 Military subdivision
41 Babysitter's headache
42 Actor Perry
44 Gal's counterpart

Across

1 Key figure of Impressionism and Manet's mentor
13 1860s presidential nickname
14 Some vowels
15 Two- or three-striper, for short
16 First tuba note?
17 Any party planner
18 SUV's cousin
20 Air setting at the service sta.
21 Calls to mind
23 Become apparent
25 Alternative to Vegas
26 Lazaretto (archaic)
27 Follower of Leno
30 It means both
34 Wad of bills
37 Places with cloisters
39 UK medal
40 Prefix for biology
41 Primary colore
42 Balance-reducing equipment, often
43 Laughably odd
45 Bitter tonic salts
47 Icelandic opus
48 Most reliable
49 Peasant
52 Alphabetic sequence
56 Inner-ear chambers
59 Gleaming
61 Suffix for potent or different

62 Resilient
64 Echo, briefly
65 Nevertheless, informally
66 Special request at a shoe store
67 When tripled, 1964 Beach Boys hit
68 Stage signal from musical director
69 Great Romantic artist famous for his optical effects and intense brushstrokes

Down

1 Adventure
2 Holding a higher position than
3 Brunch slice
4 Hardly adequate
5 Aromatic attire
6 Article for the Berlin natives
7 Without effect
8 Mere
9 Braga of Hollywood
10 Dude ranch prop
11 Legendary sewer
12 Intentionally fail to include
19 Press on or drive forward
22 Eccentric sort

24 Love handle material
26 Barn's neighbor
28 Concoction
29 Theater of old
31 Like a hard-to-hit fastball, in slang
32 Unit of eight computer bits
33 Faiths, say
34 Big name in home audio
35 Starting four
36 Bully's prey, in stereotypes
37 Bad thing to be caught in
38 Burger bread
41 Hamilton's duel foe
44 Term regarding distribution
45 Kinda similar
46 Uneasy feeling
48 Gazed rudely
50 Hall-of-Famer Merlin
51 Shoshone shelter
53 70s music
54 Jadedness
55 Overnighting option
56 Refer to as an example
57 Island near Maui
58 Drain backup cause
59 Bolivian beverage
60 Dubbing concern
63 Patriots' org.

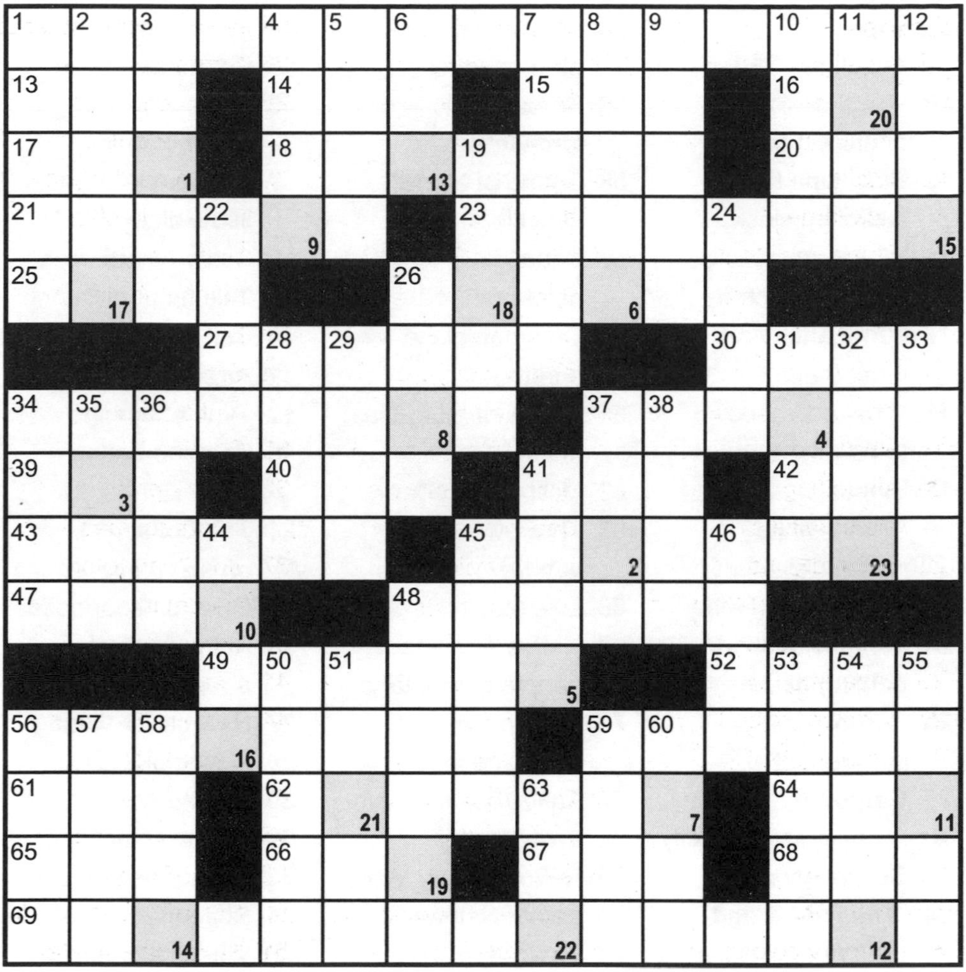

Bonus Clue

Transfer the letters from the corresponding shaded squares above into this grid to form the name of the famous work of art exhibited in the Louvre

1	2	3	4	5	6	7

8	9	10	11	12	13	14

15	16	17

18	19	20	21	22	23

Across

1 Absolute
10 Some desktop printers, familiarly
13 Busy time for a cuckoo clock
14 Well-worn pencils
15 Copycat's activity
17 20th-century art movement
18 What one needs to ride the tram
19 Blokes
20 Silvery-white metallic element
22 Gets hot on Twitter
24 Lengths of short printing dashes
25 Comparison component
26 Carpe tail?
28 Army enlistee, briefly
31 Successors
34 "The Falcon and the Winter Soldier" actress Kellyman
36 Carbo-loader's course
37 Vagrant
40 Counterbalance
44 Floor-washing robot brand
45 UK citizen
46 Alteration
47 Very important or famous
49 Sore
51 Western military alliance letters
52 Bureaucratic formulation
58 Sound of a brief chuckle
59 Squalid neighborhood
60 Common place for a tattoo
61 Cause of a big blast (inits)
63 Million preceder
65 Three-wheeled vehicle
68 Like otologists' tests
69 Native American people of Montana
71 Amazonian language
72 Takes one's breath away
73 Revolutionary War patriot Nathan
74 Fastball, in baseball lingo
75 Seabee's org.
76 Notices (archaic)

Down

1 Barely like this
2 2014 drama starring Russell Crowe
3 Customary way of doing something
4 Preposterous
5 Permeate
6 Largest of the Marianas
7 Shortened, like a dict.
8 Scary African flies
9 Title for Judi Dench
10 Bottled up
11 Arranged in advance
12 Type of admin
16 Bamboo-eating beast
21 The Colts, on a scoreboard
23 Ones on soapboxes
25 At the back of a room to swing?
27 New car sticker fig.
29 Newly baked
30 Around
32 Pet-rescuing org.
33 Anchor hoister
35 Store sign
38 Vulcan's forte
39 From Portugal or Spain
41 British boarding school
42 2002 Best New Artist Grammy winner Jones
43 Labor leaders shout
45 Remain or stay (poetically)
46 Corp. money minders

47 Command post on a ship
48 Shares house
50 Former capital of Pakistan
53 Scorns
54 Athletic event for charity
55 Clarification starter
56 Way past tipsy
57 Grand finale
62 Parishioner's 10 percent
64 Ingrid Bergman role
65 Negri of old Hollywood
66 Square dance caller
67 Pit follower
68 Tempe campus
70 Piece of siege equipment

HARD

Across

1 Cry heard after waiting
6 French currency
11 Farm structure with many layers
12 Breathe
14 Wheat, for one
15 Duties
16 Turntable part
18 Home often built in the spring
19 Deck quartet
21 State positively
24 Less tainted
28 Baby's footwear
29 Early computer called "the Giant Brain"
30 Wild and basmati
31 "No Exit" playwright
32 First group to be invited
33 Beautifies
34 Alloy of iron and carbon
36 Make followers?
40 Solve
44 States or countries
46 Binge-watcher's aid
47 Metrical foot
48 Times to call, in classifieds
49 Goes down the drains
50 Some control tower equipment

Down

1 Int. earner
2 Corrida competitor
3 Diving bird
4 Inclinations
5 Ancient war galley
6 Extrasensory perception letters
7 Abreast of
8 Ascendancy
9 Unbitten bits
10 Four of them equaled one denarius
13 Award since 1949
17 Makes a collar
20 Fisherman of old
21 Substances used for polishing
22 Burrito wrap
23 Pair in an ellipse
25 Like guinea pigs and bush pigs
26 Ceremonial
27 Acquire as someone's trust
31 Robert B. Parker's private eye
35 Do a garage job
37 Big name in espionage
38 Lay-thick connector
39 Clock's noise
41 Long live, in Mexico
42 In any circumstance
43 Erosion
45 Sighs of delight

Across

1 Money-hungry move
8 Harbor city
12 Its divided into scenes
13 Cyborg prefix
14 Sashimi fish
15 Most friable
17 Encouragement from the angler
18 Materials for securing
19 Chophouse choices
21 Direction in a score
22 Persuaders
23 Decor finish?
24 Foot of a poet
25 Take no sides
30 Asphalt mark
31 Have confidence in
32 Participant in a struggle
36 Castle material, perhaps
37 Least demanding
38 Treated with malice
40 Fashion magazine for women
41 Court battle
43 Headed for home, in a way
44 Mission-scrapping words
45 Late stage actress Hagen
46 Goes one better
47 Flowed out

Down

1 Rotating engine disks
2 Clear overlay
3 Great celebrity
4 Curmudgeonly comment
5 Caviar sources
6 Crunches strengthen them
7 Reached the lowest point
8 Part of some addresses, briefly
9 Express a viewpoint
10 Movie critic, often
11 Region near Mount Olympus
16 First lady before Michelle
20 Sir, to a Hindu
22 Restraining order of a sort
23 Medieval crossbow
24 Calligrapher's accessory
26 DC Comics superheroine
27 Get in shape
28 Let
29 Pasta preference
33 Modesto mogul
34 Yellow posy
35 Necessitates
36 Piece of flatware
38 Big video games studio
39 Beyond tired
42 Les parents give it to l'enfant

BEST ACTRESSES

Across

1 The only woman in history who won the title statuette exactly three times
15 Italian author Primo
16 Innocent person's words after "I've got nothing"
17 Apply, as a coat of paint
19 Ripping off
21 Zeniths
22 Knocker's reply, perhaps
23 Most assuredly
25 Highland haze
26 "Frasier" brother
27 Native tent
29 Gem angle
30 Opposite of cheerful
34 Lapse list
37 Divorced pair
39 Ice-rink feat
40 Z4 carmaker
42 Your, archaically
43 Lightsaber wielders
44 Poach cycling ducks
46 Lawn improvement process
50 CBS drama with DNA testing
51 Spouse's parents
52 Audiotape holder
53 Poolroom supplies
55 Foot warmer
57 Data-storage device

59 Kind of transit
62 Be corrosive
65 Requires more than one (to tango)
67 Middle Easterner
68 Charles Lamb's nom de plume
70 Start of a Chinese game
71 Puerto Rico's zone: abbr.
73 Situate
74 Costco alternative
75 Disregard
78 Bridge suit
80 In need of tidying up
82 Used colorful language
84 Coral organism
85 Lab gel medium
87 Old World prickly plants
92 Fancy
93 Portuguese good morning
95 Brilliant bird
96 Rhodes of scholarship fame
97 Drives away
98 "Tosca" solo
99 Winner of four Academy Awards who never attended the ceremony

Down

1 Custardy pastry
2 Towed-away auto, maybe
3 Diehard
4 Current Pacific El follower?
5 Each has two senators
6 Janitorial tool
7 Bishop's robe
8 Less assured
9 Honorific verses
10 Take a coffee break
11 Dress with a flare
12 Hometowners
13 Reading-impaired, in a way
14 Lowest die rolls
18 Egg creations
20 Entrails
24 BBC's nickname, with the
28 Certain flycatcher
29 Cajun milieu
30 Daytime showings
31 Beasts in a span
32 Not staged
33 Earthen jars
35 Courtroom fig.
36 Slow-witted Brits
38 Uproars
41 Finnish coin of yore
45 Business analysis letters
47 Dark wines
48 Came to earth

49 Cruel emperor
54 Brazilian musical genre
56 Overly theatrical
58 Moves with the breeze
60 Carson's predecessor
61 Scientific org.
63 Like some dessert orders
64 Part of a bank vault door
66 Responses of confusion
69 Ancient empire of Iraq
72 Fare-well connection
76 Large edible prawns
77 Encumbrance
79 Cheese city
81 Went letter by letter
83 Hidden stockpile
84 Prepare to leave
85 Cadabra preceder
86 Busy type
88 Former Swedish car company
89 Creamy white color
90 Safe haven
91 Cygnet's destiny
94 Project end?

Across

1 Trekking with a rucksack
10 Catch a criminal red-handed
12 Mercenary
13 Wretched
15 Iberian title
16 Ingenious devices
18 Oxygen-deprived
19 Backwoods folks
20 Fully horizontal
21 Time of the 90th meridian
22 Ring stats
24 "Our Man in Havana" author
26 Thrilling
28 Scoreboard tally, briefly
30 Rosie's willowy form
31 Athletics-focused channel that launched in 1979
32 Filmed over
34 Port in a storm
36 Acquire, as liabilities
39 Ageless, in poesy
41 Pen-tip material
43 Marine predators
47 Alec Baldwin's middle name
48 Move casually
49 Doesn't keep a poker face
51 Kitchen wizard Rombauer
53 Starting letters of internet protocol
54 Responding to commands, say
55 Every, in an Rx
57 Big digs
59 Elegant branched centerpieces
61 Often-misspelled contraction
62 Declining in power
63 Calculus pioneer
64 Stick nose into others business
65 Salsify

Down

2 Species of the geum plant family
3 Tomb of a sort
4 Fort near Louisville
5 Equality
6 Cry of dismay
7 Victorious declaration
8 Chinese menu promise
9 Lapidarist's object of study
10 Cell parts
11 Open-chain hydrocarbon
14 Some wind pipes
15 Rich Viennese chocolate cake
16 Billowing blasts
17 Cinematic characters, often
23 Bar accessory
25 Citadel org.
27 Evidence in some exonerations
29 Brawl souvenir
32 Out of business, for short
33 Bit of binary code
35 Sleeveless waist-length garment
37 Abduction ship, in tabloids: abbr.
38 Highway turnout
40 Monsoon occurrences
42 Stand that a politician might take
44 Harvester
45 Obtained
46 Like immature fruit
48 Combination of two videos or songs
50 Heavyweight Liston
52 Electricity usage tracker
56 Hard-drive units
58 Legendary Swiss archer William
60 NFL Hall-of-Famer Marchetti

Bonus Clue

Transfer the letters from the corresponding shaded squares above into this grid
to form the title of one of Sergio Leone's masterpieces

1	2	3	4

5	6	7	8

9

10	11	12	13

14	15

16	17	18	19	20	21	22

Across

1 Punctuation mark not found on keyboards and rarely used in print
11 Isles of the Pacific
12 Jannings of silents
13 Forebrain gray matter structures
14 Hawaiian figurine
15 Remote button abbr.
16 Mended, in a way
18 Willingly accepting
21 American deer
22 Modern zoo barrier
23 Literary framework
25 Capone and Gore
26 Light carriage
30 Grooving
32 ATM inputs
33 Largest member of the dolphin family
34 Tryout
35 Look without blinking
38 Poolside refresher
40 Stylist's concern
42 Comes before mist?
43 Root canal procedure, briefly
44 Civil War general Burnside
47 Made to last
48 First-aid applications
49 Pair of signs for enclosing extra information

Down

1 German pronoun
2 Phoenicia locale
3 Gift
4 Formally establish
5 Outer edge
6 Busting operation
7 Promise
8 Acid in protein
9 Rivals of Reeboks
10 Make an unpowered flight
11 Armchair adjunct
17 Within
19 It may be played in a pool
20 Nerve type
24 Open-sided porch
26 Small, thin scrap
27 Evenly paired
28 Present a problem
29 Country properties
31 Oxidize
34 90s video-game blockbuster
35 Rams and lambs
36 31-syllable Japanese poem
37 Helper
39 Golden Gate Bridge feature
41 Brewery dryer
45 Dashboard abbr.
46 Ave. crossers, perhaps

Across

1 Family fellows
5 Builders' sites
9 BHO's predecessor
12 And higher, in cost
13 Musical production
14 "Charlie's Angels" actress
15 Hideous
16 Time extensions
18 Enclosing in an embrace
20 Nth degree
21 ESPN analyst Dilfer
22 Fleet runner
24 Fourth notes
25 Void state
28 60's muscle car letters
29 Graph of beats
30 Of the east Mediterranean
34 Cool of Green Day
36 They come after no pain
37 Corrected
39 1990s veep
40 Cleared off
42 Be better in a no blinking contest
44 Woeful words
45 Add years
46 Gobs and gobs
47 Israeli Golda
48 Appreciative abbr.
49 Nave furniture
50 Bygone fleet, briefly

Down

1 Uncertain
2 Yarn made from hair of rabbits
3 Coarse red seaweeds
4 Keep under surveillance
5 Loughlin of "Full House"
6 Police order
7 Wolfram
8 Map dir.
9 Halberd's cousin
10 World War II era military jeeps manufacturer
11 Complete failure
17 Cymbal's sound
19 Medit. hot spot
23 Part of a polite introduction
26 Inspire
27 Crabs about to molt
28 Wire thickness measures
31 As much as is required
32 Whirlpool current
33 How pawns are arranged, at first
34 Fannies
35 Give off once more
38 Gallivants
39 One forced to take the blame
41 Department store section
43 Eavesdrop electronically

Across

1 Sent by
5 Helvetica's lack
10 Gadgets rank in cartoons: abbr.
14 Overseas coin
15 Calendario opener
16 Filmmaker Jordan
17 Memo heads-up
18 By means of
19 Bit of proofreader's notation
20 Materialize
22 Crumbled, as support
24 Flying dinosaur about the size of a modern pigeon
27 Folded-and-filled food
28 Cosmic periods
30 Addition to the staff
31 Be nitpicky
33 Family name in the Old West
36 Title before Khan
37 Fraudulent
40 Jane or John
41 Hollywood's Howard and others
43 October birthstone
44 Like honeycombs
46 Skier's way up
48 Arab leaders (var.)
49 Gentle giraffe-like prehistoric giant plant-eater
53 Thanksgiving decorations
54 Problems for orators
56 Has no entity
57 In a state of combustion
59 2008 Bond girl Kurylenko
62 World Cup objective
63 Be festive
64 Around the corner, perhaps
65 Gambling payment
66 Laments loudly
67 Assistant on the Hill

Down

1 Many a Guinness Book record
2 Forensic evidence of a wheel
3 Dinner table dropping
4 Single eyeglass
5 Weever fish
6 Happen afterwards as a consequence
7 Duplication on paper
8 Boiling blood
9 Platform at the head of the ship's frontmost mast
10 Recommend (var.)
11 Distressed
12 Heat-resistant glass
13 Responded, in court
21 Rouge destination
23 Stimpy's sidekick
24 Compadre
25 Showed a classic episode, say
26 Menace
27 Busy Midwestern airport
29 Pops the top
31 Italian resort island
32 Actress Gardner
34 Farewell, my French friend
35 Crowd clamors
38 Biblical vessel
39 Overplay
42 Give a fright
45 Non grata individual
47 A following?
48 Three-legged stands
49 Subatomic particle
50 Approach hurriedly
51 Morsel in a Greek salad
52 Song type
53 Prefix denoting a thousand million
55 Kind of package
58 Cost to hire a professional
60 Floral welcome gift
61 Have no particular place to go

Crossword Grid

1	2	3	4	■	5	6	7	8	9	■	10	11	12	13
14 (9)				■	15				(14)	■	16			(3)
17		(20)		■	18					■	19	(12)		
	■		20	21			(17)	■	22	23				
■	24	25			(18)			26						■
27	(8)					■		28			(10)	■		29
30					■	31	32		(19)	■	33	34	35	
36	(1)		■	37	38		(11)			39	■	40		
41			42	■	43				■	44	45	(16)		
	■		46	47			■		48	(6)				■
■	49	50		(15)			51	52			(22)			■
53	(21)				■	54					■			55
56				■	57	58	(5)			■	59	60	61	(2)
62			(4)	■	63				(13)	■	64			
65				■	66					■	67	(7)		

Bonus Clue

Transfer the letters from the corresponding shaded squares above into this grid
to form the monsters of "Jurassic Park"

1	2	3	4	5	6	7	8	9	10

11	12	13	14	15	16	17	18	19	20	21	22

165

Across

1 1954 film septet
7 The big leagues
13 Japanese kimono sash
14 CPR-certified volunteer
15 Witch's curse
16 Liquid coloring
17 DC lawmaker
18 Historical French province
20 "The A-Team" muscleman
21 Kazakhstan's ___ Mountains
23 Cry of despair
24 Of those who aren't clergy
25 Large hand tool with one adjustable jaw
28 Kind of effect
31 Persona-grata link
32 Apple fave
33 Forms a lap
36 Audibly reacts in surprise
40 Measly
41 Unspecified person
43 Diverse group might be a melting one
44 Reserved in advance for a price
46 In a countrified manner
48 Chaney of old chillers
49 Brought back into service
51 Restaurant serving
52 Half of the WWII bomber's name
54 Gandhi garb
55 Good, to Giuseppe
56 Green Card org.
58 Doesn't save
60 Thor's weapon used for heavy work
65 Hula movers
66 "Wayne's World" actor Carvey
67 Not leave waiting at the door
71 B-lot center?
72 Thai capital
74 Nobel physicist Tamm
75 Strong alkaline cleaner
76 Verbal contraction
77 Fair hiring letters
78 Fronted
79 Cow catchers
80 Runners of lab experiments

Down

1 Fifth player to hit 600 homers
2 Hockey Hall of Famer Sid
3 After-dinner morsel
4 Map section
5 Famous jour. publisher
6 Consoling words
7 Hypocrite, say
8 Wide fame
9 Moron's head?
10 Madison Avenue figure
11 A song or poem
12 Creepy sort
19 Like some hard soils
22 LSD and others
24 "Game of Thrones" actress Headey
26 Former key phrase in retailing
27 Aviator's acknowledgment
28 Facial feature
29 Coordinated gene cluster
30 Entertainer Rita
34 Pakistan's longest river
35 Comparatively peeved
37 Bodily blood filter
38 European nation
39 Fashion trends
42 Practice of wearing no clothes
45 Borneo swinger, for short
47 Shades of yellow
50 A monetary unit of Thailand

53 Can-opener targets
57 Get under control, in a way
59 Topped out
60 Con artist's accomplice
61 Country west of Egypt
62 Weapons with bell guards
63 Measures of horses height
64 Home or deal attachment?
68 Oven for baking ceramics
69 They are at the beginning of an idea?
70 Greets silently
72 Story of a lifetime?
73 Game-winning combination

Across

1 Absconded
5 Certain transpose of a matrix (in math)
11 Correctively
13 Front of ship
14 Resembling a spore
15 Fey of "Muppets Most Wanted"
16 Chilean seaport
18 French painter of dancers
19 Sediment formed by wind-blown dust
21 Major troubles
22 Buck of country music
24 It may come between partners?
25 Bathroom bars
26 Sub's concern
27 Nikon product, for short
29 Recipient of hospitality
30 Detective, on occasion
31 Smug look
33 Dots on a state map
34 Disembowel
37 Something heard in court
38 Really excellent
40 Distance letters
41 Less patient
42 Plaster preparations
43 TV grid rows

Down

1 Video game stat.
2 Don't remove
3 Confined
4 City where president Kennedy was assassinated
5 Seltzer lead-in
6 Easter egg colorer
7 Wall Street purchases
8 Light regulators
9 Prohibitions
10 Grounded flier (inits)
12 Readable body parts
17 Tel Aviv A
18 Belittles
20 Plays on the bagpipe
22 Britney Spears exclamation
23 Bulb measure
25 Personal ad verb
26 Foul-smelling Asian fruits
27 Made sure
28 Gridiron guards
29 Donors
30 Salutes with glasses
32 Knock-down-drag-out fight
33 Cinco minus dos
35 Statuette winner Blanchett
36 Flock contingent
37 Env. alternative
39 Med. drama settings

Across

1 Feels under the weather
5 Insights
9 Computer lab inventory
12 Crotchety sort
13 Shorthand single sign for a phrase
15 Tolkien Moria or a Lonely Mountain
17 Arabian ruminant
18 Passover
19 Lake near Nevada's capital
21 Crisis-relief org.
23 British ritual
27 Opp. of withdrawal
28 Weak
29 Orator of old
31 Bounced-check letters
32 Scorched
33 Wise guide
35 Like some ballerinas
36 Wood of the Rolling Stones
38 Opel model
42 The gods of the people of India
44 Chant
45 Archaic adverb
46 Family-friendly ratings
47 Quite a lot
48 They can't be caught indoors

Down

1 Aussie rock grp.
2 Presidential caucus state
3 Good earth for planting
4 Parts of a fugue
5 Sitcom alien
6 Arboreal bird
7 See things alike
8 They seem to live in bars
9 Surpasser
10 Fine wool
11 Texting format
14 Five-time US Open champ
16 Talents
20 Contemplation exclamation
22 Animal without feet
23 Triangle sound
24 Making safe
25 Deliberate insults
26 Mesopotamian deity
29 Tai follower
30 Uninvited guest
32 Produce from nothing
34 Mistake-canceling command
35 Sacred fig tree (var.)
37 Certain sisters
39 Byte prefix
40 Full of promise, future-wise
41 Hill inhabitants
42 Trendy
43 In need of orientation, say

Across

1 Eukaryotic 80-Across power generator
12 Bibliographical abbr.
16 Social finish?
17 16th-century collar
18 Beginning of time?
19 Second helping, to a dieter
20 Code-breaking org.
21 Ones called to an accident, shortly
22 Suit go-withs
23 Rwandan ethnic group
24 Solar eclipse phenomena
26 Common or sixth follower
27 First step
28 Desert fox
30 Bounder
32 Prize draw
35 Rene of film
38 Obvious answer
41 Keeps company with
42 Grain variety
43 Grind your teeth
44 World's largest particle physics lab based in Switz.
45 Obelisks
46 Involve, as an audience
47 Actively involved
49 Publicity ad, briefly

51 Thought over
54 Italian gentlemen
58 Violet dye obtained from lichens (var.)
62 Move to a new table
65 Large movie screen format
66 Related to form or type
67 Dependable
68 Newsroom fixture
69 Perfectly timed
70 Narrow projection from a cliff
71 One engaging in aimless activity
73 Wall St. abbr.
75 Coop up
77 Posthumously printed bio
80 Basic structural units of organisms
83 Tar
86 Ceremonial rod
87 Suitable
88 Wings, in Latin
89 Fathomed
90 Vessel by a basin
91 Coastal coaster
92 Riddick the boxer
93 Widescreen choice
94 Camera options
95 Process of copying a segment of DNA to the RNA (in biology)

Down

1 Garlic chopper
2 Make followers?
3 Certain muscle injury
4 Battlement openings
5 Opposite of cruel
6 Frequently
7 Art gallery tag letters
8 Borrower's concern
9 Get-writing bridge
10 Isolated appearance
11 Welcoming words after long time
12 Taking a breath
13 Contest
14 Focused
15 (In genetics) twisted-ladder structure
25 Hurt one's feelings
26 Racing craft
29 Lake beside Buffalo
31 A drink
33 Out yachting
34 Terrarium plant
36 Reaction to an insult
37 Crystal ball studier
39 Sheepish sound
40 Chinese menu abbr.
42 High pts.
44 Thread-like carriers of hereditary data
45 Devil's buy
46 Put off
48 An emoticon
50 Pregame ritual starter?

52 Big name in Deco design
53 Monopoly holding
55 Next-generation relatives
56 City in Russia
57 Autumn tool
59 "Rush" director Howard
60 Govt. health org.
61 Lingerers
63 Knowing fellows
64 Abandoned garden
67 More lustrous
68 Moved a lot of soil
71 Neighbor of Mozambique
72 Wickerwork cane
74 "Ivanhoe" writer
76 Tone
78 Shout very loudly
79 Wine bucket, for one
81 Croft of video-game fame
82 Country singer Anderson
84 Kind of culture
85 Wacky, in Mexico
88 Kindergarten song start

Across
1 Some cowboys
7 Crone
13 Brightest star in a constellation
14 NYC train, familiarly
16 Type of chalcedony
17 Reached, as the truth
18 English class no-no
19 Lady's companion, briefly
20 Unemotional sort
21 Ignorance-excuse bridge
22 "Jabberwocky" start
23 Whetstone, e.g.
26 Straw, essentially
29 "Trinity" novelist Leon
30 Easy wins
34 Kind of financing, for short
35 Give a reminder
36 Main route
37 Enterprising
39 Enliven
40 Disconnect, as oxen
41 Serving both men and women
42 Investigator, in old film noir
43 Italian sauce with pine nuts
44 By nature
45 Officially outlaws
46 Metric unit of length
49 Stare at in a lecherous manner
52 Radio enthusiasts
53 Legs, for ones
57 Squares on calendars
58 Question of doubt
59 Shopper's mecca of yore
60 Dagger, in Glasgow
61 Allocate
62 Lost by design
63 Tucked away
64 Calorie counters

Down
1 Stand-up comic's material
2 Not just every now and then
3 Aware of the latest developments
4 Poolside seat
5 Ship door
6 Securer for carpet
7 Sesames
8 Bond girl Shirley
9 Gentle paces
10 Over again
11 Mimicking avian
12 Nos. requested by receptionists
15 Covered with minute spines
24 Effluvia
25 Made a poor estimate, say
26 Prepare to score
27 Most easily tied
28 Barnyard sounds
31 Bombay-born famous conductor
32 Smooth one's feathers
33 Aligns in harmony
35 Grade of tea leaves
36 Negative contraction
38 Shared furniture in certain office organization system
39 Under a canopy
41 Dedicate
44 Prejudiced
45 Radiant clever
47 Big Ben sound
48 Make ecstatically happy
49 Long things for underdogs
50 Gallop, trot or canter
51 Neighbor of Cygnus
54 Seconds at the dinner table
55 Storied fox title
56 Tools that have sharp teeth

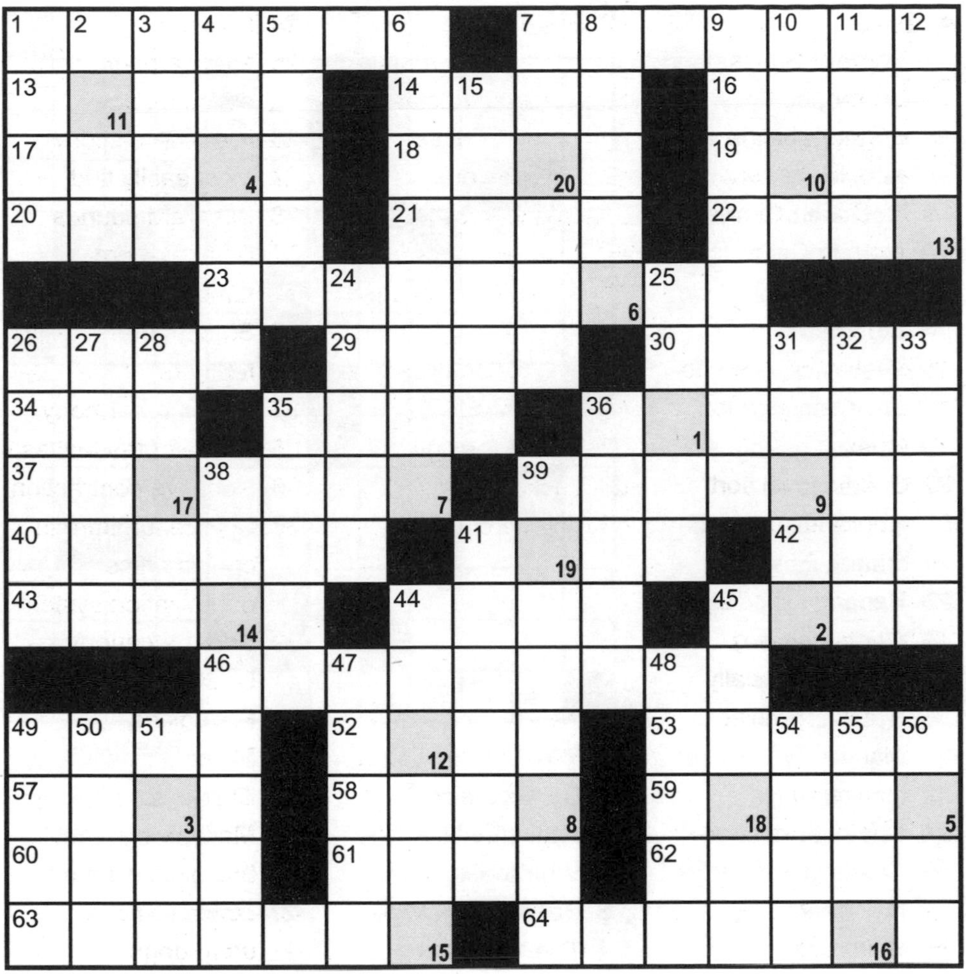

Bonus Clue

Transfer the letters from the corresponding shaded squares above into this grid to form the title of one of the most streamed Disney movies in 2021

1	2	3	4

5	6	7

8	9	10

11	12	13	14

15	16	17	18	19	20

Across

1 Winter travel method developed by northern Indigenous peoples
9 Nastase of tennis
10 God, to Gaius
12 Trapper's collection
14 Mounted
16 First track, often
18 Govt. lender
19 Current positions?
22 Buildings on the English countryside
24 Detroit music genre
26 Expand
29 Central spaces of amphitheaters
30 Set of church bells
31 Many a TikTok user
32 Hankered for
34 Apathetic gesture
35 Chess grandmaster Nakamura
36 State tree of Tex.
38 RR depot
39 Former auto make
42 Video game brother
44 Gambia money
46 Indian wise guy
49 Bit of choreography
50 Lena of "Havana"
51 Traditional form of transport of Canadian natives

Down

1 Certificate of attainment
2 Vaudevillian Olsen
3 Baseball's Hodges
4 The X-Files org.
5 Hons
6 Groom's final words
7 Safe ball
8 Emote
11 Tawdry
13 Arm-waving chilly impressions created by kids
15 Natural geothermal waters perfect for soaking after skiing
17 Beach souvenirs
20 Union
21 Guide, as a ship
23 Converse
25 Marginally ahead
27 Volcanic flowers
28 Prepare
32 Cinnamony tea
33 Fertilizing with manure
34 Ample amounts
37 Prompter's task
40 Damon of Hollywood
41 "Pinocchio" fish
43 Cry of victory
45 PD call
47 2001 boxing biopic
48 Lowest val.

Across

1 It is often padded
5 Trying ones
12 Certain navel
13 Immature parasites
14 Amused response in a text
15 Global shoe retailer
16 Homer hitter's gait
17 Words before little teapot
18 Explain in a new way
21 Urban renewal targets
22 Branch
24 OPEC member
25 Noted spokescow
26 Historical community
30 Pollux's twin
31 Chichen Itza natives
32 Fen
33 Chain crossed by Hannibal
34 One spelling for large rounded rocks
39 An abnormally low body temperature
41 It follows yoo
43 The Explorer of kiddie TV
44 Mild oath
45 Canteen initials
46 Egyptian solar disk
47 Capital of Latvia
48 Chastised
49 Musk of Twitter

Down

1 Cause of an adrenaline rush
2 Prone to leaking
3 Non-studio film, briefly
4 Bright lights in Las Vegas
5 Intestinal
6 Yes follower
7 Transit map markings
8 Study of the heavens, for short
9 Snobbish
10 Bulg. neighbor
11 Drool
19 Talks up
20 They follow Ks
23 Italian possessive pronoun
25 Great Seal feature
26 Freeway misadventure
27 Evil computer of moviedom
28 Eastern tropical storm
29 Hassle-free
30 Helper on a drive
32 Indian fig plant
34 Fair structure
35 Enimem mentor
36 You might be copied on one
37 Beatle behind the others
38 "Cosmos" author Carl
40 BlackBerrys, e.g.
42 Big Ten inits

Across

1 Most common order in a US coffeehouse
12 Broad hollow
13 Peel
14 Actor Bates
15 Ready to be eaten
16 Causes of a painful blinking
18 Gentle
19 Way to fry
21 Astronomical cloud's name
22 New Year abroad
23 Nutmeg-flavored drinks
25 Lung compartment
28 Cork shooter
31 Stripe of contrasting color
33 Dec. 24, notably
34 Russian country cottage
36 Bit of philately
39 Grades below the curve, perhaps
41 Utility-bill measure
43 Words that come after your time
44 Miscalculation, for example
46 Bright flashes
48 Nittany Lions sch.
49 They may be girded
51 Momentarily, informally
53 Reverberations
56 "Gotcha, daddy-o"
57 Spanish 101 article
58 Hero war pilots
61 Indian Zoroastrian
64 Party that might turn into a chaos
65 "WarGames" setting
67 Animated fellow
68 Rubik of cubes
69 Casual farewell in Rome
70 Jolly syllables
71 Layered java drink often served in a shot glass

Down

1 "Bittersweet" and "Quiet" writer Susan
2 Basset's bowlful
3 Tipping
4 Gee preceders
5 Voices between sopranos and tenors
6 Rochester clinic
7 Observer
8 High notes male singers of old
9 Lotion botanicals
10 90s trade pact
11 Can. province
12 Drip-brew coffee with three shots of espresso
17 Ninja projectile
20 At great volume
24 Element of an annoying cloud
26 MS web server software
27 Morning energizer with steamed milk foam
29 Division of play in cricket
30 Classmate, e.g.
31 Casts off
32 Shipping deduction
35 Bottom of one's face
37 Egyptian biters
38 Inspiring one
40 Baseball homer type
42 Domestic of a sort
45 Anonymous Wade opponent
47 Cut corners
50 This-outrage link
52 Mystery woman?
54 Bow of the silents
55 Does not possess, for short
56 Designer Mizrahi
59 Natural stimulant
60 "The Very Busy Spider" author Carle
62 Canine anchor
63 London club district
64 Loudness unit
66 "I goofed!"

Bonus Clue

Transfer the letters from the corresponding shaded squares above into this grid
to form the **names of two must-see attractions of Rome**

1	2	3	4	5	6	7

8	9	10	11	12

13	14	15	16	17

18	19	20	21	22	23	24	25

Across

1 Billiard stroke
6 Compressed video format
10 Wall St. figures
14 Small piece of land surrounded by water
15 Fashion's Chanel
16 Southeastern Conf. powerhouse
17 Evidence of mowing
18 Warm spot for a sleeping cat
19 Carelessly reveal secrets
20 Union issue
22 Like rushing swine
24 Tehran citizen
26 Having no blood vessels
30 Have a stab at the answer
34 Stitch's cartoon partner
35 Mafia bosses
36 Prefix with coastal or mural
37 Novelist Bellow
38 Instinct source
39 Emphatic agreement
40 Scooter's cousin
42 Highway warning
43 A natural talent
45 Judo setting
46 Poisonous lily
49 Give a rude awakening to
50 Bridal gown decoration
51 Collaborative website
52 Brief aides?
53 Ways into buildings
55 Speedy warship
57 Little European grebe
61 Boon of the NHL Hall of Fame
65 Lay the groundwork
66 Change for the bettor?
68 Major cocoa producer
69 Popular Indian destination
70 Words before angel or fool
71 Villain in a Christmas tale
72 End of many company names
73 "A Beautiful Mind" role
74 Mission start?

Down

1 Certain table distribution slips
2 Even-speak link
3 Poetry-reading competition
4 Caterpillar's hair
5 Cuisine category
6 Ones making introductions: abbr.
7 Painfully emotional
8 Cream pastries
9 First name in Israeli statehood
10 For short, for short
11 Poetic place between hills
12 Federal agent
13 Homebuilder's need
21 Does monotonous work
23 Cardiac complaint
25 How not to talk in libraries
27 Going through, on a travel plan
28 Graduate
29 Star of the recital, perhaps
31 Open
32 Of an anesthetic
33 Full house sign letters
39 No longer the same
41 Sudden overthrow attempt
42 Trivia answers
43 White-bearded relatives
44 Aurora's Greek counterpart
45 Dummy
47 Maui music-maker

48 Wrongly advises
50 Cornea defect
54 Correctly, old-style
56 "Breaking Bad" poison
58 2012 political thriller about the Canadian Caper
59 Capital of Switzerland
60 Some tax advisers, shortly
62 The Goddess of Pop
63 Former "American Idol" judge DioGuardi
64 Aware of
67 Theater in Tokyo or Osaka

HARD

Across

1 Film maker's handheld
11 Hillbilly
12 Introverted
13 Whisper sweet nothings to
14 Price hike, briefly
15 Cruise site
16 Dorm people
17 Medieval helmet
19 Sacrificial stack
20 Early Englishmen
22 Persian emperors
25 Dimensions
29 Hint
30 Baker's dozen
32 Part of a microscope
34 Acronym to an oversharer
35 More shiny, as a fruit on a shelf
36 Alaska on a map, sometimes
38 It's big in Latin America
40 Passing crazes
43 Five-year period
47 Associated with us
48 Augment
49 Poi, essentially
50 Coy conclusion?
51 Neurologist's tool, shortly
52 Navel discovery
53 Strategic video game category

Down

1 Nursery furniture
2 Soviet moon-probe program
3 Rudimentary teachings
4 Succumb
5 Super Six, of old autodom
6 Oratory
7 Lose-whisker link
8 Not straight
9 Beastly noise
10 Remedy ration
18 Much less nice
19 Exam for jrs
21 Calypso and her sisters
22 Hasenpfeffer or bouillabaisse
23 Casual greeting
24 Culmination
26 Doesn't disallow
27 Funny image, e.g.
28 Bit of sulkiness
31 Proclaimed
33 Truffle hunters
37 Stinging plant
39 Poke
40 Pedal pusher
41 Limo, for instance
42 Barrymore or Carey
44 Come down
45 Garden ornaments
46 Iota
48 Flying prefix

Across

1 Very dark
8 Battle souvenir
12 Verb-forming suffix
13 Theban god
14 Big swing state
15 Monastic bro
16 Cheerleader uniform's element
17 50+ percent
18 Celestial traveler and wishes fulfiller
21 Safari sight
22 Bottle up
24 Having feeling
28 Baby grand, e.g.
29 Brute
30 Canceling key
32 Evening hour
33 Islamic center
36 Challenge for mice, at times
39 Fishers
41 Louis or Carrie
42 Where to go to buy a fortune for a few coins
47 Road to the Forum, e.g.
49 Ending for peek
50 Scooby follower?
51 Reddish steed
52 Sean in Hollywood
53 Pension letters
54 Bobbles the ball
55 Projecting beyond

Down

1 Wink
2 Cornell's Cornell
3 Wild duck
4 Thin plate
5 Words after wait or laugh
6 DC bunch
7 Samosa relative
8 From Mogadishu
9 Backboned animals' phylum
10 Three-toad sloth
11 Compound used to treat scabies
19 Some no longer manufactured smartphones
20 Apex
23 Don Juan's mother
24 Seacoast plant that is sometimes pickled
25 Fencing style
26 Ties, for example
27 Subj. for US immigrants
31 Large artillery pieces
34 Scot. terriers
35 Mult.-choice selection
37 Long past
38 Cat's cry
40 One can get into it sweating
43 Mountain goat
44 Toolbar heading
45 Tribal traditions
46 Stow cargo
48 Rocky knoll

Across

1 Sea of fine particles in the galaxy
14 "Little Women" woman
15 Rob of "The West Wing"
16 Down in pillows
17 Electrical resistance unit
19 1950 noir classic
20 Right side of a famous racehorse?
21 Accused's excuse
22 Word of disgust
23 Former gridiron org.
24 Novel ID
25 Shampoo follow-up
26 Picnic intruder
27 Users resources
29 IRS form fig.
31 Nickname for a noncom
34 Catch some rays
37 Puts into groups
41 Cheery sounds
44 Henry VIII's Catherine
46 TV Guide letters
47 Tree trunk bulge
50 Summer, in Bordeaux
51 Zola portraitist
52 Orbison or Rogers
53 Swarms on
54 Pollen producer
56 Pro bono promise
58 "Moneyball" star Hill
59 Engineer or suit
60 Disinfest
61 Marinara must
62 Chem. table component
63 Whittle
64 Skinny sort
66 Trim
67 Discontinued iPod
68 Old record label
69 Classy
70 "Chicago" actor
71 Rat fink
74 Casino card holder
76 Kenyan tribesman
79 Advisory group to POTUS
81 Genealogy abbr.
84 Antepenultimate mo.
85 Mountain spurs
89 State of affairs preceders
92 Incredibly long time
94 Boston Bobby
95 Flat sign, maybe
96 End of a bartender's question
97 Bygone cable inits
98 Recent prefix?
99 Like solo sailors
100 Messy barbecue meal
101 Shooting marble
102 Systematic search conducted by NASA

Down

1 Exit line
2 Large antelope
3 Romance novelist James
4 Cornfield creation
5 Mop, as decks
6 Shore birds
7 Becomes informed
8 Caron film of 1953
9 Game point situation
10 Gray uniform wearers
11 Having the least rainfall
12 Up till now
13 Individual object
14 Toothpaste-approving grp.
18 Often destructive rocky rain from the cosmos
28 NFL hurlers
30 Tailor, humorously
32 Dad's words
33 Earth orbiter in its first or last quarter
35 Wing measurement
36 Topeka's loc.
38 Duration
39 Tubular instrument
40 Charles or Bradbury
42 Hun leader
43 Utter delight
45 Order for more issues
48 Undistinguished

49 Nullifier, at law
51 Gibson or Brooks
55 Type of acacia
57 Roman symbol
of power
58 Slight push
60 1920s art style
61 RPM indicator
63 Coverage provider,
briefly
65 Tasty Otto's head?

70 Grand opening?
72 Racecourse
semaphore
73 Top of the foot
75 Most unusual
77 Real estate units
78 Sharpen with a belt
80 Hub on the Nile
82 Start in earnest
83 Movie barbarian
86 Audition assignment

87 Common tissue
additive
88 Boomers' babies,
in brief
90 Cause trouble
91 "Dancing Queen"
band
93 Wind hdg.

Across

1 Common online interruptions
4 Fans' place
10 Having colored patches
14 Understand, as a concept
15 Half the distance
16 Minestrone ingredient
17 Imitations
19 Potential limb
20 Gave to charity
21 Drawing with acid
23 Shoulder band
25 Winnie-the-Pooh's favorite snack
26 Self-indulgent shopping binge
29 Like a nasal membrane
32 South Dakota's capital
34 Sales rep with a fixed line of travel
38 Lee who directed "Life of Pi"
39 The offense and the defense
41 Just-expected joiner
42 Ferrari competitor
45 Carry off
48 Matisse, Derain and others (painters)
50 Real estate attachments
51 Spruce (up)
54 Canada's leaf
56 Total screwball
59 Fodder holders
63 Black gold gp
64 Of a particular French emperor
66 Cash-register output
67 Balanced conditions
68 Call-day link
69 Workout makeup
70 Filmdom awards
71 Frequent college funding source

Down

1 Allowed to mellow
2 Car for a test drive
3 Strike dumb
4 Modest knowledge
5 Titration unit
6 Avia alternative
7 "Hollywood" Hogan's wrestling org.
8 Caroline Wozniacki, by birth
9 Routine, briefly
10 Asphalt fault
11 Novelist Shaw
12 Web periodical
13 Pooch, to a tyke
18 Holography tool
22 Songbird of the thrush family
24 Daily
26 Bane of cyberspace
27 Colada intro
28 Partner of rules, informally
30 "Lenore" poet
31 Certain incisor
33 Jenkins with a 1966 VW Bus
35 Bison feature
36 Strong-ox bridge
37 Squeaks by in competition
40 British channel
43 Rubs out
44 Great quantity
46 Indisposition
47 Soccer legend Maradona
49 Filled Indian pastry
51 Casino temptation
52 Cocooned bugs
53 Bungle-prone
55 More wan
57 Far front?
58 Andrew Lloyd Webber musical with feline characters
60 Actress Graham of "Mare of Easttown"
61 2005 hurricane
62 Pompano relative
65 DC lobby

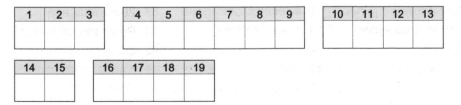

Bonus Clue

Transfer the letters from the corresponding shaded squares above into this grid
to form the title of a comedy adventure movie about animals in NYC

1	2	3

4	5	6	7	8	9

10	11	12	13

14	15

16	17	18	19

Across

1 Sort of short and spiky men's coiffure
10 New Delhi noblewoman
11 Corral call
12 Casual attire
13 Bitter, in a way
15 Change decor
16 Barks
17 Emmy-winning science series
19 Oklahoma tribe
21 Buenos Aires loc.
24 Machine part fastener
27 Many Founding Fathers, religionwise
29 Golf legend Walter
30 Flood prevention barrier
31 Scribble on
32 Exhaust
34 Big inits in news
35 Decimal meas.
36 One of Christopher Columbus' crafts
38 They're thrown
40 Island off Java
43 Outline
46 Poked fun
47 Saintly glows
48 Decrees
49 Chic updo for formal occasions

Down

1 At no charge
2 Cape Town cash
3 Bulb used by cooks
4 Card type
5 Lure and catch
6 Unwilling to listen
7 Packs, as sardines
8 Starter, in brief
9 Letter after upsilon
12 Tresses popular among Rastafarians
14 Timeless hairstyle perfect for weddings
16 Actress Gardner and others
18 Band of eight
19 Pipes in church
20 Begin a course
22 Steward
23 Assumed fact
25 Detailing result
26 Villain
28 Sun. oration
31 Wheel-shaped cheese
33 Liquid, say
37 Chinese calculators
38 Oscar winner Laura
39 Apple for sale
41 Some rentals, briefly
42 In the event that
44 Kaiser or Maxwell
45 Shade of color
46 Uppercut's target

HARD

Across

1 Being seen via
   the small screen
5 Drink, casually
7 Cover the road
11 End of rugby match
13 Stays in another
   location, maybe
15 Last word of
   Kansas' motto
16 Opposite of
   tumultuous
17 Stanza of some
   sonnets
18 Licoricelike spices
19 Troubled thoughts
21 Egg-white protein
25 Comment section
   disclaimer
29 13th undisputed
   World Chess
   Champion
32 Lets up
33 Meet again
34 Palate protrusions
37 Imperial measure
   of liquid
40 Calculating
44 Milky Way
   constellation
45 Shredder
46 Long distance
   athlete
47 Esteem highly
48 Summoned
49 End of spam?
50 Distort the truth

Down

1 Where theater
   actors perform
2 Margin of victory
   at the track
3 Olive oil amts.
4 Nam lead-in
5 50s bohemian
6 MasterCard
   alternatives
7 Macron, for one
8 Makes quite
   an impression on
9 Arrow site
10 Centers of
   hurricanes
12 Inspiring reverie
14 En route
20 Tree knot
22 Research setting

23 Returning soon,
   in online shorthand
24 Schoolteaching nun
26 X-ray kin
27 Recent,
   as an escapee's trail
28 Exceeded one's
   balance
30 Beach find
31 Shoved
35 Field mouse
36 Strip of weapons
37 Style of apparel
38 Miami Dolphins
   uniform hue
39 Bergman in
   "Casablanca"
41 Smashes into
42 Nordic name
43 No longer are

Across

1 Holiday treat with layer of chopped candy canes
12 Atlas stat
13 Whale chaser
14 Humvee forerunner
16 Recital pieces
17 Bulgars, for ones
18 Point-return bridge
19 Tiny crustacean with a bivalve carapace
21 Accept without objection
22 Solo in movies
23 Animal known for stubbornness
25 Manx male
26 Christmas recipe popular especially in the UK and Ireland
32 Clock-radio button
33 Expiable
37 The original place (with in)
38 Billing date
40 Agronomist's study
41 Picking on
43 Wooded regions
44 Winter drink topped with whipped cream or marshmallows
47 Text digitization meth.
50 Metaphor phrase
51 Fish in backyard pools
52 Trombone section
54 Small pastries
59 Greek letter before kappa
60 Dual contraction
62 Shoe named after the Latin for bird
63 Furry Endor denizen
64 Dublin's land, to natives
65 Undesirable engine sound
66 Sweet treats with a whimsical name

Down

1 El follower, in Texas
2 Mischievous bow wielder
3 Strike, as with hailstones
4 Low hand
5 Court great Karl
6 Preceded a hunch?
7 Maritime org.
8 Conan O'Brien's outlet
9 What one could land
10 Size again
11 A martial art
15 Metrical composition
17 Many a get-rich-quick scheme
20 Contrived cough
21 Speller's clarification
23 Courtroom figs
24 Identify the precise location
26 Distillery mixture
27 Pelvic bones
28 DC baseball players, for short
29 Beat by a mile
30 Pirate's cry
31 Three-legged prop for an artist
34 Ball-rope missile
35 Bouncy step
36 Alternative word
38 Is appropriate
39 Old-time Peruvian
42 Clark's co-worker
43 Darer's shout
45 Given the nod
46 Appliance part
47 Off-Broadway award
48 Gloats
49 Betray, in a way
53 Literary Munro
54 Guam, to the US
55 Southern Calif. cops
56 Malignity
57 Barbecue tool feature
58 Gives a little
60 Shatner's sci-fi drug
61 Get a move on, quaintly

Bonus Clue

Transfer the letters from the corresponding shaded squares above into this grid
to form the **names of two traditional delicacies**

1	2	3	4	5

6	7	8	9	10	11	12

13	14	15

16	17	18	19	20	21

22	23	24	25

Across

1 Novel about Hercule Poirot enjoying a cruise down the Egyptian river
13 Part of some fruit drink names
14 Most fit to fight
15 Author Ephron and others
16 Wild party
17 Pudding ingredient, perhaps
18 Fixes, as a horse
19 Totally understood
21 Colorado winter sports town
23 Conflict-preventing skill
25 Firstborn sibling
29 Sends out, like gamma rays
33 Repairs
35 Hot tub sigh
36 Best vision spot
37 Estimating words
38 Prepare for preservation
39 Brief romance
40 Attention-grabbing sound
41 It may be required for entrance
42 Cinematic snippet
44 Absorbs, as a loss
46 Vincent van Gogh's brother
49 Bits of roasted cocoa beans
51 Karma believer
54 Electrified particles
55 Lawyers levies
56 Sorry souls
57 Parking reg., e.g.
58 Peter of "Casino Royale"
59 Entertain in a humorous way
60 Nextel Cup org.
62 Treasure chest contents, maybe
64 Cuban dance music
66 Relative of a niqab
70 Present for rejection or acceptance
73 Made in the US
75 100 Turkish kurus
76 Lose strength, as a storm
77 Hi, in Honduras
78 Canvas cover for a diamond
79 Book titled after a nursery rhyme and a fingerplay

Down

1 Kind of race or queen
2 Wasps nest location, sometimes
3 Turn-profit bridge
4 Leafy garden plant
5 Out-limb link
6 Naysaying types
7 Eponymous New Mexico tribe
8 Associate of Karl Marx
9 To a great extent
10 Dublin's country, in the Olympics
11 Address at a Scottish pub
12 Suffix with seer or lion
13 Literary genre in which felony is central to the plot
20 They precede your fault?
22 Jai alai or its ball
24 More variable
26 Parisian waters
27 Teasdale of poetry
28 West End show based on this puzzle theme penner's work
30 Game developer's alteration
31 Wall greenery
32 Phone conferences, briefly
34 Tax payer, e.g.
38 Element used in atomic clocks
43 Give the facts
45 Defeat utterly

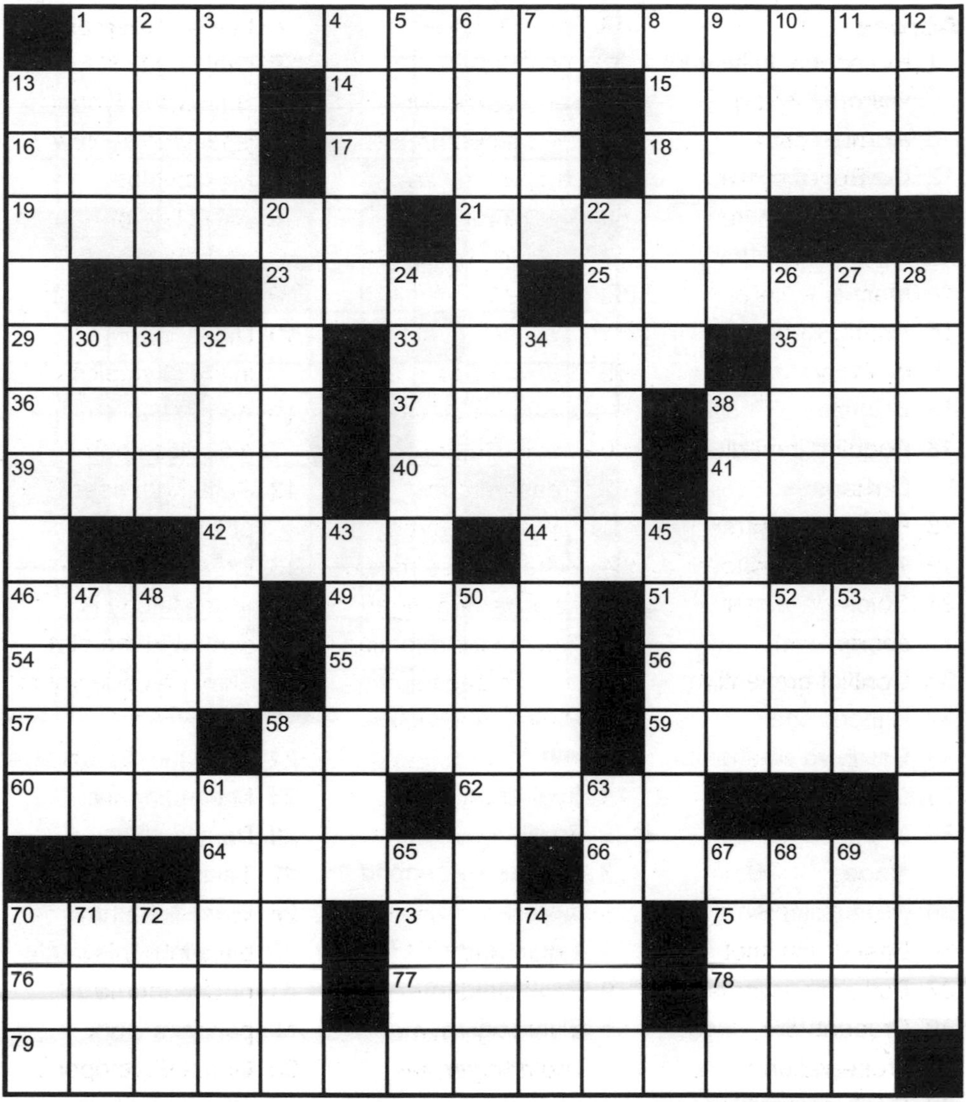

47 Jewish wedding musical ritual
48 Machiavellian justification
50 Fine pear
52 Fresh, to Friedrich
53 Red Cross workers, for short
58 Victory emblem
61 Mediterranean tourist attraction
63 Jazz legend Carmen
65 Thai dough
67 Certain singers
68 Chess bishop's trajectory: abbr.
69 Hockey's Bobby and Colton
70 Goon
71 Dept. of Justice arm
72 Best-liked, informally
74 Right-angled pipe joint

HARD

Across

1 Play at the maximum volume
6 Arouse
12 Cowboy's home
13 Nothing further
14 They come after shame
15 Attack verbally
16 Suitably
17 Dreams up
18 Peculiar quality
20 Confesses
22 Product of some worms
26 Truck
27 Angel
30 Type of arrow
32 Historic chairman
33 Sarajevo combatant
34 Cut loose
36 In the beginning stages
39 John Peterson novel, with the
42 Put a cover on
45 Defense line made of felled trees
46 Carlo or Cristo opener
47 Steep in hot water
48 Capital on the Gulf of Guinea
49 Warehouses
50 Young Aussie hoppers

Down

1 Beat head?
2 Bowling channel
3 For even a second more
4 Takes to task
5 Datebook abbr.
6 Slyly cutting
7 Learned works
8 Stalemate in negotiations
9 Overwhelming victory
10 Strongly encourage
11 Ballpoints, e.g.
17 Ideas offered
19 Annual charge
20 Globes, e.g.
21 Birds perch, perhaps
23 Impending evil
24 Be a slacker
25 Macrame feature
28 Gives a hand
29 GPS input, slangily
31 Lookout, maybe
35 Furniture style
37 Carroll's heroine
38 Stops working
39 Tykes
40 Doubting riposte
41 Meat-filled tortilla
43 Response to a compliment
44 Rural expanses
46 Coll. focus

FINGERS OF LAND

Across

1 Cape located in the Nordic region
10 Members of Saruman's army
11 Kung-chicken link
12 Center opening?
14 Kill the dragon
15 Black magic
17 Ghostly gathering
19 Immobilize in chess
20 Temporary beds
22 Obviously stunned
25 Four-song records, perhaps
28 Boss
30 NASDAQ debuts
31 Peninsula in the Southeast Asia
34 Talk tipsily
35 It may be worn after traveling
36 Wall St. initials
38 Birdbath scum
40 Necklace part
42 Hand-held organizer
44 Cesspool
47 To a degree
51 Sneak about
52 Buff ending
53 Mideast map abbr.
54 Horrific smell
55 The easternmost projection of the second largest continent

Down

1 Anatomical pits
2 Gardner of fiction
3 Org. for student sports
4 Boy band of the 90s
5 1040EZ expert
6 50+ org.
7 Finnish mobile phone maker
8 End of cash?
9 Perfectly put
13 Falklands, e.g.
15 Perceive
16 Harmon of TV
18 Small Pacific salmon
21 Indian title
23 Lhasa ___ (dog)
24 Minstrel, e.g.
26 Bit of medicine
27 Cozy room
29 Point the way
32 Window treatment option
33 "Hud" actress Patricia
34 Authorization, informally
37 Spiritual center, in yoga
39 Astronomer Hubble
41 Sorrow
43 Cry of enlightenment
45 Auto on the autobahn
46 Gator's cousin
48 Circus attender's sound
49 Dialer's 6
50 Boxer's hello

Across

1 Hold the interest of
6 NY Mets stadium
9 Bakery preparations
14 Moment off
the ground
15 Without purpose
17 Save for later,
in a way
19 Confident to
an extreme
20 Put together
21 Lashed
22 Gaming cube
23 A/C opening
24 Took legal action
25 Proven
26 Experimental efforts
28 Athlete's beads
30 Seeks water
31 Smartphone's brain
34 Bunker of TV
36 Bollywood musical
tunes
40 Author of the Rebus
novels, Ian
42 Applelike fruit
46 Cairo cobra
47 Shuttle path
48 Singing A follower?
50 Resort of a sort
51 Blood worry
52 Type of track?
53 Vinegar variety
55 Indo-Iranian
language
57 No longer fresh

58 "Deadwood" actress
Jewell
59 British musician
Brian
60 With public excluded
62 Charmer
63 Channel for
cinephiles
64 More gung-ho
65 Elders
66 He once worked
for Edison
68 Chemist Mendeleev
71 Consonantal trio
72 Owns up or lets in
76 Trapper John
portrayer
78 Draw nearer to
81 Dunderhead
82 Having two bands,
like car radios
86 Graph maximum
87 Roarer in film intros
88 Chinatown gang
89 Stable female
90 Amorous skunk
in cartoons
91 USCG officers
92 Affectionate gift
93 Hula strings
94 Shovel-like tools
95 Sigmoid swimmers
96 Does a greenhouse
job

Down

1 Charitable gifts
2 Dandy
3 Sushi bar drink
4 Pundits' pieces
5 Bird of the frozen
North
6 Nancy Drew, e.g.
7 Jekyll's other
personality
8 Expand,
as a collection
9 Bride's purchase
10 Issuance from an
American embassy
11 FBI agents, slangily
12 At an impasse
13 Ones ranked
above cpls
16 Paul who won
a Nobel in Physics
18 Hotel room asset
27 Lands of Latin
29 Be stalled in a line
30 Hardly superficial
31 Davy of the frontier
32 Vernacular
33 Reveals
35 Bratty kids
37 Monthly reading
material?
38 Some tablets
39 Most stupefied
41 Friends
43 Block, legally
44 Andean wool
provider

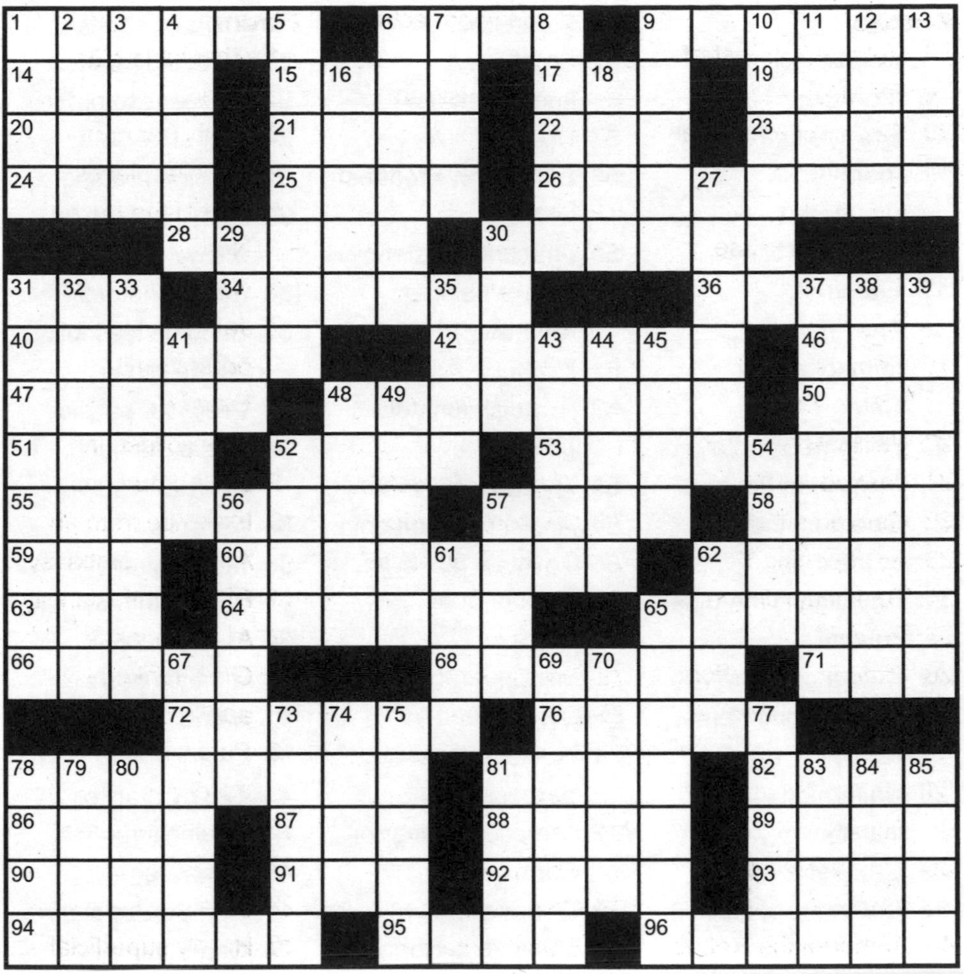

45 Partner in war
48 Greek temptress
49 Seoul man
52 Not just eat
54 Admirer's words after what
56 Japanese emperor's title
57 Pathogen
61 Prescriptions, informally
62 Bedspring's shape
65 Menial work enforcer
67 Went frolicking
69 Homes with domes
70 Roger Rabbit and friends
73 Selling points
74 Tracy Marrow's stage name
75 Demonstrative pronoun
77 Stop from flowing
78 Dev teams products
79 Minimal protest
80 Hemingway's nickname
81 PC key under Shift
83 Mackerel shark
84 Guitar part
85 Embarrassing situation

Across

1 Celestial shadows
6 Indweller
13 Feature of a messy room
14 Greet, in a way
16 Heavenly bangs
17 Elated
18 The final word, to theologists
19 Calm
20 Philip who wrote "American Pastoral"
21 One from the top of the map
23 Anything in the plus column
25 K, to a goldsmith
26 Good or bad name, for short
28 Uniformed troops, initially
29 Croquet area
32 Catherine of Russia and others
36 Oscar-winning actress Minnelli
37 X-ray
38 Musical interval
41 Fashionable
42 Pluses
44 Told the cops everything
45 Supplier of a tight squeeze
46 Battery term.
47 Blemishes
49 Plane tracker
52 Small wind instruments
57 Up-good link
58 Bar patron's request, with the
59 First choice, slangily
60 Before being renamed, in brief
61 Mantel
62 Swedish furniture giant
63 Icy coating
64 Ancient Roman coin
65 Toyota rival

Down

1 Newer software, perhaps
2 "Amadeus" director Forman
3 Calf cries
4 Misleading clue
5 McGregor of "The Men Who Stare at Goats"
6 Too old
7 Moderate views holders
8 Fluid
9 Beneficiaries of Robin Hood
10 Amway competitor
11 Celebrity decorator Berkus
12 Mideast capital
15 All over the place
22 Chooses to order
24 Pint-size
27 LA clock setting
29 They carry on a legal contest
30 Black Sea gulf
31 Become less full, as the moon
33 Prefix for physics
34 Hacienda hand, maybe
35 Narcotic
36 Metric quart, approximately
39 One-third of a movie dog's name
40 Ovary output
43 Grainy cracker
44 Downhill run
45 Illegalize
47 Rex Stout sleuth
48 Computer menu option
50 Day of movies
51 Jungian archetype
53 US Open stadium namesake
54 Paris street grid components
55 Shake alternative
56 Bean of "Game of Thrones"

Bonus Clue

Transfer the letters from the corresponding shaded squares above into this grid
to form the **dieting advice by Miss Piggy**

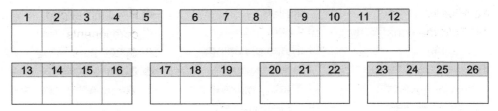

1	2	3	4	5		6	7	8		9	10	11	12

13	14	15	16		17	18	19		20	21	22		23	24	25	26

178

HARD

Across

1 Explorer Boone
7 Defensive trenches
12 Kind of sausage
13 Coastal bay
14 Preliminary outlines
15 Liquid dynamite, for short
16 King known for his wealth
18 Valiant's boy
19 High tennis shot
20 How squatters live
22 Oscar winner Burl
24 Male parent of an animal
25 Onionlike bulbs
27 Calfskin parchment
31 Flowchart symbols
33 South American grassland
34 Circus crowd sounds
36 Prehistorical novelist
37 Sledders starting points
41 Fight unit, briefly
42 Black cuckoo
43 Trained
45 Make it through to
47 Thin puree
49 Actor Kovacs
50 University of Oregon home
51 Census Bureau accumulation
52 Deepen waterway

Down

1 CD successor
2 Support for ground troops
3 Prohibition Era brew
4 Mole's quest
5 Come onstage
6 Highlands girls
7 Singer of folk songs
8 Covert maritime org.
9 End of the wedding march
10 Land, in Lyon
11 Piece of curling equipment
17 Prof's employer
19 Philanthropist Wallace
21 Chap
23 Danish toast
26 Fabric samples
28 Adorned, in a way
29 Continual
30 Penicillin was created from it
32 Dismissive remark
35 Spread out
37 Rabbit-like creatures
38 Unable to move
39 Tarzan's swing
40 Clean with hard rubbing
44 Quite significant
46 Abbr. in the footnote
48 Receive

Across

1 Story spanning decades
5 Dale, hill or valley
12 Center of rotation
13 Words of witness
14 Geese formation shape
15 Painting van follower?
16 Most important
18 Cheaper, for now
20 Tries to be seductive
21 Chinese dynasty
23 Delicately patterned
24 Evaluated
28 Notified
30 Apollo's moon lander
31 Punishment related
33 Puzzle-ster link
34 Palindromic title
36 Sleepers
38 Thin cut
40 Lawyer: abbr.
41 Suspend
43 Component of a compass
46 Line of gunfire
48 Clinton adviser Panetta
49 Puppet end?
50 Some bedroom sharers, informally
51 Alt-rock singer Tori
52 Plasterboards
53 Film editing technique

Down

1 Source of a dried starch used in textile industry
2 Neural transmitter
3 Jobs in clubs
4 Unfortunate news
5 Driving needs
6 Contents of a BBQ pit, often
7 Trusting sort
8 Live
9 Vanquish
10 Designed anew
11 New York MLB squad
17 Regal order
19 Baby-talk trait
22 Columbus's birthplace
25 Chef, at times
26 Young fishes
27 London insanity
29 Give to others
32 Subject to a penalty fee, perhaps
35 Certain conservative skirt
37 Rule made by a local authority (var.)
39 Oklahoma city in a Clapton tune
41 Pay attention to, as advice
42 Water carrier
44 Actress Moore of "The Scarlet Letter"
45 Noose
47 Baseball two-bagger, briefly

180 CUTE ANIMALS

Across

1 Rabbit relatives known for large size of its hind feet and a winter camouflage
12 Acknowledged
13 Put up for display
14 Announces
16 Pre-storm atmosphere
17 Tony nominee O'Shea
18 Traffic delay
19 Story of hidden meaning
21 Nix
22 Not shes
23 Big Red rivals
24 Hereditary social classes
28 Assured vigor
29 Atlas ref.
31 Watergate investigator
32 Off-road rides, in brief
33 Beloved bear
34 Certain collector of acorns living in pine and fir forests
37 Skillfully
38 Illness end?
39 Ancestor
41 Ware lead-in
42 Ivy climber, briefly
43 Moon goddess
44 Boxing champ Max
45 Advanced degree
46 Keep safe
49 Like whiteboards
53 Bring to bear, as pressure
54 Car rental chain
55 Metaphor for an opportunity
56 Musical extravaganza
57 Tall ship pole
58 Marina greeting
59 Furry burrowing rodent endemic to Washington state

Down

1 It signifies approval
2 Dickensian teen heroine
3 Free, as a drink
4 Uninteresting types
5 Lashes makeup
6 Simply unique
7 High self-image
8 Reach or succeed in accomplishing
9 Steed steerers
10 Type of engineering, for short
11 Veer sharply (var.)
12 Not at all plentiful
15 Enter the pool
20 Belgian city
21 Hand grip
23 Graceland icon
25 Caribbean cruise stop
26 Drivel
27 Requiring an optical enlarger to see
28 Body of moral principles
29 Paris newspaper, with Le
30 Subway fare
32 Stage coach user, possibly
33 Magnetism
35 Focused
36 Earned wages (archaic)
37 Bank of America co-founder Giannini
40 Daydream (var.)
42 Diminutive
43 California mountain
44 Juniper fruit
45 Light splitting crystal device
47 Former Montreal baseball player
48 Use your fingers
49 Rescue op
50 "Wealth of Nations" author Smith
51 Nonconformist writer
52 Pilfered stuff
54 Defensive question

Crossword Grid

Across/down numbers in grid: 1, 2, 3, 4, 5, 6, 7, 8, 9, 10, 11, 12, 13 (13), 13, 8, 14, 6, 15, 16, 4, 17, 18, 9, 19, 20, 27, 25, 21, 21, 22, 23, 24, 25, 26, 27, 3, 28, 22, 29, 30, 31, 28, 32, 5, 2, 33, 12, 34, 35, 19, 36, 37, 14, 38, 39, 40, 41, 24, 42, 23, 20, 43, 17, 44, 7, 45, 46, 47, 48, 49, 15, 50, 51, 52, 53, 10, 54, 55, 18, 56, 11, 57, 1, 58, 59, 16, 26

Bonus Clue

Transfer the letters from the corresponding shaded squares above into this grid to form the **names of two adorable creatures**

1	2	3	4	5	6	7	8	9	10		11	12	13	14

15	16	17	18	19	20	21	22		23	24	25	26	27	28

Across

1 Language spoken by Jesus
7 Catchy tunes
13 Fishing spot in Scotland
14 Devoid of any pleasure
16 Uncertain
17 Animated bug film
18 Bias
19 Bubblehead
20 Infamous Ugandan Amin
21 Admit to the premises
22 First name in flagmaking
23 Opposite of whole, milkwise
25 Boycott-sparking Parks
27 Ship's stores of old
29 Body's failure to react to an antigen
33 Fabric for a professor's jacket
36 Declared
39 Rolls in a field
40 Barbara or Conrad
41 Rock type
43 Good-sized piece of meat
44 Comic strip about the Patterson family
45 Sot
46 Rose of baseball

47 "Roots" author Haley
48 Treasure hunter's quest, perhaps
49 Pea pod, e.g.
51 Speculators' considerations
52 Tree producing senna
53 No longer in business
55 Doublet
58 Skilled ones
62 Drum major's topper
66 Member of the familia
68 Old-school show of support
69 Canine in Oz
70 Sparkler
71 Desert of Asia
72 Any of several Norwegian kings
73 Introduction for English
74 Have sovereignty
75 Seance leaders
76 Given, as custody

Down

1 "Scorpio" co-star Delon
2 Sonata movement
3 Protein found in muscles

4 VHF unit
5 Atlas close-ups
6 NFL player from Indianapolis
7 Shrugger's comment
8 One may be returned for a TD
9 Daily ebb and flow, at the beach
10 Start to please the court?
11 Some amphibians
12 Eclipse cause
15 On the foul line, ironically
21 Gives kudos
22 Group of outlaws
24 Giveaways (var.)
26 Finnish steam bath
28 Occult or secret matter (var.)
30 Meringue requirement
31 Depends (upon)
32 Home of 34-Down Airport
33 Cookbook abbr.
34 Polish Peace Prize winner Lech
35 Fills with excitement
37 Andersen's countrymen
38 Evil spells
42 Zingers
44 Chinese gambling region

48 Like oil directly from a well
50 Playful prank
52 Bespoke
54 Jean of the early screen
56 Church assents
57 Hip-hop pal
59 Full of self-esteem
60 Array of figures
61 Acted alarmed, as a horse
63 Gopher's opening
64 Little amount
65 Former UN leader Annan
67 It joins two cremes
70 Jazz club session
71 Warning from a boxer

Across

1 "The Island of the Day Before" writer
4 Action-packed
12 Litmus test nos.
13 Latin name for Ireland
14 Am-risk link
15 Conjures up in the mind
16 Garden tool
18 Tampa Bay team, familiarly
19 Dancer de Mille
20 2000s Disney Channel star, to fans
21 Green lookalikes
22 Grain layer
24 Humble dwelling
25 Boastful person
29 Immaculate
31 Magnetic prefix
32 Rendell of whodunits
33 Toothed device
34 Ham sandwich specification
37 Wrestling rounds
38 It comes in cakes or bars
39 Capital of Georgia
41 Halloween outfits
43 Jersey plaint
44 Climber
45 Reaction participant
46 Repeals, as a ruling
47 Weigh station wts

Down

1 Grave messages
2 Load batteries
3 Continuous rhythm
4 Door-holding wedges
5 Caustic substance
6 Place where guy walks into in jokes
7 Gig fraction
8 Buying favors from an official
9 Void, as a marriage
10 Female kin
11 Bombastic, in slang
17 Parisian possessive
20 Kiosk display
22 Maverick of "Maverick"
23 Overly hasty
25 Sea color
26 18 or older provision
27 In a minute, say
28 Twisting forces
30 Of a pancreas' enzyme
33 Country lass
34 Actor's dream
35 Dangerous loop
36 Grates harshly
37 Symbols of strength
39 Tax cheat chaser, briefly
40 Modify, as rules
42 Mysterious Geller

Across

1 Focused gazer into a round crystal
12 Emu relative
13 MPEG alternative
14 The hot center of the earth
15 Such-is bridge
16 Morse Code syllable
17 Snoop on stage
18 Type of industrial connectors
20 Air pollution
21 Desert refuges
23 Makes finer
27 Not those
31 Person seeing the hidden things
32 Romantic emoji
33 Du Pont trademark
35 Start of a French oath
39 "Dracula" author, Stoker
43 Like some doors
47 Caribbean nation
48 List of chapters, briefly
49 Cartoon Betty
50 Love, to Latin lovers
51 GOP org.
52 Composer of fugue fame
53 Moving of objects with the mind only

Down

1 Swiss coins
2 Emphatically
3 Restraint
4 Uses a sewing shuttle
5 Skater Komanechi
6 Demonic deeds
7 Name of a movie
8 Watch displays, for short
9 Weaver's tool
10 As a result, in logic
11 Jamaican export
19 Speculates
22 Arranged
24 Jewels, slangily
25 Tampa's st.
26 Road sealer
28 Farm gathering

29 SASE, for one
30 Narrow passage of water, briefly
32 Decorative wheel cover
34 Talmud letters
36 Houston MLB player
37 Heavy dull sound
38 Fashion designer Stefano
40 Molasses-based beverages
41 Birth announcement words
42 Anthony or Chagall
44 Cleric in Cannes
45 Burlesque wraps
46 Points in math class

Across

1 Checkout option
6 Pizza unit
11 Ridiculous
17 Maui greeting
18 Adjuncts
19 Swing bowler
20 Jellyfish defense
21 Not accidental
22 Wine amount by which a cask falls short of being full
23 First lady of the 1950s
25 Chest sculptures
27 Oldies refrain syllable
28 Plumbing unit
29 Contorts
33 As originally placed
37 Promotional mailing
39 Actor Scott
40 Area where trees grow
41 Hollywood legend Marilyn
43 South African entrenched position
45 Organized fighting force
46 Underwear with underwire
47 Most reserved
49 Perceive through the nose
51 Engineering detail
53 Choy root?

54 It can appear after a while
56 Salad inventor Bob
58 Strikebreakers
63 Happening
68 Strove for superiority
70 Lingerie section designation
71 National personae non gratae
72 French fine
74 Happy cat's sound
75 Fish breathing organ
76 Swollen parts
78 Uneven, as a performance
80 Oktoberfest souvenir
82 Point of view, metaphorically
83 Keypad trio
84 Swimming or floating
86 Investigate
91 Neighbor of Montenegro
94 Bedevil
96 Gourmet burger condiment
97 Comparatively compliant
98 Sow's sniffer
99 Citizen of Zagreb
100 Like a lea
101 How to say alas
102 "Amazing Grace" and others

Down

1 TV's Letterman
2 Atlas abbr.
3 Fide preceder
4 Blue-roofed eatery chain
5 Least threatening
6 American Pacific territory
7 Creditor's claim
8 Lupino of the screen
9 Peruvian coin
10 Prevented legally
11 Eee computer company
12 Not on deck
13 Taqueria fixture
14 Thurman of filmdom
15 Suit spec
16 Dr. of rap
24 Any compass point
26 Seminarian's subj.
28 Astronomical length
30 Mania
31 Crusty desserts
32 Excel function
33 "Tennessee Waltz" opening
34 Acceptable standard
35 Any number of
36 Pastoral poem (var.)
37 Hypnosis ender
38 Red "Sesame Street" puppet
42 "Citizen Kane" poster name
44 Stocky diving birds

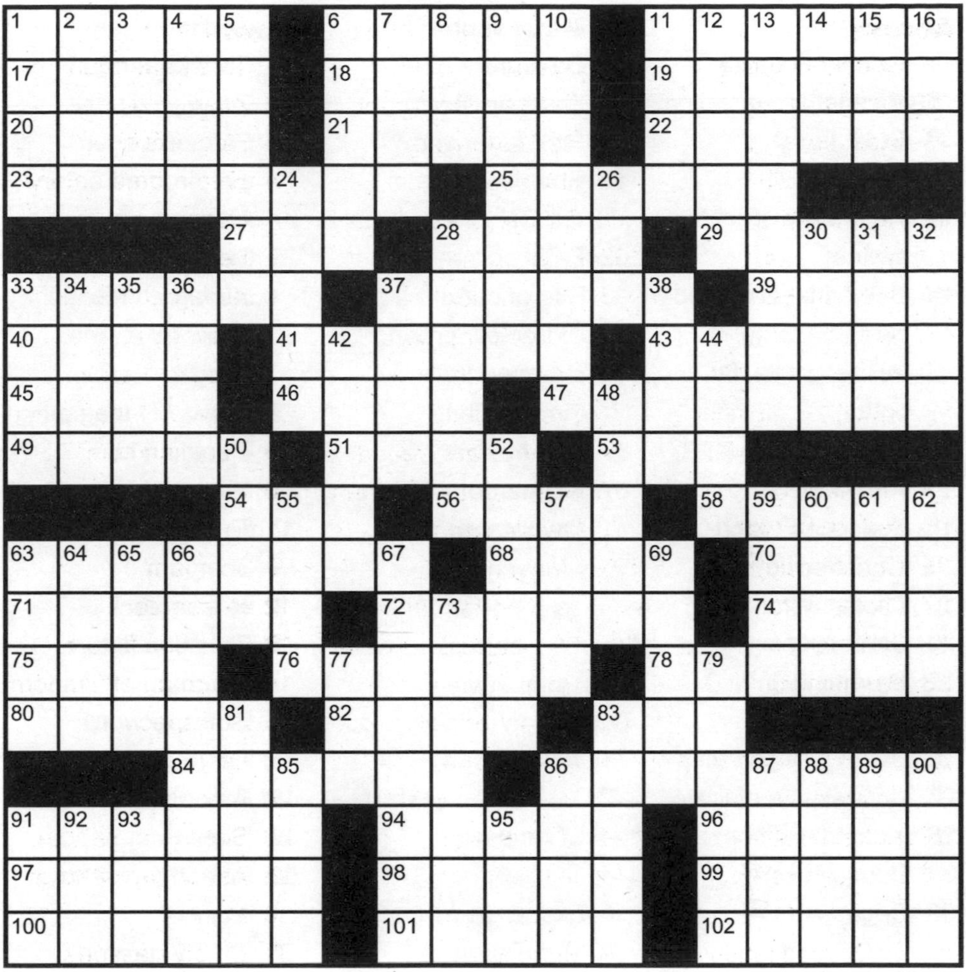

48 Flowed back
50 Load at the docks
52 Forms a layer over
55 Main point
57 Rubbermaid wares
59 Crime bigwig
60 Above the rest preceders
61 Bacharach or Ward
62 Lively and active
63 Tries for a treat
64 Stage direction
65 Backsplash square
66 US state and river
67 Willingness
69 Newsroom array
73 Butte setting
77 Form follower
79 Interlace
81 Areas for worshippers
83 Wharf
85 British conservative
86 Ramirez of tennis
87 Bright and breezy
88 Hotel offering
89 Genealogist's study
90 Internet page visits
91 Barrel to tap
92 Dinghy propeller
93 Certain rhetorical device, initially
95 Male fox

Across

1 Taunting remark
5 Joke teller's question
10 Govt. farming monitor
14 Mainframe operating system
15 Like critters counted at night
16 Vessel with a flat bottom
17 Balance beam surrounders
18 Seasons French fries, maybe
19 Charge list
20 Confectionary
22 Passes by, as time does
24 Island groups (var.)
27 Undesirable place
28 Industrial action
31 Doesn't own
33 Ceded a seat
34 USCG rank
38 Checks for fingerprints
40 Impediment to advancement
41 Makes level or uniform
43 Foot specialists?
45 Examine methodically
47 Sudden increases
51 Urban variety of a football's relative
53 Malevolent
55 Devourers (suffix)
57 Just shy of shut
58 Postgame show
61 Rodolfo's love in "La Bohème"
62 Fatal poison
63 Site of current flow
64 Extremely proper
65 Dropped from the schedule
66 Cut, in a way
67 Kangaroo pouches, for instance

Down

1 Jaw covering
2 To a certain extent
3 Chompers
4 Cut out
5 Exchanged rumors
6 Mrs. Peron
7 Poetic contraction
8 Spy's acquisition, informally
9 Magnetic flux measures
10 Flash drive connections
11 Splitting
12 One-time Clinton challenger
13 Handy tools for cobblers
21 God in Asgard
23 Catalysts, for short
25 Pictured model
26 Patronizes a restaurant
27 Air conduits
29 Big name in campgrounds
30 Beats by a small margin
32 Assembly stages
35 Electric curve
36 Marsh plant
37 Seesawed
39 Sharpened, as a razor
42 Feudal class member
44 Example word
46 Nerve-related
48 Rascals
49 Flight from danger
50 Relating to sandy regions
52 2010 Supreme Court appointee Kagan
53 Sponge cake soaked in rum syrup
54 Cleanser named for a Greek hero
56 Virtual people in a series of video games
59 Long-leaved lettuce
60 Citrus drink suffix

Bonus Clue

Transfer the letters from the corresponding shaded squares above into this grid
to form the title of an award-winning wuxia movie directed by Ang Lee

1	2	3	4	5	6	7	8	9

10	11	12	13	14

15	16	17	18	19	20

21	22	23	24	25	26

209

HARD

Across

1 Closely pursued
10 Always, in scores
11 Site of the 2022 World Cup
12 Inner selves
13 Hit the town
15 Hospital colleagues of MDs
16 Failed to be
18 Matter under investigation
20 Drop in the ocean
21 Monk's title
23 "The Commuter" star Neeson
25 White bird
26 Spanish silver
29 Lapwing (var.)
31 Some Chinese teas
33 In a way, slangily
34 Score followers?
35 Dogs with square muzzles
37 USAF bigwig
38 Hardly radiant
39 Little cry
42 Blanketed
45 Laotian language group
46 Drinks from a flask
48 Reddish-brown hair color
50 Gunpowder holder
51 Understanding
52 All the same

Down

1 Body art dye
2 Slightly odd
3 Dashboard abbr.
4 Do a sketch
5 Euro forerunner in Spain
6 Neatened the lawn
7 On the horizon
8 Discredited
9 Essence, in perfume names
10 Mummy's grave
14 Scheduling
17 Smoothed-out stairs
19 "Candle in the Wind" singer John
22 "Ars Amatoria" poet
24 Creator of M and Q
25 Religious belief of a sort
27 Harp-like instrument
28 Capital city of Paraguay
30 Heart test
32 Footwear altercation
36 Feeling of discomfort
38 Had no existence
40 Places for pins
41 Gives a yellow flag
43 Fairy-tale heavy
44 Sword fight
47 Basic question
49 Buzzing colonist

Across

1 Farm mail designation
4 Integrated circuit
11 Rocker Morissette
13 Greek's "unlucky" letter
14 Small book
16 1830s revolution site
17 Propel oneself in water
18 Major endocrine gland
20 Assault
22 Software no.
23 Geometry symbols
25 Comic Silverman
27 Dark quaff
28 Whimsical
30 Mexican waterways
32 1999 Exxon merger partner
33 Hit sketch show since '75, initially
34 Article in Berlin
35 Chipmunk of song
38 Geisha's instrument
41 Soul vocalist Gray
42 2006 Winter Olympics host
43 Finished in the top three
45 Actress Slezak
46 Japanese living art form
47 Army quitters
48 Abbr. on food labels

Down

1 Ones who send cut and paste letters, perhaps
2 Gone
3 Miles of music
4 Part of a Pentagon web address
5 One of las Canarias
6 Weasel's cousin
7 Julie of "The Talk"
8 Any insect
9 Letters written sloping to the right
10 Ballerina's step
12 Arch enemy
15 Kind of 21-Down on goods (as a percent of value)
19 Detox setting
21 Type of payment to the IRS
24 Go in without a suit
26 "Can't Fight the Moonlight" singer LeAnn
27 Hotel employee
28 Underwater missile
29 Aunt, in Acapulco
31 Protect against possible loss
34 Iran currency
36 French dance
37 Tool for a mountaineer
39 Eavesdropping aid
40 Neighbor of Colo.
42 2012 movie about a stuffed bear
44 Don'ts companions

Across

1 Use persuasive flattery
8 President before Buchanan
13 Off in the distance
14 Flier in a V formation
16 Fossil fuel mined in West Virginia
17 Long, thin part of a guitar
18 Etcher Albrecht
19 Exerts dominance over, in slang
20 Came in
22 Metro gates
24 Suitable's opposite
26 Colin of "Apartment Zero"
28 Nursery needs
32 Loses on purpose
34 Trap, so to speak
36 Sloth
40 Rush
41 Young's accounting partner
43 On the money
44 Cart's wheel attachment
46 Standing up
48 Fire engine accessories
50 Basketball's Shaquille
52 Leader of Jewish congregation
56 Treatise
58 Piddling
60 Crowd disperser
64 Digits with nails
65 Major maker of beverage cans
67 Calamities
68 Things we share
69 Appears bigger and bigger?
70 All you need, per the Beatles
71 Straining one's patience
72 Vassal

Down

1 Most rational and reasonable
2 "Inside Man" actor Clive
3 Non-fiction
4 Story time listener
5 Epigrammatist Nash
6 Barbary sheep
7 Favor preceder?
8 Irreverent
9 Bacteria to avoid
10 Oar handler
11 Are able, archaically
12 Building wings
15 Octave followers, in sonnets
21 Lack of practice, metaphorically
23 Conditional phrase
25 First of a kind
27 Baseball Hall-of-Famer Wilhelm
29 Platinum Card co.
30 Lie about
31 Like many a viral animal video
33 Latin music's Puente
35 Person who earns a military medal
37 Takes back gun
38 Daughter of Nereus
39 Fake fanfare
40 90s sitcom star
42 Model afresh
45 With-ring link
47 Dissenting words with a chance
49 Zen achievement
51 Drop
53 French affair
54 Noah of film
55 Often villainous operatic roles
57 Call it quits
59 New Year's Eve song word
61 Get one's blood boiling
62 Purloin
63 Suffragette Belmont
64 Stroller occupant
66 Baltimore legend Ripken

Bonus Clue

Transfer the letters from the corresponding shaded squares above into this grid to form the **inspirational quote by Oprah Winfrey**

1	2	3	4		5	6	7	8		9	10	11	12	13	14

15	16	17	18		19	20	21	22	23	24

189 WORDS DERIVED FROM TOPONYMS

Across

1 Traditional wool hat named after a royal Scottish residence
13 Particle in electrolysis
14 Printing color
15 Boneless fish inside the f-ed?
17 Celebrity chef Oliver
18 State that borders three Can. provinces
19 Very deep sleep
20 "Space Invaders" company
21 Ferrari who founded Ferrari
22 Cal. marking
23 Rowing machines, casually
25 Most ancient, for William Wallace
27 Dig find
30 Soprano Te Kanawa
31 Fictional giant
32 Surrender formally, as land
34 Cease holding
38 Bond girl Hatcher
40 Goes public with
42 Novak Djokovic, at times
43 Patio furniture item and a massif in northeastern New York
47 Commotions of yore
48 Emphatic typeface: abbr.
49 Flight hub for Norwegian
50 Carnivore with sloping body
51 Bird venerated by the Egyptians
53 Cornerstone letters
54 Accrue
57 Causes of some night frights
59 Antlered animal of the Old World
63 Element in Chinese medicine
64 Image quality issue
65 Lightest coin
67 Construction rod
71 Submit to authority
72 Important vows
73 Nullify
74 Way to learn
75 Late-July babies
76 Make comparisons
77 Fermented liquid condiment invented in England

Down

1 Mexican peninsula
2 Subj. for a surgeon
3 Home of the oldest university in the Americas
4 Watery silks
5 Relating to dreams
6 Tippy-tops
7 City on the Rhone
8 War cry
9 Traveling theatrically
10 Energy acronym
11 Blow off the big wedding
12 Interim workers
16 Skin ornament
24 Pick up slowly
26 Door-yard bloomer, in a poem
27 Greek diner staple
28 Sometime soon
29 Footstep
30 Hair protein
33 Conn of "Shining Time Station"
35 Audio feedback, of a sort
36 Coquettes
37 Young salmon
39 Golf selection
41 Evidence of a recent scrape
44 Truman Dam river
45 Kevin in the American Theater Hall of Fame
46 Starts to attract flies, say
50 Ship-anchoring area
52 Light reddish-brown horses

55 Official of ancient Rome

56 Eye portions (var.)

58 Portugal + Spain

60 Joint where the funny bone is

61 By reason of

62 Water extractor

63 Hermann, author of novels "Siddhartha" and "Knulp"

66 Not worth talking about

68 Port on the Caspian Sea, capital of Azerbaijan

69 Words after gimme or wait

70 Actor Auberjonois of "Boston Legal"

215

HARD

Across

1 Low opera voices
7 Greedy king
12 Bull-themed tequila brand
13 Followers of Jakob Ammann
14 "Dynasty" character
15 Doesn't die
16 Member of a corp. board
17 Puzzle variant
19 Stimulus receptors in the brain
21 Boolean operators
23 Places for some patches
24 Trifle
25 Futuristic knight
28 Hang back
30 Sealed
33 Construction co. job
34 Ensured: abbr.
35 Bellini work
38 Comic Caesar of 1950s TV
39 Hideous
43 Lay
45 Lea sound
46 Argentinian leader
47 Steak choices
49 Tomb marker
50 Certain Christian
51 Ritual combustible stacks
52 Mascara targets

Down

1 Units of sweat
2 Kate's sitcom friend
3 Howard of XM radio
4 Red or White team
5 Poet's prayer
6 Last words of an uncertain person?
7 Digestive enzyme
8 Wishy-washy response
9 Sale of assets
10 Small orbiting object
11 Calls for silence
18 Berlin suds
20 Record problem
22 Like lyrics
25 Moonshine vessels
26 Wholeness
27 Unsteady one
29 Future CEOs degrees
31 Firehouse vehicles
32 Ancient Scandinavian
36 Contrite
37 Mideast holy city
40 West Indian witchcraft
41 Far from shiny
42 Smooths the way
44 Exclusive
46 Old Sony handheld console
48 Tulipe relative

SOLUTIONS

SOLUTIONS

1

```
A D D E D
D R I V E
M O P E S
I N I N K
T E N T S
```

2

```
  T E A S
D E V I L
E R O D E
A S K E D
N E E D
```

3

```
B   A M P
A U D I O
T R U C E
O G L E S
N E T   Y
```

4

```
W A G   F
O P I N E
M E D A L
A D D T O
N   Y O N
```

5

```
B E G S
O G L E R
O R A T E
M E R I T
  T E N D
```

6

```
A P R O N
D R I P
V I S T A
  D E E D
K E N D O
```

7

```
C U R L   A R T S   I B M
F R E E   D E E M   D U O
O N C E   M I S S P E N D
    E R R A N T   L A S E
R A P   O N S A L E
E X T R A   T E A P O T
B L O O D P R E S S U R E
S E R B I A     S E R G E
    B E R A T E   I S M
L O S E   T I R E O F
A P P R A I S E   A I D S
W E E   L A L A   T E A K
N N W   F L E D   H D M I
```

8

```
S W E A R I N   E S P N
A H A   A R E   A P I E
Y E S   R E V E R E N T
S T Y L E   E X A C T S
    G A S T R I C
A D O P T S   S H I R E
L E I   A L T E R E D
S E N S O R Y   R A G
O R G A N   R E M A D E
    R I P E N E D
H O O D O O   A N I S E
A R M I N A R M   A L A
L E A N   C U E   T A T
L O N E   H E L M E T S
```

SOLUTIONS

9

R	O	S	E	S	■	P	A	S	S	I	N	G
A	P	P	■	P	R	O	M	■	E	C	R	U
P	E	A	G	R	E	E	N	■	T	E	A	M
S	C	R	E	E	N	T	E	S	T	S	■	T
■	■	■	L	E	T	■	S	E	E	K	E	R
H	I	P	S	■	■	L	I	N	E	A	G	E
E	R	R	■	A	H	E	A	D	■	T	I	E
L	O	O	T	B	A	G	■	L	E	S	S	■
I	N	D	I	C	T	■	G	A	S	■	■	■
P	■	U	N	D	E	S	I	R	A	B	L	E
A	R	C	H	■	F	I	R	S	T	A	I	D
D	A	T	A	■	U	N	D	O	■	L	E	D
S	Y	S	T	O	L	E	■	N	E	E	D	Y

10

P	I	L	E	U	P	■	A	D	D	O	N
U	N	E	A	S	E	■	C	A	R	R	Y
S	C	A	R	E	S	■	T	R	E	E	S
H	I	N	D	■	T	E	E	N	A	G	E
■	T	E	R	N	■	E	D	E	M	A	■
S	E	D	U	C	E	R	■	D	O	N	E
M	■	M	A	N	I	C	■	■	F	O	G
O	P	P	■	A	T	L	A	S	■	■	O
G	I	L	L	■	O	Y	S	T	E	R	S
■	R	E	A	L	M	■	H	E	R	E	■
B	A	D	D	E	B	T	■	R	A	C	E
A	N	G	L	E	■	A	R	I	S	E	N
S	H	E	E	R	■	R	E	L	E	N	T
S	A	S	S	Y	■	E	X	E	R	T	S

11

J	U	G	S	■	M	A	R	T	■	V	I	A
O	G	L	E	■	O	L	I	O	■	E	N	D
B	L	A	N	C	D	E	B	L	A	N	C	S
S	I	M	I	L	E	■	S	L	I	D	■	■
■	■	■	L	A	R	D	■	S	M	E	L	T
H	O	M	E	W	A	R	D	■	S	T	A	Y
I	P	A	■	S	T	E	E	P	■	T	S	K
F	E	N	D	■	E	S	C	A	L	A	T	E
I	D	I	O	M	■	S	A	N	E	■	■	■
■	■	F	E	E	D	■	D	I	G	E	S	T
P	R	E	S	T	I	G	E	C	U	V	E	E
H	I	S	■	A	K	I	N	■	M	I	R	E
S	A	T	■	L	E	N	T	■	E	L	A	N

12

A	N	D	R	E	A	G	A	S	S	I
N	O	N	E	■	A	L	P	A	C	A
S	T	A	S	H	■	P	L	A	N	E	S
W	■	T	I	B	I	A	■	D	D	T
E	T	C	■	K	E	N	Y	A	■	E
R	H	Y	M	I	N	G	■	W	E	A	R
S	E	C	O	N	D	■	C	A	M	P
■	S	L	U	G	■	F	I	S	C	A	L
S	E	E	N	■	S	O	T	H	E	R	E
Q	■	D	O	N	O	R	■	E	T	A
U	S	B	■	N	A	D	I	R	■	D
A	T	O	M	I	C	■	C	O	A	T	I
B	E	D	E	C	K	■	M	I	E	N
■	P	E	T	E	S	A	M	P	R	A	S

13

F	O	R	G	E
■	W	E	E	K
U	N	P	E	G
S	E	A	S	■
D	R	Y	E	R

14

T	A	B	O	O
H	■	L	A	B
A	B	A	T	E
W	A	R	■	Y
S	T	E	M	S

15

A	B	O	U	T
L	O	W	■	A
P	A	N	T	S
H	■	E	E	K
A	I	D	E	S

SOLUTIONS

16

```
T O D   T H O U   A F A R
A V E   H E W N   M A R E
R E F E R E E S   A C E S
O R A T E D   A B S E N T
  A C H E   A L L S T A R
A L T O   M I T E     O
B L O S S O M E D I N T O
U     T O A D   N O R M
N A S C E N T   U R S A
D R E A M S   P S E U D O
A G E D   H I R E D G U N
N U D E   O D O R   A C T
T E S T   T O P S   R E V
```

17

```
A D J   M E R I D I A N
L I E   O D E   O S H A
A S E P T I C   C L O P
S C R A T C H   K E Y S
      N O T A T E
T Y P E     R U T T E D
C A L L S I G N   H A Y
B L U   T R E A S U R E
Y E S T E R     U S S R
        S W I N G S
C A G E   G O A H E A D
H U R T   A N T I W A R
I R I S   T O E   E R A
N A M E L E S S   S P Y
```

18

```
R E D T A P E   A S K E W
O V E R L A Y   C H I M E
C A B O O S E   P O L A R
  L A W N S   L O U N G E
P U R E E   Y O W L
E A R L   N O S E D I V E
R T E   F O Y E R   N I X
M E D I A T O R   P U C E
    M U M S   F O N T S
S A M P L E   R O N D O
C L O U T   Y A R D A R M
A G A T E   A S C E T I C
B A T E D   W H E R E A S
```

19

```
A B Y S S   B L A M E S
F L O A T E R   N A V Y
F O R G O N E   O X E N
A W E S O M E   N I N E
I       D I Z Z Y   R
R U N S   T E E M I N G
  P A T S Y   T O D A Y
M O G U L   H A U L S
I N S T A T E   S E A R
T   T W E R P     U
T A K E   N E U T R A L
E W E R   N O T R A C E
N O P E   I N T E G E R
S L I D E S   Y E A R S
```

SOLUTIONS

20

S	A	B	L	E		B	A	L	L	A	D	S
O	C	E	A	N		U	S	A		L	I	T
S	L	E	P	T		S	I	M	P	L	E	R
O	U	T	S	E	T		A	P	E	S		I
		E	R	R	S		R	A	P	I	D	
A	B	C	S		Y	U	L	E	T	I	D	E
C	O	O		F	O	R	A	Y		C	O	N
H	O	L	D	I	N	G	S		B	E	L	T
I	N	D	E	X		E	S	P	Y			
E		C	L	A	P		O	I	L	R	A	G
V	A	U	L	T	E	D		V	I	O	L	A
E	X	T		E	R	Y		O	N	T	O	P
R	E	S	I	D	U	E		T	E	S	T	S

21

C	L	A	S	S	I	C		S	T	A	G	
R	U	N	U	P			I	N	L	I	N	E
A	T	O	N	E		G	U	I	L	T	Y	
S	E	N	S	E		A	D	D	L	E	S	
H			D	I	R	G	E				E	
E	G	O	I	S	M		E	R	R	O	R	
D	A	R	N		I	S	S	U	E	D		
	L	A	T	I	N	O		L	E	D	S	
M	A	L	E	S		O	R	E	L	S	E	
A		S	L	A	T	E						C
R	E	N	T	A	L		A	I	M	E	R	
A	D	D	I	N	G		C	R	I	M	E	
U	G	A	N	D	A		T	A	C	I	T	
D	Y	K	E		E	N	S	N	A	R	E	

22

	F	U	R	
S	A	L	E	S
O	C	T	E	T
N	E	R	D	Y
	S	A	Y	

23

I		S	H	E
L	A	N	D	
L	O	O	T	S
	N	O	V	A
D	E	P		E

24

P	A	D		F
	C	I	A	O
S	H	A	V	E
P	Y	R	E	
F		Y	R	S

25

T	H	E	E		A	P	P	E	A	R	E	D
R	A	C	K		R	O	A	N		E	D	U
A	L	O	E		B	U	T	S		F	I	N
C	O	N	S	P	I	R	E		B	I	T	E
T			U	T	E	N	S	I	L			
O	R	D	E	R	E	D		P	O	L	E	S
R	A	I	D	E	R		C	O	M	E	U	P
S	N	A	G	S		B	O	N	E	D	R	Y
	G	E	T	T	I	N	G					G
B	A	R	D		I	N	T	E	R	N	A	L
I	R	A		W	A	D	E		I	A	M	A
D	I	M		W	R	E	N		D	A	I	S
E	A	S	T	W	A	R	D		E	N	D	S

26

A	N	A	L	O	G		S	A	B	E	R	
L	A	M	E		A	C	H	I	E	V	E	
U	T	E	S		N	O	O	D	L	E	S	
M	I	N	T		G	R	E	E	T		U	
N	O	D		U	S	E	S		O	I	L	
I	N	S	E	R	T			D	U	C	T	
			A	N	E	C	D	O	T	E	S	
C	R	O	S	S	R	O	A	D				
R	I	F	E		A	T	O	N	A	L		
I	M	F		S	A	L	E		E	P	A	
T		S	C	E	N	E		T	W	I	N	
T	O	I	L	E	T	S		A	B	E	D	
E	N	D	E	M	I	C		L	I	C	E	
R	E	E	F	S		E	X	C	E	E	D	

SOLUTIONS

27

S	L	I	M		M	I	S	H	M	A	S	H
C	A	M	E		O	N	T	O		C	P	I
U	S	P	S		U	F	O	S		R	U	T
F	E	A	S	T	S		O	T	T	E	R	S
F	R	I		O	S	T	L	E	R			E
	G	R	A	T	E	R		D	I	G	I	N
D	U	E	L		I		B	A	N	D		
I	N	D	I	A		T	A	P	E	R	S	
M			A	C	C	E	D	E		D	U	G
P	H	Y	S	I	O		U	N	W	E	L	L
L	E	O		D	U	L	L		I	N	T	O
E	F	G		I	G	E	T		L	I	E	S
S	T	I	T	C	H	E	S		L	A	D	S

28

O	P	T	I	C	S		K	A	Y	A	K
B	O	R	N		C	O	I	N	A	G	E
I	N	I	T		H	A	N	G	D	O	G
T	Y	P	E	S	E	T		R	A	G	S
			R	E	M	E	D	Y			
E	T	C	E	T	E	R	A		G	O	P
B	O	O	S	T		S	U	P	I	N	E
A	R	C	T	I	C		N	O	B	E	L
Y	E	A		N	A	S	T	I	E	S	T
		A	G	R	E	E	S				
F	L	A	X		E	N	D	O	R	S	E
A	I	M	L	E	S	S		N	U	L	L
I	M	M	E	R	S	E		E	L	E	M
L	O	O	S	E		S	C	R	E	W	S

29

A	M	I	C	A	B	L	E		F	E	A	R
B	A	S	H		A	I	M		E	X	P	O
R	U	N	E		R	O	U	L	E	T	T	E
A	L	T	S		O	N	S	I	D	E		
		T	E	N	S		N	E	R	V	E
P	L	A	S	M	A		H	E	R	N	I	A
E	O	N		I	G	L	O	O		A	S	S
A	S	T	U	T	E		M	U	L	L	E	T
S	T	I	N	T		M	E	T	E			
		D	I	E	S	E	L		A	V	O	W
P	R	O	T	R	U	D	E		G	A	M	E
T	O	T	E		C	I	S		U	S	E	D
O	W	E	D		H	A	S	B	E	E	N	S

30

M	A	U	L	E	D		C	L	O	A	K
I	M	P	A	L	E		R	A	B	B	I
L	I	C	H	E	N		A	T	O	L	L
E	G	O		C	O	G	W	H	E	E	L
S	O	U	R		T	A	L	E			J
		N	I	N	E	S		G	O	O	
C	A	T	C	H		H	O	O	R	A	Y
A	F	R	E	S	H		T	R	E	K	S
T	R	Y		Y	U	C	C	A			
A		R	A	M	P		A	T	O	P	
C	O	M	E	I	N	T	O		D	U	E
O	P	I	U	M		A	V	I	A	T	E
M	A	N	S	E		K	E	N	N	E	L
B	L	E	E	D		E	N	T	E	R	S

31

	M	E	S	H
M	I	X		A
A	L	I	G	N
P		L	A	G
S	H	E	D	

32

C	R	U	D	
Z		T	O	S
A	R	I	A	L
R	E	L		O
	D	E	F	T

33

		M	I	D
S	P	A	C	E
O	L	D	E	N
F	E	A	S	T
T	A	M		

SOLUTIONS

34

A	S	H	C	A	N		O	U	S	T	E	D
B	C	E		F	E	L	L		P	E	A	R
A	R	C		R	A	I	D		L	A	T	E
S	E	T	F	O	R	T	H		A	S	I	S
H	E	A	L			H	A	S	T	E	N	S
	C	R	E	S	C	E	N	T				E
S	H	E	A	T	H		D	O	L	L	A	R
T			A	I	R	S	P	E	E	D		
O	B	S	E	R	V	E			G	I	M	P
R	O	I	L		A	M	B	R	O	S	I	A
A	X	E	D		L	I	E	U		U	R	L
G	I	V	E		R	T	E	S		R	E	M
E	N	E	R	G	Y		R	E	F	E	R	S

35

C	A	S	H	I	E	R		S	T	I	R
A	N	T	E	N	N	A		O	H	N	O
S	K	I	L	L	E	T		D	I	V	A
T	A	N	D	E	M		M	A	N	E	S
E	R	G		T	Y	P	O		A	R	T
R	A	Y	S			A	D	V	I	S	E
			P	I	O	N	E	E	R	E	D
O	R	G	A	N	I	S	M	S			
V	E	R	N	A	L			T	O	G	A
A	P	E		N	Y	P	D		C	O	T
T	R	A	C	E		R	E	P	E	A	T
I	O	T	A		C	O	L	L	A	T	E
O	V	E	R		I	N	T	O	N	E	S
N	E	R	D		D	E	A	D	S	E	T

36

V	I	B	E		A	B	S	T	R	A	C	T
A	D	A	Y		T	A	M	E		F	A	R
L	O	D	E		W	R	A	P		I	P	O
U	S	E	D	T	O		S	E	P	T	E	T
A			A	R	C	H	E	R				
B	L	E	M	I	S	H			I	D	E	S
L	O	C	A	L	T	I	M	E	Z	O	N	E
E	G	G	S			R	E	V	E	N	G	E
			T	R	I	P	L	E				D
P	A	S	S	O	N		A	S	T	R	A	L
A	G	A		A	T	T	N		W	A	N	E
L	U	G		C	R	A	G		O	R	E	S
L	E	E	S	H	O	R	E		S	E	W	S

37

C	P	A		S	P	A	N	K	I	N	G
O	U	R		C	O	D	A		C	E	O
M	R	I		E	N	V	Y		A	A	A
A	L	D	E	N	T	E		I	N	T	L
			A	T	O	N	E	S			
A	B	B	R		O	T	T	O	M	A	N
M	A	R	L	I	N		C	L	O	S	E
P	L	A	I	N		T	H	A	N	K	S
S	I	D	E	C	A	R		T	O	S	S
			S	H	R	I	N	E			
F	I	S	T		A	B	I	D	E	B	Y
I	C	U		A	B	U	T		P	I	E
F	O	R		P	I	N	E		E	L	L
E	N	F	O	R	C	E	R		E	E	L

SOLUTIONS

38

S	H	O	W	S		S	U	B	L	I	M	E
C	O	P	I	L	O	T		M	E	T	E	R
A	R	I	Z	O	N	A		W	A	S	T	E
L	M	N		E	L	K	S		F	O	R	M
D	O	I	N		Y	E	L	P		K	O	I
	N	O	E	S		S	A	I	L			T
G	E	N	R	E	S		P	E	O	P	L	E
L		F	E	E	L		S	O	L	O		
A	W	E		D	E	E	P		T	A	U	T
R	A	N	T		R	A	I	L		N	D	A
I	F	N	O	T		S	T	A	R	T	E	R
N	E	U	R	O		E	A	S	I	E	S	T
G	R	I	N	N	E	D		S	O	R	T	S

39

L	U	C	I	D		C	L	A	M	O	R
I	N	O	N	E		L	A	C	U	N	A
S	T	I	N	G		A	D	D	S	U	P
T	O	N	E	R		N	I	C	E	S	T
E			R	E	I	G	N				U
D	I	M	M	E	R		G	A	M	E	R
	K	I	O	S	K	S		L	A	N	E
P	E	N	S		S	E	W	I	N	G	
H	A	I	T	I		C	H	E	E	R	Y
R			G	E	T	I	N				A
A	R	M	I	N	G		T	A	G	O	N
S	E	A	D	O	G		E	B	O	O	K
A	D	M	I	R	E		S	L	O	P	E
L	O	A	D	E	D		T	E	N	S	E

40

P	O	P		
A	N	I	M	E
L	I	N	E	D
S	T	O	N	E
		N	U	N	

41

C	O	G	S	
D	A	R	T	
S	T	O	I	C
	H	U	L	A
	S	P	E	D

42

	G	L	A	D
	H	E	R	O
M	O	V	I	E
S	U	E	S	
G	L	E	E	

43

G	L	U	E		Y	O	U	F	I	R	S	T
N	O	N	S	T	O	P		I	D	A	H	O
U	P	S	T	A	G	E		S	E	T	O	N
		P	A	G	A	N		H	A	S	T	E
S	P	O	T	S		T	O	E	S			
L	A	K	E		D	O	R	Y		O	B	I
U	N	E	S	C	O		B	E	D	P	A	N
M	T	N		L	O	T	S		R	U	I	N
		F	E	M	A		B	I	L	L	S	
U	M	B	R	A		B	R	A	V	E		
S	A	L	O	N		L	I	C	E	N	S	E
E	L	I	T	E		E	T	H	I	C	A	L
R	E	P	H	R	A	S	E		N	E	C	K

44

E	V	A	D	E	S		S	P	R	I	G
M	E	R	E	L	Y		E	R	A	S	E
B	E	R	L	I	N		L	O	G	O	N
				E	X	C	E	L	L	E	N	T
C	A	C	T	I		R	O	I			
O	T	H	E	R		R	U	F	F	L	E
N	E	O		V	E	T	E	R	A	N	
G	A	R	B	L	E	D			A	N	D
O	M	E	L	E	T		S	L	I	C	E
		E	S	C		P	I	L	E	D	
M	A	I	N	S	H	E	E	T			
A	B	O	D	E		M	E	T	A	L	S
N	O	W	I	N		I	C	E	T	E	A
S	W	A	N	S		T	H	R	E	A	D

224

SOLUTIONS

45

```
H O L E U P ■ T U R T L E
T H I N ■ A R E A ■ H E Y
M I N D ■ P I N E T R E E
L O G O T Y P E ■ O U S T
■ ■ W I R E T A P ■ ■ E
E G G ■ P U N ■ R I D G E
S L E E P S ■ D O C E N T
T O N A L ■ S U M ■ M P H
R ■ ■ T E S T B A N ■ ■
A P S E ■ N U I S A N C E
N O O N T I M E ■ C A L M
G E M ■ A P P T ■ R I O T
E M E R G E ■ Y I E L D S
```

46

```
B E E F T E A ■ H O B O
E N D U E ■ B R A C E R
A G I L E ■ R A T T A T
N A T ■ S P O N S O R ■
■ G O D H E A D ■ P E P
S E R R I E D ■ S U R E
H ■ I R K ■ P O S S E
O W L E T ■ E R N ■ V
C H A R ■ C L E A N S E
K E Y ■ N O S T R I L ■
■ R E F E R E E ■ C I A
R E T O O K ■ N E E D S
A T T U N E ■ D A T E S
D O E R ■ D I S T O R T
```

47

```
Y A P ■ R O A D ■ P U M A
E X U D E ■ L E B A N O N
T I R E D ■ P L A Y B O Y
I S R A E L ■ I S E E ■ W
■ L E A P ■ T E A C H
S C R I M M A G E ■ T H E
P E E N ■ P R O ■ H E I R
A L L ■ A S S U R A N C E
C L E F T ■ E R A S ■
È ■ G E O L ■ D I S C U S
B O A T M A N ■ S L U N K
A R T I S T S ■ E E R I E
R E E D ■ S A S S ■ B T W
```

48

```
A R C A D E ■ S O F A S
R E A L ■ S T O M A C H
M E R E ■ T R A I N E E
E V E R ■ H E R S ■ E
N E T T L E S ■ S A L T
I ■ I T S ■ I B I S
A S S U M E ■ C O I F
■ P A P A ■ H U N T E D
P I N S ■ K I T ■ E
I N S T ■ O M E L E T S
E ■ A A A S ■ A D O S
C U B I C L E ■ T U N E
E T E R N A L ■ I C E R
D E N S E ■ F I N E S T
```

49

```
C O A L S
A N N I E
D O G M A
I N U I T
Z E S T S
```

50

```
■ B L A T
M E A T Y
O L D E R
C I L I A
K E E N ■
```

51

```
U ■ P O X
S P U M E
H E M I N
E R A T O
R P S ■ N
```

SOLUTIONS

52

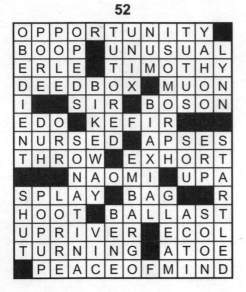

O	P	P	O	R	T	U	N	I	T	Y	
B	O	O	P		U	N	U	S	U	A	L
E	R	L	E		T	I	M	O	T	H	Y
D	E	E	D	B	O	X		M	U	O	N
I		S	I	R		B	O	S	O	N	
E	D	O		K	E	F	I	R			
N	U	R	S	E	D		A	P	S	E	S
T	H	R	O	W		E	X	H	O	R	T
		N	A	O	M	I		U	P	A	
S	P	L	A	Y		B	A	G			R
H	O	O	T		B	A	L	L	A	S	T
U	P	R	I	V	E	R		E	C	O	L
T	U	R	N	I	N	G		A	T	O	E
	P	E	A	C	E	O	F	M	I	N	D

53

S	P	A	N	I	S	H	A	M	E	R	I	C	A	N
T	O	D	O		I	O	U	S		E	M	O	T	E
R	O	A	M		L	O	P	E		P	A	R	T	S
A	L	M	S		A	P	A	C	H	E		F	A	T
T		G	I	G	L	I		I	N	C	U	R	S	
A	T	A		T	E	A	R	I	N	T	O			
G	A	L	L	O		S	I	D		S	P	A	S	
E	X	P	O	R	T	S		S	U	B	M	E	N	U
M	I	S	O		O	O	H		I	O	N	I	C	
		F	O	R	D	A	B	L	E		N	S	C	
D	E	C	A	F	S		S	O	I	L	S			E
I	R	L		F	I	R	I	N	G		N	A	M	E
C	O	O	P	S		A	D	I	N		A	P	O	D
E	D	D	I	E		S	I	T	U		F	A	V	E
D	E	S	K	T	O	P	C	O	M	P	U	T	E	R

Mystery Words: MAXIMUS DECIMUS MERIDIUS

54

M	A	R	C	E	L	S		A	P	R	I	L
A	M	O	R		I	L	L	T	R	E	A	T
A	B	O	O		P	R	O	T	E	S	T	S
M	I	D	S	T	S		S	I	F	T		
			B	A	Y		S	C	A	R	A	B
B	A	R	Y	O	N	S			B	A	C	O
I	L	E		S	C	H	W	A		I	M	O
A	M	A	N			U	R	B	A	N	E	R
S	A	L	U	K	I		E	B	B			
		I	B	I	D		C	A	Y	M	A	N
B	A	S	I	L	I	S	K		S	O	H	O
E	N	T	A	N	G	L	E		M	O	M	S
A	S	S	N	S		O	D	Y	S	S	E	Y

55

S	P	E	E	D	B	O	O	S	T	E	R	
T	U	L	S	A		G	O	U	R	D	E	
A	P	I	S	H		R	O	B	U	S	T	
G			A	L	A	E		V	E	E	R	
N	A	R	Y		M	I	S	E	R	L	Y	
A	G	E		B	A	S	E	R				
T	A	U	P	E		H	O	T	T	E	R	
E	L	P	A	S	O		U	S	U	R	Y	
			R	E	N	A	L		P	O	E	
S	P	U	R	T	E	D		L	I	S	T	
M	A	R	Y		M	A	G	I			O	
A	L	B	I	N	O		E	V	I	T	A	
L	E	A	N	E	R		R	E	B	U	S	
L	O	N	G	T	E	R	M	D	E	B	T	

SOLUTIONS

56

H	A	D		C	L	O	S	E	U	P		A	T	T
I	G	O		N	E	C	T	A	R	S		R	H	O
G	R	O	U	N	D	C	O	R	I	A	N	D	E	R
H	O	R	N		T	U	N	A	S		O	O	R	T
			A	H	O	L	I	C		B	O	R	E	S
A	M	I	G	A		T	E	H	R	A	N			
R	E	T	E	L	L		R	E	E	K		V	G	A
C	A	R	D	I	A	C		S	I	L	K	I	E	R
S	L	Y		F	I	R	M		D	A	R	E	N	T
		C	A	R	E	E	R		V	A	S	E	S	
R	E	D	O	X		A	N	O	R	A	K			
A	V	I	V		U	M	A	M	I		O	O	Z	E
F	I	V	E	S	P	I	C	E	P	O	W	D	E	R
T	A	E		S	T	E	E	R	E	D		E	E	N
S	N	D		H	O	R	R	O	R	S		S	S	E

Mystery Words: SOUP IS ALWAYS A GOOD IDEA

57

I	C	A	N	T	S	T	A	Y	L	O	N	G
S	E	Q		A	T	A	N		E	R	N	O
I	N	U	N	I	S	O	N		F	R	E	T
S	T	A	I	N			E	S	T	E		
			C	T	N	S		H	I	R	E	D
W	I	R	E		C	A	P	O	E	I	R	A
A	D	E		M	O	P	U	P		E	I	N
G	E	O	D	E	S	I	C		A	S	E	A
E	A	R	E	D		D	K	N	Y			
		I	L	S	A			A	E	G	I	S
R	H	E	A		M	I	L	K	S	O	P	S
C	O	N	N		O	D	I	E		N	O	N
A	C	T	O	F	K	I	N	D	N	E	S	S

58

K	A	Y	O		E	P	I	L	A	T	E
I	G	O	R		M	A	R	I	N	E	S
N	A	D	A		P	I	E	T	I	E	S
G	R	A	N	T	E	R		E	T	T	E
C			G	U	R	U		R	A	H	S
R	I	C		P	O	P	P	A			
A	N	T	H	E	R		S	T	I	N	K
B	A	N	A	L		D	A	I	M	O	N
		B	O	W	E	L		P	R	E	
H	O	R	A		R	P	M	S			E
I	V	A	N		A	U	S	T	R	A	L
F	A	K	E	D	I	T		R	U	D	E
I	T	E	R	A	T	E		U	B	E	R
S	E	R	A	P	H	S		T	E	S	S

59

S	G	T	S		D	E	L	E		S	T	A	L	E
H	E	A	P		A	R	U	M		T	I	G	O	N
E	T	N	A		W	I	S	P		I	N	E	P	T
D	I	S	T	I	N	C	T	I	V	E	N	E	S	S
S	T	Y	E	S				R	I	S	E			
			U	N	O	P	E	N		R	O	B	S	
D	I	A	S	P	O	R	A		A	S	K	I	N	
A	C	A	T		H	A	L	O	E	D		A	S	A
R	E	C	R	U	I	T		B	L	O	O	P	E	R
N	A	H		S	T	E	R	E	O		R	I	C	K
E	X	E	C	S			B	A	P	T	I	S	T	S
R	E	N	E		N	O	S	H	E	R				
			L	E	E	R				A	L	E	P	H
I	N	D	E	P	E	N	D	E	N	C	E	D	A	Y
N	O	I	S	E		A	U	D	I		G	E	L	D
C	A	R	T	E		T	E	N	T		A	M	E	R
R	H	E	A	S		E	T	A	S		L	A	R	A

60

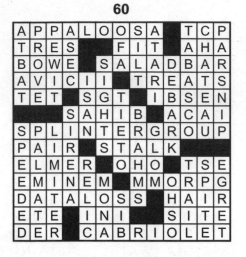

```
A P P A L O O S A ■ T C P
T R E S ■ F I T ■ A H A
B O W E ■ S A L A D B A R
A V I C I I ■ T R E A T S
T E T ■ S G T ■ I B S E N
■ S A H I B ■ A C A I
S P L I N T E R G R O U P
P A I R ■ S T A L K ■
E L M E R ■ O H O ■ T S E
E M I N E M ■ M M O R P G
D A T A L O S S ■ H A I R
E T E ■ I N I ■ S I T E
D E R ■ C A B R I O L E T
```

61

```
O H A R A ■ A N G O R A
K I L O S ■ P U L L O N
A D I O S ■ O B O I S T
P E A F O W L ■ B O S E
I ■ T R O U P E ■ C
■ C A R T O N S ■ O P E
A R N E ■ E Y E L I D
C O D E C S ■ M A T E
C C S ■ T H E G I F T ■
U ■ D R A W L S ■ A
S C A R ■ D E I S T I C
E L N I N O ■ T A R O T
R A N L O W ■ C R A N E
S M A L T S ■ H Y P E D
```

62

```
D A Y O F F ■ A D D I N S ■ I N S P
O V A L ■ I R M A ■ R O T ■ M I L A
F A R E ■ B I O L ■ I T Y ■ P T A S
F I N G E R P R I N T E X P E R T S
S L S ■ R I P E ■ O I D ■ A R O S E
■ B I L L ■ S R S ■ D P I
M I M I C ■ E D A M ■ D E P L E T E
O N A P A R ■ A R A B I C A ■ N O X
I L I E ■ E S T A ■ L O O S E N U P
R I D D A N C E ■ B O N D ■ D U P E
E E E ■ B E A R P A W ■ E G G I E R
S U N D O W N ■ R E N O ■ R E S E T
■ E R S ■ D O R ■ R B I S
T E S L A ■ V O L ■ A T E E ■ S S S
I N T E L L I G E N C E A G E N C Y
F O R T ■ I A M ■ E E G S ■ R E A R
F L U E ■ R N A ■ B R A T ■ T E R I
S A M S ■ A D S O R B ■ S H E R P A
```

63

```
P A T S ■ E M B O S S E D
E R S E ■ V O O ■ C O C O
S T A R L E T S ■ O U R S
T Y R A N N O S A U R U S
■ P G S ■ H T C ■ I
A S H E ■ O M I S S I V E
C H A ■ E N E R O ■ N C R
T R Y I N G T O ■ M G R S
U ■ B C C ■ N G O
A V A I L A B L E S O O N
T I L E ■ S A U T E R N E
O L E S ■ T I N ■ Y M C A
R E S T R I N G ■ S E E P
```

SOLUTIONS

64

B	E	N	C	H		T	O	W	A	G	E	S
A	M	P	H	O	R	A		E	L	I	D	E
L	O	R	E	L	E	I		L	I	N	D	A
L			N	E	A	L		S	T	A	Y	S
A	T	O	N		D	O	N	H	O			
D	E	W	A	R		R	A	M		I	B	F
R	E	L	I	E	F		N	E	C	T	A	R
Y	D	S		P	A	M		N	O	S	E	E
		C	R	A	I	G		D	O	Z	E	
C	A	P	R	I		D	O	U	G			Z
A	L	A	I	N		O	B	V	E	R	S	E
U	P	S	E	T		F	I	E	R	I	E	R
L	O	A	D	S	O	F		A	S	S	T	S

68

C	H	I	C	K	E	N	C	O	O	P	
H	O	S	A	N	N	A		F	R	A	G
A	T	O	M	I	C	S		H	A	R	I
I	S	L	E	T		A	L	O	N	S	O
	P	A	L	S	Y		A	N	G	E	R
O	U	T	S		O	P	P	O	S	E	D
D	R	E		P	U	R	E	R			A
D		B	E	V	E	L		M	I	N	
B	E	T	I	D	E	S		P	A	L	O
A	R	O	M	A		S	H	E	L	L	
L	A	B	E	L	S		O	P	T	E	D
L	S	A	T		P	A	S	S	A	G	E
S	E	G	A		A	R	T	I	S	A	N
	S	O	L	A	R	P	A	N	E	L	S

65

I	R	S		B
R	E	T	R	O
I	C	E	I	N
S	T	A	N	D
H		K	G	S

66

C	I	G	S	
O	N	E	O	F
A	D	E	L	E
T	I	N	E	S
	C	A	S	T

67

R	E	A	D	S
I	A	G	O	
P	R	A	Y	S
	L	I	L	Y
A	S	N	E	R

69

A	D	I	M		S	H	I	V	A		N	A	G	S
R	O	T	O		A	U	D	E	N		E	T	A	L
A	U	T	O		S	M	E	L	T		V	I	V	E
B	R	O	N	C	H	O		V	S	H	A	P	E	D
		B	L	A	R	N	E	Y	E	D				
B	A	B	O	O		S	I	T		A	A	H	E	D
O	B	I	W	A	N		G		A	D	N	A	T	E
G	I	G		K	A	S	H	M	I	R		S	H	A
E	D	G	A	R	S		T		D	E	F	T	E	R
Y	E	S	N	O		A	I	G		S	L	Y	L	Y
		C	O	O	P	E	R	A	T	E				
B	A	T	H	M	A	T		A	B	S	C	I	S	E
O	R	E	O		S	E	E	D	Y		K	A	L	I
A	G	E	R		I	S	L	E	S		E	T	O	N
R	O	N	S		S	T	O	R	M		D	E	B	S

70

L	E	T	S	G	O		S	A	M	O	S	A
A	V	A	T	A	R		T	R	O	P	E	S
L	A	R	R	U	P		E	A	T	E	R	S
A	N	T	E	C	H	A	M	B	E	R		I
			W	H	A	T		S	L	A	N	G
S	E	A	S	O	N	E	D		S	H	I	N
A	M	C		S	E	L	E	S		A	L	E
R	I	C	H		D	I	G	E	S	T	E	R
A	R	E	A	S		E	R	G	O			
T		P	R	O	G	R	A	M	M	E	R	S
O	C	T	A	N	E		D	E	A	R	I	E
G	L	O	R	I	A		E	N	L	I	S	T
A	R	R	E	A	R		S	T	I	N	K	S

Mystery Words: BRIDGE OVER TROUBLED WATER

SOLUTIONS

71

T	A	M	A	B	L	E		H	A	R	P
C	H	A	B	L	I	S		A	G	E	S
M	I	G	R	A	N	T		L	O	B	E
		G	A	Z	E	R		F	R	A	U
A	S	I	D	E		A	B	O	A	R	D
F	R	E	E		S	N	O	R	E		O
F	A	Q		L	O	G	I	C			N
I			F	I	D	E	L		T	V	Y
L		B	O	L	A	S		C	H	E	M
I	N	A	R	O	W		W	H	I	T	S
A	I	L	S		A	F	I	R	E		
T	H	E	A		T	I	P	O	V	E	R
E	A	R	L		E	L	E	M	E	N	T
D	O	S	E			R	E	R	E	D	O	S

72

M	I	R	A		O	G	D	E	N		A	N	K	A
U	T	I	L		P	R	I	M	O		L	E	I	A
T	A	L	K		T	I	T	A	N		F	I	N	S
E	L	L	A	F	I	T	Z	G	E	R	A	L	D	
			L	E	N	T			O	L	L	A	S	
D	A	V	I	T		Y	E	A	R	O	F		E	
I	P	E	C	A	C		P	R	O	F	A	N	E	D
G	I	N		P	H	O	N	E		O	L	A		
R	E	I	S	S	U	E	D		S	P	O	I	L	T
A		T	A	S	S	E	L		O	N	R	Y	E	
M	A	J	O	R		A	U	R	A					
	L	O	U	I	S	A	R	M	S	T	R	O	N	G
A	T	I	T		P	R	O	B	E		O	B	O	L
C	O	N	E		E	I	D	E	R		L	I	T	E
U	S	S	R		W	E	E	D	S		L	E	A	N

Mystery Words: DUKE ELLINGTON
ORNETTE COLEMAN

73

A	S	O	N	E		P	S	Y	C	H	I	C
T	A	U		M	S	R	P		A	E	R	O
S	W	I	T	C	H	E	D		M	A	I	D
U			Y	E	A	S		B	E	T	S	Y
N	E	G	L	E	C	T	F	U	L			
S	M	E	E		K	O	A	N		M	E	S
E	M	E	R	I	L		S	T	P	A	U	L
T	A	S		W	E	N	T		O	K	R	A
		L	A	D	I	E	S	R	O	O	M	
P	A	C	E	S		G	N	A	T			B
O	S	H	A		D	I	E	T	S	O	D	A
K	I	E	V		U	R	D	U		B	I	N
E	F	F	E	N	D	I		P	R	O	N	G

74

G	A	S	P		H	I	G	H	H	A	T
A	R	I	A		E	S	E		A	L	A
E	N	V	I	S	I	O	N		L	D	L
L	O	A	D	E	D	P	I	S	T	O	L
I			V	I	R	A	L			E	
C	L	A	V	E		E	L	E	C	T	S
	O	B	E	R	O	N		I	L	E	T
E	B	A	N		V	E	G	G	I	E	
N	O	T	I	C	E		R	H	O	M	B
D		C	A	R	P	I			A		
O	B	S	E	S	S	E	D	O	V	E	R
W	O	W		H	O	R	S	I	E	S	T
E	D	U		I	L	K		L	I	S	A
D	E	M	A	N	D	S		S	N	O	B

SOLUTIONS

75

S	A	P	S		N	U	R	S	E		D	O	M	E
T	R	I	E	D	O	N		A	R	B	I	T	E	R
A	N	T	E		E	L	A	B	O	R	A	T	E	D
B	I	C	Y	C	L	E	S		D	E	S	O	T	O
	C	H	O	Y		A	S	P	E	R				G
L	A	Y	U	P		R	I	O	S		B	E	T	A
E			R	I	N	G	S		D	A	Y	A	N	
O	R	D	A	I	N		N	E	M	E	S	I	S	
S	E	A	G	O	E	R		D	I	P	I	N	T	O
	P	R	E	T	Z	E	L		C	O	N	G	E	R
I	R	E	N	E		H	E	M	A	N				C
C	O	S	T		R	A	G	A		I	T	E	M	S
E			C	A	B	I	N		N	E	R	O		
A	L	P	H	A	S		O	L	I	G	A	R	C	H
X	Y	L	O	P	H	O	N	E	S		B	A	K	E
E	R	U	P	T	E	D		S	T	R	A	T	U	S
S	A	G	S		S	A	Y	S	O		G	A	P	S

76

I	M	A	G	O	E	S		G	A	B	L	E
R	O	B	O		M	I	N	O	T	A	U	R
A	D	E	N		E	X	E	R	T	I	N	G
N		Y	E	A	R		S	K	A	T	E	S
I	N	A	R	T	I	S	T	I	C			
A	Y	N		M	E	M			H	E	R	B
N	E	C	E	S	S	A	R	Y	E	V	I	L
S	T	E	P			R	E	O		A	N	O
			S	W	A	M	P	L	A	N	D	S
E	S	P	I	A	L		R	O	M	E		S
N	A	I	L	F	I	L	E		I	S	N	O
C	U	L	O	T	T	E	S		S	C	A	M
E	D	E	N	S		E	S	C	H	E	W	S

77

C	H	A	M	O	I	S		P	A	R	A
R	E	C	O	N		H	I	L	L	E	D
I	N	T	O	W		R	H	U	M	B	A
T	R	O	T	H		I	A	M	A		P
T	I	N	S	E	L	E	D		N	U	T
E			E	E	K		E	A	R	S	
R	I	B	A	L	D		C	O	C	A	
	B	U	C	S		M	U	E	S	L	I
L	A	S	H		J	U	T				C
I	R	T		C	O	M	E	H	O	M	E
N		A	V	E	C		N	A	M	E	D
G	I	G	O	L	O		E	B	E	R	T
A	D	U	L	T	S		S	I	N	G	E
M	O	T	E		E	A	S	T	S	E	A

78

D	E	E	P	T	I	S	S	U	E	M	A	S	S	A	G	E
I	N	R	E		B	E	T		P	A	R	E		C	A	D	S
S	Y	S	T		E	N	E		I	G	O	T		E	M	I	L
K	A	T	A	K	A	N	A		Z	E	U	S		T	U	T	U
			A	M	A	D	E	O		S	H	E	A	T	H	E
A	S	H	E	N			S	A	G	E	O	I	L	
S	M	A	R	T	A	L	E	C		A	S	T	R		N	E	V
C	E	R	N		T	U	V	A	L	U		E	B	O	L	A
R	A	V	E		T	R	I	P	O	D	A	L		I	S	B	N
I	R	E	S		S	E	L	E	N	I	T	E		S	H	O	E
B	E	S	T	S		E	D	G	E	I	N		H	A	W	S
E	D	T		P	L	A	Y		A	R	E	A	C	O	D	E	S
		I	C	E	B	E	R	G			O	P	E	R	A
O	V	E	R	A	T	E		E	O	C	E	N	E	
A	R	C	O		I	T	S	A		O	X	I	D	A	N	T	S
T	O	O	N		T	T	O	P		S	U	N		D	O	H	A
S	O	L	I		G	E	R	E		T	R	E		D	R	E	W
	M	I	C	R	O	D	E	R	M	A	B	R	A	S	I	O	N

SOLUTIONS

79

```
S A B B A T H S   L I M O
T B A R   I M I T A T E D
A L S O   M O N O T O N Y
N E S T L E   A M E N D S
  C H A L K I E R     S
C O L   V A N     A R T E
A V E R A G E S A L A R Y
S A F E   E H S   B I S
T   M A C L A I N E
O A F I S H   P A E L L A
F L E X T I M E   G A I N
F I R E O P A L   R I F T
S E N D   S T Y L I S T S
```

80

```
L I A M   O V I F O R M
A L B A   F A B   M O E
P I E R   F L E N S E D
B A T T L E A X E     I
O   Y A R N   E L B A
A P A R T   C I D E R
R O W   E V E R Y M A N
D I A G N O S E   M C A
  S C O T T   N B A E R
T E S T   E D I E   R
A   I N D O C H I N A
C A N N O N S   A S I T
O B E   R A E   V A N E
S A S H A Y S   E Y E S
```

81

```
B U R R O
  S U E Z
T E N D S
B U O Y
A P N E A
```

82

```
P H A G E
A   F R Y
S C O P E
T S O   U
E A T U P
```

83

```
S K I R T
H I M   O
A D M E N
L   I C Y
L E X U S
```

84

```
R A K I S H   J A D E S
A G A T H A   O V E R T
D O R I E S   H E N N A
C R A N   S P A R S E R
L A T   L E N S E S
I   S A B E R S   S T K
F   B A D   S I T O N
F E M U R   G O N   I
E X O   R H O N D A   G
  P R A Y E D   I S H
A L A R M E D   B R U T
P O L I O   E P I C A L
T I L E R   S H R O V E
S T Y L E   S I D N E Y
```

85

```
I A M B   L A P L A N D E R S
A V I A T E   L O K I   M A L
L A S S I E   A N A L E M M A
  S T E E R I N G   M Y S T
E   H O Y T   E A R P
A C T I N   A U D I O T A P E
G L U T   M L K   L A Y E R S
L O T   K A Y A K E R   S A S
E A T S I N   S Y D   I O T A
S K I N D I V E R   M O P E Y
  I S A W   I P A D   S
A L E C   G R E E N I S H
C O C K A T O O   T E D E U M
C R O   P A L L   I D E A T E
T E N D E R F E E T   S L U G
```

Mystery Words: YOUR ONLY LIMIT IS YOUR MIND

SOLUTIONS

86

V	E	R	B		R	I	N	G	T	O	S	S
I	M	H	O		I	C	A	N		A	E	I
S	U	E	D		D	I	V	A		H	T	S
C	L	O	S	E	D	C	I	R	C	U	I	T
I	S	S		A	L	L	E	L	E			E
D	I	T		S	E	E	S		D	E	E	R
	F	A	T	E				G	E	N	X	
M	Y	T	H		S	A	G	O		A	P	P
A			A	M	E	L	I	E		M	E	R
M	A	R	I	O	N	B	A	R	T	O	L	I
M	B	A		I	S	I	N		A	R	L	O
A	R	I		R	O	O	T		P	E	E	R
L	A	N	T	E	R	N	S		A	D	D	Y

87

C	O	A	S	T	E	D		L	O	I	S
O	N	S	T	A	G	E		I	N	F	O
B	O	T	U	L	I	N		B	A	N	A
R			P	O	S	T	E	R	I	O	R
A	D	M	A	N			M	A	R	T	S
K	R	I	S		M	E	I	R			
A	I	L		D	O	O	R	Y	A	R	D
I	B	E	R	I	A	N	S		M	A	A
			W	E	T	S		A	I	R	Y
D	U	C	A	T			O	R	D	E	R
E	V	E	N	S	O	N	G	S			A
R	E	N	D		M	O	L	E	R	A	T
M	A	T	A		A	D	E	N	I	N	E
A	S	S	N		R	E	S	E	A	T	S

88

B	L	O	N	D	E	B	O	M	B	S	H	E	L	L
L	E	S	S		D	O	R	A		H	A	N	O	I
A	T	T	Y		D	A	Z	E		A	N	G	S	T
C	O	E	N		A	T	O	N	E	R		R	T	E
K	N	O	C	K			A	L	E	S				R
E			A	C	C	E	D	E		T	I	N	A	
R	O	D		P	A	A	R		C	R	U	R	A	L
	H	A	P	P	Y	B	I	R	T	H	D	A	Y	
I	N	S	E	A	M		K	I	R	I		S	S	T
B	O	H	O		A	B	A	D	A	N				R
E		N	A	N	O			E	L	U	D	E		
R	D	A		T	S	U	R	I	S		E	Z	R	A
I	O	T	A	S		R	I	N	K		O	B	I	T
A	D	O	R	E		S	T	A	Y		N	E	V	E
N	O	R	M	A	J	E	A	N	E	B	A	K	E	R

Mystery Words: SOME LIKE IT HOT
                  MONKEY BUSINESS

89

U	M	I	A	K		E	S	C	R	O	W	S
N	I	C	H	E		A	L	I		F	E	E
S	K	E	I	N		S	O	T		F	I	N
T	E	S	T	T	H	E	W	A	T	E	R	S
O				A	U	S	T	I	N			E
P	I	L	E	D	U	P		I	N	D	U	S
	P	A	N	E	L		L	O	G	E	S	
C	O	D	E	R		G	E	N	E	R	A	L
R		S	M	I	L	E	E					O
U	G	L	Y	D	U	C	K	L	I	N	G	S
M	A	O		I	N	K		A	G	A	R	S
B	E	V		N	C	O		V	E	N	U	E
S	L	E	I	G	H	S		S	T	A	B	S

90

```
O N T H E L A S T D A Y
  B W A N A     N E A R
S A I N T S     E A T O N
T     D I S     A R E N A
E T C   C O O K         T
A B A S E     A S T H M A
M O N I S M S     R O U T
I N T L     O T H E L L O
R E S O R B     R Y D E R
O       E S P Y     S S I
N A I V E   I V S       U
S I S A L     A N A D E M
  D A L E     N I T E R
W A T E R C O A S T E R
```

91

```
B A C K P E D A L S     S L A M
A L O E   R O M E O     P O L O
A T O P   N O R A S     Y U A N
S O L I D I   I N O F F I C E
        R E C T O     R I S K Y
S E T A E   H A N S E L
A L E W I F E     P O M A C E
H E R E   L A W M A N   C O N
A V E S   O P T I C     O H M S
R E D   C R O S S E     L I E U
A N O M I A     E X E G E T E
      U G L I E R     T A R O S
P A S T A   B A S I C
E U M A R K E T     T H I R D S
A D I T   O R E O S   D O I T
C I T E   H I R A M   I P O D
H O E D   L A Y R E A D E R S
```

92

```
  B A C K S T R E E T S
A L T A   K O I   C R A M
R U N T   E O N   C I A O
C R O O N I N G   L O B S
H       O N S I T E     Q
A G L E T S   N A S S A U
E B O N Y       M I A M I
O S A G E S   B E A T I T
L     E T C H E S       O
O P E N   A U S T R I A N
G I L D   M R T   A S W E
Y A L E   P T O   C L O T
  F E R R I S W H E E L
```

93

```
O C T E T S     T U M I D
P I O N   P O M P A N O
A C I D   A R A L S E A
H A L L U C I N A T E
  D E E P E N   N O D S
H A D S T   O D D I T Y
Y       S I N C E   D O N
A C C   C O O E R     O
T R A C K S   M U S E D
T U B A   T H E B E S
  C O N T R A D I C T S
R I O T O U S   C O H O
G A S L A M P   O N E S
B L E E D   S A N D R A
```

SOLUTIONS

94

```
B R I D G E T J O N E S S D I A R Y
L O C O ■ ■ O O N ■ S O P ■ ■ J O E
A S I N ■ A N A T O L I A ■ C A S A
B I E N ■ D I N A R ■ ■ S C O R E R
S E R A P H ■ P A J A M A S ■ ■ L ■
■ ■ S O W N ■ C U D ■ P E R C Y ■
H I G H S C H O O L M U S I C A L ■
E L I O T ■ O N R E P E A T ■ V I M
S L R S ■ L A O S ■ ■ S A B I N E
S W A T H E ■ ■ T A C H ■ L O G S
E I S ■ A V E M A R I A ■ M O L T O
■ L O S T I N T R A N S L A T I O N
A L L O T ■ I N G ■ T E A L ■ ■ ■
D ■ L E A D S U P ■ ■ D I S A R M
O S C A R S ■ E A R L E ■ E L I A
B O H R ■ T E A S P O O N ■ P I C T
E I O ■ ■ R E T ■ A L C ■ I B E T
S L U M D O G M I L L I O N A I R E
```

95

```
S L A N T ■ A C C U R S T ■
T I T E R ■ ■ T O R ■ E P I ■
U L T R A ■ E R A ■ ■ F U L ■
C I N D Y C R A W F O R D ■ ■
C ■ ■ ■ ■ ■ P A L L O R ■ E
O U T D R A W ■ S U M O S ■
■ L O R E S ■ W I N E D ■ ■
C A P E D ■ M A N D R E L ■
O ■ H A W S E R ■ ■ ■ ■ O
N A O M I C A M P B E L L ■
F U N ■ N A T ■ R O Y A L ■
I T O ■ G N U ■ O B E S E ■
T H R U S T S ■ P O R E D ■
```

96

```
A P I C E S ■ O B R I E N
Y U M A ■ A M B ■ E N D O
U M P S ■ L I L ■ S T E T
R A S H D E C I S I O N S
V ■ ■ ■ I M A G O S ■ ■
■ E D I T S ■ S E A T I N G
D E T E R S ■ S N O R E R
A L V E O L I ■ D R A C O
■ ■ T B O N E S ■ ■ T
S T R E E T P R O P H E T
P O U R ■ T U N ■ R E P O
A P S E ■ E T S ■ A L E E
N E E D E D ■ T H Y M E S
```

100

```
A D D R E S S B O O K ■ ■
C R E E ■ E ■ T O N E
I S A A C ■ I T C H E S
D ■ ■ P A T S Y ■ S E P
I P S ■ L A M P S ■ ■ I
C A N U C K ■ E L S I E
■ R O G U E ■ W O U N D
A T O L L ■ W R E N S ■
L Y D I A ■ E I S N E R
L ■ S T I L T ■ I T E
I B M ■ O D D E R ■ ■ N
E L Y T R A ■ R I L E D
S O N Y ■ H ■ G I V E
■ C A R B O N P A P E R
```

97

```
■ F O P ■
A L A R M
T U T O R
V I E W S
■ D S L ■
```

98

```
W ■ S R I
I C K Y ■
G R I E F
■ A P S O
O W S ■ O
```

99

```
T E K ■ N
■ L E V Y
O S M I C
N A P A ■
T ■ T L C
```

101

M	M	S		F	L	I	P	P	E	R		C	S	T
V	O	C	A	L	I	C		O	X	A	L	A	T	E
P	R	O	D	U	C	E		U	T	T	E	R	E	D
S	E	T	A		I	C	O	N	S		V	E	N	D
		P	E	T	A	R	D		D	I	T	S	Y	
S	A	L	T	S		P	I	E	C	E	S			
U	B	I	E	T	Y		G	R	A	B		F	P	S
R	O	E	D	E	E	R		S	T	U	D	I	E	S
F	W	D		F	L	E	W		E	N	R	A	P	T
		L	A	P	D	O	G		K	I	T	E	S	
H	O	P	I	N		B	R	U	I	S	E			
A	X	E	S		B	E	N	I	N		D	A	N	G
M	E	A	L	I	E	R		T	U	B	U	L	A	R
M	Y	C	E	N	A	E		A	R	A	P	A	H	O
Y	E	E		F	U	T	U	R	E	S		W	S	W

Mystery Words: THERE IS NO SIN EXCEPT STUPIDITY

102

H	U	G	O		W	E	D		A	V	G	S
A	S	A	N		A	Y	E		B	O	R	A
D	E	M	I		S	E	C		A	C	E	D
A		E	T	O	N	C	O	L	L	E	G	E
D				S	T	U	D	I	O			
A	D	A	P	T		P	E	N	N	A	M	E
T	U	M	U	L	T		R	E	E	L	I	N
E	N	T	R	E	E	S		A	S	T	O	N
			P	R	A	T	E	R				O
A	L	T	O	S	T	R	A	T	U	S		B
L	E	A	S		R	I	G		C	T	R	L
F	A	C	E		A	V	E		L	A	C	E
A	R	K	S		Y	E	R		A	G	T	S

103

G	M	T		T	E	E	N	M	A	G	S
L	I	O	N	E	S	S		A	C	N	E
A	T	W	O	R	S	T		S	H	U	N
D		S	C	R	E	E	N	T	E	S	T
S		A	E	N	E	A	S				
T	O	W	N		C	M	S		J	A	B
O	N	E	D	G	E		A	G	I	L	E
N	Y	L	O	N		O	L	I	V	E	S
E	X	T		A	F	C		N	E	X	T
		T	W	E	A	K	S				I
T	A	P	E	S	T	R	I	E	S		R
A	S	O	N		T	I	N	N	I	E	R
L	A	S	S		E	N	D	G	A	M	E
E	P	H	E	D	R	A	S		M	I	D

104

A	M	E	R	I	C	A	N	D	O	G	W	O	O	D
P	A	L	E	O		E	O	S			N	S	A	
O	M	I	T	S		K	A	L	E		P	E	A	T
P	A	S	O		N	O	T	E		A	L	I	K	E
		O	H	I	O		U	V	U	L	A	S		
A	P	P	L	E	B	L	O	S	S	O	M			
D	O	E	S	T		U	T	E	N	S	I	L	S	
A	C	E		P	O	T	U	S		M	E	I		
M	O	N	O	C	L	E	D		A	B	N	E	R	
	C	H	E	R	O	K	E	E	R	O	S	E		
C	A	N	T	A	B		A	G	R	A				
O	R	E	A	D		B	E	R	G		C	C	C	P
L	E	W	D		B	E	L	A		C	E	L	L	O
I	C	E		A	A	A		O	R	I	O	N		
C	A	L	I	F	O	R	N	I	A	P	O	P	P	Y

Mystery Words: MOUNTAIN LAUREL
SCARLET CARNATION

236

105

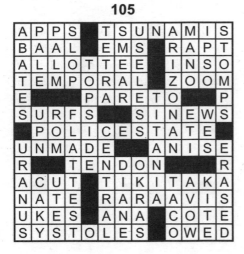

```
A P P S _ T S U N A M I S
B A A L _ E M S _ R A P T
A L L O T T E E _ I N S O
T E M P O R A L _ Z O O M
E _ _ P A R E T O _ _ P
S U R F S _ S I N E W S
_ P O L I C E S T A T E _
U N M A D E _ A N I S E
R _ T E N D O N _ _ R
A C U T _ T I K I T A K A
N A T E _ R A R A A V I S
U K E S _ A N A _ C O T E
S Y S T O L E S _ O W E D
```

106

```
P A G A N _ C H R O M A
O R E G A N O _ E W A N
T A T U M _ A P P E N D
P L A Y A _ T E E N S Y
O _ _ S P I E L _ _
U P L A T E _ P L E B E
R A I S E R S _ A X O N
R I O T _ K E R N I N G
I N N E R _ G U T T E R
_ _ R A D O N _ _ O
S P L I C E _ O V E N S
A L A S K A _ V I R U S
W O N K _ L E E T I D E
S P A S M S _ R A K E S
```

107

```
F O R B I D D E N F O R E S T
O B O E _ O I L E R _ A R E S
R E I N _ G O T T A _ V I C E
K Y L E _ E R O S _ T A C E T
_ _ S T A I N _ C I G A R S
P V C _ A R T _ D E M E S N E
R E A C T _ E L A T E _ _
I N R U S H _ I T E R A T E S
C O I L _ A R O A R _ S E A T
E M B L A Z O N _ A T E A S E
_ _ L A P S E _ O A K E N
H I S T O R Y _ R R R _ S L O
O N H A N D _ T R I E R _
O S A G E _ D E A N _ E M U S
R I M E _ C E R T S _ S I N E
A T A N _ E E R I E _ E S T E
H U N D R E D A C R E W O O D
```

108

```
H E R A L D I C _ V I C I
U V U L A E _ A P E M A N
B A N A N A _ S E E O F F
S P A R E R _ C O R N E L
_ E L M S _ C A P S _ E
P R O S _ F U R L _ L E X
H O N _ A U R A E _ O T E
A N G _ T E E S _ T V A D
N _ G O L D _ D R E G _
T I T A N S _ V O I L E S
A V O U C H _ E N T I R E
S E N S E I _ T O O F E W
M S G S _ P O O R N E S S
```

109

O	M	B	R	E	S		B	A	T	H	E
F	O	R	E			U	P	B	R	A	I	D
F	L	E	E		P	I	C	T	U	R	E
B	E	E	C	H	E	N		I	T	E	M
E			H	O	R	A	C	E			A
A	B	L	O	O	M		R	S	V	P	S
T	I	A		R	E	B	A	T	E	D	
	G	R	O	A	N	E	D		T	A	C
O	D	D	L	Y		G	L	A	S	S	Y
X			I	S	S	U	E	D			P
C	C	T	V		W	I	D	O	W	E	R
A	R	R	I	V	A	L		R	I	L	E
R	E	U	N	I	T	E		E	P	O	S
T	W	E	E	D		S	I	R	E	N	S

110

A	T	K	I	N	S	D	I	E	T		D	O	U	B	L	E	S
Z	A	P		O	T	O		N	U	K	E		N	A	U	R	U
A	B	M		U	N	D		C	R	I	B		I	R	A	N	I
L	U	G	E	R		G	O	I	N	T	O		T	R	U	S	T
E		R	I	S	E	U	P		T	N	T	S		E
A	T	R	E	S	T		T	H	R	E	E	S		T	H	I	S
	M	O	C	H	A		L	E	O	N		K	R	A	I	T
D	I	N	T		C	H	A	R	T		A	S	E	P	S	I	S
E			S	K	I	S		E	N	T		G	E	S	S	O
M	A	F	I	A		L	T	R		E	E	L	S			L
S	E	I	S	M	A	L		U	P	E	N	D		S	F	P	D
	O	R	I	E	L		A	S	A	D		O	F	A	G	E
A	N	E	T		T	I	S	H	R	I		P	U	L	S	A	R
L			L	I	N	K		A	N	N	A	L	S			E
N	A	F	T	A		S	M	O	G	G	Y		F	A	I	N	T
I	L	I	E	D		T	O	N	O		A	N	I		N	E	A
C	A	D	R	E		A	M	E	N		L	O	L		O	W	N
O	N	O	R	D	E	R		A	S	S	A	I	L	A	N	T	S

111

M	A	N	D	A	T	O	R		U	R	S	A
A	T	C		M	I	N	E		N	O	E	S
S	E	A	E	A	G	L	E		V	O	W	S
H	E	A	L	T	H	Y	D	I	E	T		E
			K	I	T		G	I	B	E	S
P	C	T	S		W	I	G	G	L	E	R	S
L	A	H		C	A	S	E	Y		E	T	E
A	V	O	G	A	D	R	O		B	R	E	D
C	A	R	A	T		R	H	O			
E		A	S	H	W	A	G	A	N	D	H	A
B	A	C	H		E	V	I	L	D	O	E	R
O	D	I	E		D	I	A	L		G	N	C
S	A	C	S		S	A	N	E	N	E	S	S

112

N	A	I	L	S	C	I	S	S	O	R	S
A	N	G	E	L		D	C	A	R	E	A
T	O	N	G	A		E	O	L	I	A	N
I	D	I	O	M		A	U	K	S		D
V	A	T		M	A	L	T		O	R	C
E	L	E	V	E	N	S		W	N	B	A
			E	R	Y		P	O	S	I	T
F	E	R	N	S		F	E	R			
I	M	E	T		H	O	T	D	O	G	S
S	B	A		C	U	B	E		P	A	P
S		S	W	A	M		R	H	O	N	E
U	P	S	I	D	E		P	U	R	G	E
R	O	A	M	E	R		A	N	T	E	D
E	G	Y	P	T	I	A	N	G	O	D	S

SOLUTIONS

113

```
  A S H Y
Y U K   A
A X I O M
W   E P S
S U D S
```

114

```
I N G A
M   R X S
A T A L L
M V P   I
  S H I P
```

115

```
      R R S
U B O A T
T A W N Y
A D A G E
H U N
```

116

```
O M N I B U S   U S D A
C O U N T R Y   P O U T
C O L D W A R   S U M O
I D L Y   N U M E R A L
P     Z I P I T     L
U M B R I A   S T E P S
T U R E E N   F I D E
  L I N G   B I N G E S
H E G E L   A R G Y L E
E   G E N I E       M
A P P A R E L   J U D I
D U A D   R O P E S I N
O L D E   D U O D E N A
F E S S   S T R I D E R
```

117

```
P R I N C E C H A R M I N G
L U C E   N O U N   A D I O S
A L I A   C A R T   M O N E T
C E N T   A X L E   B L A S E
A R G O T S   S N O       A
R     R E A R   A S H R A M
D E I C E   M E T A   T U G S
  C O O K I E M O N S T E R
H O U R   T R I G   E P S O M
A L S A C E   T O B E     E
S     E R R   A N I M A S
S T A T S   A G A L   M A T S
L I A R S   B O O R   A C T I
E T H A N   A S N O   G A I A
  O S C A R T H E G R O U C H
```

Mystery Words: EMMA STONE
SUSAN SARANDON

118

```
G R I N   T E D S   C U P
H O N E   E T I O L A T E
O A F S   C O N T E S T S
S C O T C H   G O A T E E
T H R E A D S     D I R T
    G R E W U P   L E A
S T A G E M A N A G E R S
C A M   S O R T I E
O V U M   M I N S T E R
R E L I S H   M E T A X A
P R E M I E R E   A B I T
I N T E G R A L   L O S E
O S S   N A V Y   T O T S
```

119

```
R U M B A E D   C H A P
U S E A B L E   H O B O
S U N R O O F   R Y A N
    T E M P I   Y A R D
S T A   B E E T S
C O L A   D R E A D E D
A W A I T   S A L I V A
B I G M A C   M I S E R
S T E L L A R   S P R Y
    E L V E S   O Y L
S U B S   O V A L S
A S U S   R E T E A C H
G A L L   T R I F L E S
A F L Y   S T E T S O N
```

SOLUTIONS

120

A	S	S	U	A	G	E		R	E	G	A	T	T	A
T	O	U	R		L	U	T	E		A	R	G	O	N
L	U	L	L		A	R	U	N		S	T	I	N	T
A	S	K	S	I	N		A	T	P		I	F	S	O
N	A	Y		S	C	O	R	S	E	S	E			N
T		C	R	E	P	E		A	I	R	D	R	Y	
A	L	C	O	A		A	G	E	R	S		I	U	M
	O	R	W	E	L	L		A	S	S	I	S	T	
I	D	A		L	I	S	T	S		Y	A	C	H	T
M	E	G	R	I	M		R	E	S	I	N			R
P		E	S	P	O	U	S	E	S		S	C	I	
A	M	O	S		S	U	M		T	H	E	T	A	S
R	O	W	E	R		Z	A	P	S		F	O	N	T
T	U	N	N	Y		O	N	T	O		T	A	D	A
S	E	S	T	E	T	S		A	N	I	S	T	O	N

Mystery Words: WHEN WORDS FAIL MUSIC SPEAKS

121

D	U	N	E		C	U	B	A	T	U	R	E
A	L	U	M		A	P	E	D		T	U	G
K	A	T	E		P	I	A	M	A	T	E	R
O	N	S	E	T	S		T	I	M	E		E
I		R	A	U	L		T	E	R	M	S
T	D	S		F	L	I	T		B	I	O	S
	C	O	N	T	A	M	I	N	A	N	T	
H	U	L	A		R	O	M	A		G	S	M
E	P	I	C	S		S	I	P	S		A
L		C	H	U	M		D	E	A	L	I	N
P	R	I	O	R	A	T	E		Y	A	N	G
M	G	T		L	U	I	S		H	I	K	E
E	S	S	A	Y	I	S	T		I	D	Y	L

122

H	A	S	H	E	S		A	B	E	T	S
A	T	T	I	C	A		R	E	L	I	T
C	H	O	C	O	L	A	T	E	B	A	R
K	E	A		T	U	S	S	O	R	E
E	N	T	I	R	E	L	Y		W	A	T
D	A	S	T	A	R	D		B	E	E	T
		C	D	S		K	I	D	D	O
L	O	C	H	S		T	A	D
I	V	E	Y		V	I	N	E	G	A	R
P	E	D		C	A	T	E	N	A	T	E
B	R	I	T	I	S	H		M	O	C
A	L	L	O	T	T	E	D	T	I	M	E
L	I	L	L	E		R	E	I	N	I	N
M	E	A	D	S		S	E	L	E	C	T

123

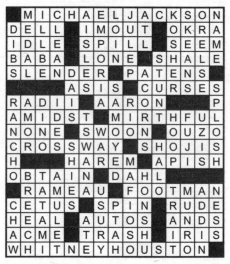

	M	I	C	H	A	E	L	J	A	C	K	S	O	N
D	E	L	L		I	M	O	U	T		O	K	R	A
I	D	L	E		S	P	I	L	L		S	E	E	M
B	A	B	A		L	O	N	E		S	H	A	L	E
S	L	E	N	D	E	R		P	A	T	E	N	S
			A	S	I	S		C	U	R	S	E	S
R	A	D	I	I		A	A	R	O	N			P
A	M	I	D	S	T		M	I	R	T	H	F	U	L
N	O	N	E		S	W	O	O	N		O	U	Z	O
C	R	O	S	S	W	A	Y		S	H	O	J	I	S
H			H	A	R	E	M		A	P	I	S	H
O	B	T	A	I	N		D	A	H	L
	R	A	M	E	A	U		F	O	O	T	M	A	N
C	E	T	U	S		S	P	I	N		R	U	D	E
H	E	A	L		A	U	T	O	S		A	N	D	S
A	C	M	E		T	R	A	S	H		I	R	I	S
W	H	I	T	N	E	Y	H	O	U	S	T	O	N	

240

SOLUTIONS

124

Y	E	L	L	O	W	J	A	C	K	E	T	S
A	C	E	Y		Y	O	G	A		N	O	U
L	A	D	E		O	Y	E	R		V	O	N
T	R	U	S	S		F	O	S	S	I	L	S
A	D	P		P	O	U	F		H	O	K	E
		C	A	R	L		F	R	U	I	T	
A	R	M	I	N	G		G	U	E	S	T	S
L	O	A	N	S		S	E	E	K			
L	O	R	D		G	I	R	L		C	D	T
S	T	A	Y	S	O	N		S	C	O	U	R
T	A	N		I	N	N	S		L	O	G	E
A	G	T		K	N	E	W		A	K	I	N
R	E	A	C	H	A	D	E	A	D	E	N	D

125

S	M	O	G	S		N	I	K	I	T	A
L	I	Z		C	H	A	N		N	A	L
O	R	O		H	E	C	K		D	M	V
W	O	N		M	A	R	I	P	O	S	A
		E	V	I	D	E	N	T			
A	P	H	I	D	S		D	O	R	S	A
S	H	O	O	T	U	P		M	E	L	T
K	I	L	L		P	I	C	A	D	O	R
S	L	E	E	T		G	A	I	E	T	Y
		N	E	W	L	I	N	E			
B	L	O	T	C	H	E	S		M	G	R
O	O	F		H	I	T	S		E	A	U
G	U	M		I	M	S	O		R	P	G
S	T	E	R	E	S		N	O	S	E	S

126

S	E	A	M		L	I	L	A		G	R	A	B	A	C	A	B
U	L	N	A		I	N	A	C	T	I	O	N		R	A	G	U
M	E	T	R	O	N	O	M	E		S	S	A		A	T	A	D
A	N	I	L		D	R	A	T		M	A	T	T	R	E	S	S
C	A	S	A	V	A		R	I	C	O		I	A	N	S		
		A	N	A	R	C	H		R	E	D	T	A	I	L		E
A	S	P	I	R	E	R		O	V	U	L	E					E
T	W	I	C	E		O	N	E	L	A	N	E		I	S	L	A
T	A	L	E	S		D	O	W	E	L		V	O	D	K	A	S
A	Z	O	R	E	S		B	A	R	O	N		D	E	A	T	H
B	I	T	S		H	I	L	L	A	R	Y		E	S	T	E	E
O			G	A	V	E	L		N	E	S	T	E	R	S		
Y	A	R	D	A	G	E		E	T	H	Y	L	S				
	M	O	O	N		E	T	U	I		M	A	M	B	A	S	
T	E	L	E	G	R	A	M		S	P	A	T		E	L	M	O
I	L	L	S		I	S	I		S	P	I	R	I	T	U	A	L
L	I	E	N		F	O	L	K	L	O	R	E		E	N	Z	O
T	A	R	T	U	F	F	E		E	S	S	E		S	T	E	N

127

	S	L	I	C	E	O	F	P	I	Z	Z	A
C	E	O	S		S	H	O	O		O	O	P
A	L	B	S		C	O	R	L	E	O	N	E
S	L	O	U	G	H		C	E	A	S	E	S
S			E	Y	E	T	E	S	T			
O	C	D		M	A	E			A	B	E	D
C	H	R	I	S	T	M	A	S	T	R	E	E
K	A	Y	O			P	C	T		A	R	P
		N	E	U	T	R	A	L				R
D	E	S	I	S	T		O	B	L	I	G	E
E	X	A	C	T	I	O	N		A	M	E	S
L	E	T		E	L	L	Y		N	A	N	S
I	C	E	C	R	E	A	M	C	O	N	E	

129

```
T I C
A F R O S
S I E G E
S T A R T
    M E H
```

130

```
K I S S
M O T H
S W O R E
  A W E D
  N E W S
```

131

```
  A B B Y
  Z U L U
D U R U M
A R M S
Y E A H
```

128

```
A C C E S S   E I T H E R
T A B   A C H Y   W O K E
O V E R D O   E L I T E S
Z E R O I N   C A N S
    B E E F U P   A D C
B L O B   E P I C U R E
L A T E C L A S S I C A L
A M O R O U S   D E W S
M P S   O N T I M E
    C A K E   M A R K U P
P R O U S T   A R S I N E
J A P E   T U M S   W I T
S H E L V E   S H R I V E
```

132

```
S H O T   M I S H A P S
T O P E K A   Q U I E T
A P E M E N   U D D E R
R E D P A N D A   S K A
C     T A I L S   I
H D T V S   M O U T O N
Y O R E   B E R L I N
  V I S T A S   F E U D
D E P T H S   T A R S I
O   S E R V E   S
O T B   R A I L I N G S
D O L C E   B E M I R E
A T O M S   E X O T I C
D O G D A Y S   K E P T
```

133

```
A M B E R   S W A G   C O M E
G O U G E   T O G A   A D A Y
A P R O N   R O O M   S I Z E
P E N N A M E S   B O T N E T
A   M A P   C O O S   E
E M O T E S   B A L M   T U E
  A H H   C E L L   P R I N T
G I B E D   L A V   H E A T H
O Z O N E   L I E S   F R I
L E Y   B I E R   V I S A E D
G   F I N N   D E B   R
O W L E T S   B O N I F A C E
T O U T   I H O P   S A M O A
H O S E   S A N E   E M E N D
A D H D   T H O R   S E X T S
```

134

```
D A C T Y L S   T U P A C
A W O K E   E R I T R E A
M A L T A   V E N E E R S
P R O   S W E P T   P A H
S E N A T O R S   G A T E
    L I K E   A R R O W
A M B L E S   B R I E R S
R A R E R   C O I F
C R A Y   H A R D T I M E
L I V   S T E E N   L A G
A N A D E M S   E W I N G
M E D U L L A   S W A G E
P R O O F   R E S I D E D
```

Mystery Words: LITTLE HOUSE ON THE PRAIRIE

SOLUTIONS

135

C	H	E	V	I	O	T	■	R	O	D	E
L	O	G	A	N	■	I	C	E	B	O	X
A	L	G	I	D	■	M	A	S	O	N	S
S	T	Y	L	I	■	B	A	I	L	E	E
P	■	■	■	C	O	R	N	S	■	■	C
E	M	I	R	A	T	E	■	T	O	R	T
D	O	Z	E	N	S	■	M	I	M	I	■
■	L	O	F	T	■	P	A	V	A	N	E
A	L	D	A	■	R	E	S	E	N	D	S
V	■	■	S	P	E	N	T	■	■	■	T
E	T	C	H	E	D	■	O	L	D	I	E
S	A	L	I	N	E	■	D	O	U	S	E
T	R	I	O	D	E	■	O	C	C	A	M
A	N	O	N	■	M	O	N	K	E	Y	S

136

S	O	A	K	■	M	U	M	P	S	■	H	A	K	A
H	A	Z	Y	■	A	N	G	L	E	■	O	V	I	D
A	S	T	O	■	N	A	M	E	R	■	W	I	L	E
D	I	E	T	E	D	■	T	A	G	S	■	A	O	N
E	S	C	O	L	A	R	■	T	E	N	O	N	■	■
■	■	■	A	R	A	B	■	S	U	B	I	T	O	
H	A	L	F	L	I	V	E	S	■	B	E	Z	E	L
A	C	A	I	■	N	E	G	E	V	■	L	E	N	D
G	R	U	F	F	■	N	A	T	I	V	I	S	T	S
S	E	N	T	I	N	■	T	O	R	I	■	■	■	
■	C	H	E	A	P	■	N	A	N	N	I	E	S	
B	A	H	■	F	I	R	S	■	G	E	O	R	G	E
U	T	I	L	■	L	O	T	T	O	■	M	A	G	E
M	O	N	O	■	E	V	O	K	E	■	A	T	O	M
P	E	G	S	■	R	E	P	O	S	■	D	E	N	S

Mystery Words: BEING NORMAL IS VASTLY OVERRATED

137

F	A	T	S	■	U	P	S	T	A	I	R	S
L	U	R	E	■	P	O	K	Y	■	R	O	T
A	R	O	W	■	F	L	I	P	■	I	W	O
C	O	I	N	C	O	L	L	E	C	T	O	R
O	R	K	■	O	R	E	L	■	O	I	N	K
N	A	A	C	P	■	N	E	G	U	S	E	S
■	■	R	E	B	■	D	O	G	■	■	■	
A	D	D	E	D	U	P	■	W	H	E	R	E
L	E	I	A	■	F	A	W	N	■	K	A	L
L	A	C	K	O	F	R	E	S	P	E	C	T
I	R	T	■	W	O	O	L	■	Y	O	K	O
E	M	U	■	L	O	L	L	■	R	U	E	R
D	E	M	E	S	N	E	S	■	O	T	T	O

138

A	L	A	C	A	R	T	E	M	E	N	U
L	O	T	U	S	■	B	R	E	T	O	N
L	O	O	T	S	■	A	N	G	E	R	S
U	S	D	■	U	P	R	E	A	R	■	A
R	E	D	C	R	O	S	S	■	N	E	V
E	N	S	U	E	D	■	T	H	A	N	E
■	■	B	R	I	O	■	B	L	V	D	
P	A	R	A	■	A	T	W	O	■	■	
O	M	E	N	S	■	H	A	M	P	E	R
S	O	C	■	O	V	E	R	B	I	T	E
T	■	I	D	C	A	R	D	■	P	U	B
D	E	T	A	I	L	■	E	V	A	D	E
O	P	E	R	A	S	■	N	I	G	E	L
C	A	R	E	L	E	S	S	N	E	S	S

139

	A	R	C	H	A	E	O	L	O	G	I	S	T	
S	A	I	L		T	A	P	I	R		C	O	A	L
N	A	D	A		B	R	I	N	Y		E	L	B	A
A	S	S	N		A	N	N	E	X		U	F	O	S
R			G	E	Y	S	E	R		O	P	A	R	T
F	I	D	E	L			S	S	N	S				
	M	A	D	E	D	O			E	X	I	L	E	D
O	P	T		N	O	M	A	D	S		M	A	X	I
F	A	S	H	I	O	N	D	E	S	I	G	N	E	R
F	L	U	E		D	I	V	E	I	N		D	D	E
S	A	N	D	A	L		R	E	U	T	E	R		
			B	E	B	E				S	O	D	A	S
T	I	B	I	A		O	R	A	T	E	D			H
O	L	E	G		T	O	R	S	O		E	C	H	O
M	I	L	L		O	B	I	T	S		A	L	E	C
B	A	C	O		T	O	N	I	C		T	U	R	K
	C	H	O	R	E	O	G	R	A	P	H	E	R	

140

F	O	M	E	N	T	E	D		F	L	A	G
U	V	A		O	R	M	E		L	I	S	A
N	E	D		F	O	P	S		I	N	I	T
T	R	O	J	A	N		P	S	E	U	D	O
O	R	N	O	T		C	O	A	R	S	E	R
D	U	N	G		C	H	I	P				
O	N	A	S	M	A	L	L	S	C	A	L	E
			B	R	O	S			A	V	I	V
M	C	S	H	A	N	E		C	R	I	M	E
A	R	I	O	S	E		B	A	D	G	E	R
G	A	D	S		G	O	O	N		N	A	E
M	I	L	T		I	T	T	O		O	D	S
A	G	E	S		E	T	H	E	R	N	E	T

141

S	H	I	A		A	S	S	I	S	T	S
C	O	M	B		U	N	O		T	W	O
A	W	A	Y	F	R	O	M		A	I	M
P	L	Y		R	O	O	M	E	T	T	E
E			M	A	R	T	E	N			O
S	C	H	E	M	A	S		C	A	P	N
	H	O	T	E	L		R	O	X	I	E
B	O	O	R	S		C	E	D	E	S	
R	O	T	O		H	U	M	E	R	A	L
O			I	S	O	P	O	D			I
C	R	E	D	I	T	O	R		B	Y	S
A	U	G		G	A	L	A	X	I	E	S
D	I	A		M	I	A		L	E	T	O
E	N	D	E	A	R	S		S	L	I	M

142

D	I	S	S	E	D		M	U	D	S		P	A	S	T	A	S
A	N	N	U	L	I		E	P	I	C		A	T	T	I	R	E
S	H	A	N	I	A		A	L	L	I		S	T	O	P	I	N
H	A	R	D	E	N		L	O	L	A		H	A	R	P	O	N
E	L	L	A		A	S	T	A		T	S	A		M	E	S	A
R	E	S	E	E		T	I	D	B	I	T		M	S	D	O	S
			A	J	A	M		A	C	U	T	E					
P	E	M	B	R	O	K	E		L	A	B	O	R	C	A	M	P
I	T	O	O		G	E	S	T	S		U	V	U	L	A	R	
S	T	A	L	A	G		Y	A	T	E	S		F	A	D	E	
H	A	N	D	C	L	A	S	P		U	G	L	I	F	I	E	S
			R	E	N	E	E		R	E	E	F					
C	A	C	A	O		N	A	B	O	B	S		I	R	V	I	N
H	E	L	L		Y	O	W		J	U	T	S		H	A	R	E
O	R	I	O	L	E		A	R	I	L		T	H	E	L	A	W
S	A	C	H	E	M		R	O	B	E		R	E	S	I	D	E
E	T	H	A	N	E		D	O	W	N		A	M	U	S	E	S
N	E	E	S	O	N		S	K	A	T		W	I	S	E	S	T

SOLUTIONS

143

B	L	A	C	K	H	O	L	E		M	A	G
B	A	R	R	I	O			C	H	I	N	O
L	Y	R	I	S	T	S		L	E	N	D	L
	L	A	N		S	A	L	A	R	I	E	D
B	A	S	K	S		G	A	T		S	A	E
R		L	I	N	E	R		D	U	N	N	
O		P	E	S	O		D	R	I	B		E
W	H	O	D		V	I	S	T	A			R
N	E	S		R	A	D		S	T	O	M	A
B	A	E	D	E	K	E	R		O	H	I	
E	R	U	P	T		M	I	S	M	A	T	E
A	T	R	I	A			F	A	I	R	E	D
R	H	S		G	R	E	E	N	C	A	R	D

144

A	R	C	T	I	C	C	I	R	C	L	E
T	O	R	O	N	T	O		I	L	E	X
M	O	O	R	I	N	G		V	I	D	A
S	T	U	N	T	S		T	U	N	I	C
	C	P	U	S		S	I	L	E	N	T
D	R	I	P		P	A	G	E			
T	O	E		K	I	T	E	T	A	I	L
S	P	R	I	N	T	E	R		B	M	I
			M	O	A	S		V	E	I	N
A	D	A	P	T	S		H	I	R	T	
L	I	V	E	S		C	O	N	R	A	D
I	P	A	D		T	H	R	O	A	T	Y
V	I	S	E		W	A	D		T	O	A
E	N	T	R	E	P	R	E	N	E	R	D

145

G	A	S	S	T	A	T	I	O	N		D	E	P	T
O	U	T	P	O	U	R		L	O	B	B	Y	E	R
A	B	A	L	O	N	E		D	R	O	S	E	R	A
D	A	L	I		T	E	R	E	S	A				V
E	D	I	T	H		E	N	E	R	V	A	T	E	
D	E	N		O	R	F	F		D	O	Z	E	S	
			O	P	U	L	E	N	T		C	U	R	T
T	E	R	R	I	T	O	R	I	A	L	A	R	M	Y
I	T	O	R		S	E	A	C	R	A	B			
A	N	D	I	E		B	E	S	T		P	G	A	
M	A	S	S	M	A	I	L			S	C	A	R	S
A			B	E	D	E	W	S		I	G	O	T	
R	O	O	K	E	R	Y		A	P	P	R	O	V	E
I	M	P	E	R	I	L		G	U	A	R	D	E	R
A	G	E	R		E	S	S	E	N	T	I	A	L	S

Mystery Words: TATE MODERN
                MADAME TUSSAUDS

146

A	P	H	R	O	D	I	S	I	A	C	
	L	A	I		R	U	N	D	L	E	
S	A	I	D		T	E	E	T	H	E	
E	N	R	O	B	E	S		R	O	A	M
R		F	I	R		S	A	C	R	A	
O	J	S		G	R	O	A	N			G
T	A	H	I	T	I		L	E	N	I	N
O	N	O	N	E		S	U	T	U	R	E
N		H	A	B	I	T		I	S	S	
I	S	L	A	M		T	E	A			I
N	A	I	L		B	I	R	D	F	L	U
	S	N	A	P	O	N		D	O	O	M
P	H	E	N	O	L		E	R	A		
	A	N	T	I	O	X	I	D	A	N	T

SOLUTIONS

147

```
M T G   G L A D D E N E D
O R I   R O B E D   E X E
D I F F I C U L T   P A W
U P T O D A T E   M A L E
L O B E     G U I L T Y
E L O   T R I A G E
S I X T E E N T H N O T E
    H E A V E S   R E X
I M B E D S     M G R S
N A R Y   S U B L E A S E
A R I   G U N R U N N E R
L I E   U M I A K   I S T
L A F A Y E T T E   C T S
```

148

```
C A M I L L E P I S S A R R O
A B E   A E I   N C O   O O M
P O L   M I N I V A N   P S I
E V O K E S   M A N I F E S T
R E N O   S P I T A L
    O B R I E N     A M B I
B A N K R O L L   A B B E Y S
O B E   E X O   B L U   A T M
S C R E W Y   Q U I N I N E S
E D D A   S U R E S T
    C O T T A R   C D E F
C O C H L E A S   A S H I N E
I A L   S P R I N G Y   S N D
T H O   E E E   F U N   C U E
E U G E N E D E L A C R O I X
```

Mystery Words: LIBERTY LEADING THE PEOPLE

149

```
U N M I T I G A T E D   H P S
N O O N   N U B S   A P E R Y
D A D A   F A R E   M A L E S
R H E N I U M   T R E N D S
A   E N S   A S A   D I E M
P F C   D E S C E N D A N T S
E R I N   P A S T A     R
D E R E L I C T   E V E N U P
  S C O O B A   B R I T O N
C H A N G E   H I S T O R I C
F   I R K E D   N A T O
O F F I C I A L E S E   H E H
S L U M   A R M   T N T   A
  O N E I N A   P E D I C A B
A U R A L   C R O W   T U P I
S T U N S   H A L E   H E A T
U S N   A N I M A D V E R T S
```

150

```
A T L A S T   E U R O S
C O O P   R E S P I R E
C R O P   I M P O S T S
T O N E A R M   N E S T
      T R E Y S     E
A F F I R M   P U R E R
B O O T E E   E N I A C
R I C E S   S A R T R E
A L I S T   P R E E N S
D   S T E E L
A H I T   U N R A V E L
N A T I O N S   T I V O
T R O C H E E   E V E S
S I N K S   R A D A R S
```

SOLUTIONS

151

```
C A S H G R A B ■ P O R T
A C T ■ R O B O ■ O P A H
M E A L I E S T ■ B I T E
S T R A P S ■ T B O N E S
■ A D U E ■ C O A X E R S
A T O R ■ I A M B ■ ■ ■ A
R E M A I N N E U T R A L
B ■ ■ S K I D ■ R E L Y
A G O N I S T ■ S A N D
L A X E S T ■ S P I T E D
E L L E ■ O N E O N O N E
S L I D ■ N O G O ■ U T A
T O P S ■ E M A N A T E D
```

152

```
F R A N C E S M C D O R M A N D ■ O
L E V I ■ T O H I D E ■ L A Y O N
A P I N G ■ A P I C E S ■ I T S M E
N O D O U B T ■ M I S T ■ N I L E S
■ T E E P E E ■ B E V E L
M O R O S E ■ E R R A T A ■ E X E S
A X E L ■ B M W ■ T H Y ■ S I T H
T E A L S ■ A E R A T I O N ■ C S I
I N L A W ■ R E E L ■ C U E S ■ N
N ■ S O C K ■ D I S K ■ R A P I D
E A T ■ T A K E S T W O ■ O M A N I
E L I A ■ M A H ■ A S T ■ B A S E
S A M S ■ P A S S B Y ■ H E A R T S
■ M E S S Y ■ C U S S E D
P O L Y P ■ A G A R ■ T E A S E L S
A D O R E ■ B O M D I A ■ M A C A W
C E C I L ■ R E P E L S ■ A R I A
K ■ K A T H A R I N E H E P B U R N
```

153

```
B A C K P A C K I N G ■ N A B
■ V E N A L ■ W O E F U L
S E N O R A ■ G I M M I C K S
A N O X I C ■ U N S ■ F L A T
C S T ■ T K O S ■ G R E E N E
H E A D Y ■ P T S ■ O S I E R
E S P N ■ R E S H O T ■ E
R ■ H A V E N ■ I N C U R ■ O
T ■ E T E R N E ■ F E L T
O R C A S ■ R A E ■ M O S E Y
R E A C T S ■ I R M A ■ T C P
T A M E ■ O M N ■ E S T A T E
E P E R G N E S ■ T H E R E S
■ E B B I N G ■ E U L E R
P R Y ■ O Y S T E R P L A N T
```

Mystery Words: ONCE UPON A TIME IN AMERICA

154

```
■ I N T E R R O B A N G
O C E A N I A ■ E M I L
T H A L A M I ■ T I K I
T ■ R E C ■ D A R N E D
O P E N T O ■ M O O S E
M O A T ■ P L O T
A L S ■ S T A N H O P E
N O T C H I N G ■ N O S
■ O R C A ■ T E S T
S T A R E ■ I C E T E A
H A I R D O ■ A T O ■ T
E N D O ■ A M B R O S E
E K E D ■ S P L I N T S
P A R E N T H E S E S
```

SOLUTIONS

155

D	A	D	S		L	O	T	S		G	W	B
O	N	U	P		O	P	U	S		L	I	U
U	G	L	Y		R	E	N	E	W	A	L	S
B	O	S	O	M	I	N	G		H	I	L	T
T	R	E	N	T		U	S	N	A	V	Y	
F	A	S		E	M	P	T	I	N	E	S	S
U			G	T	O		E	C	G			H
L	E	V	A	N	T	I	N	E		T	R	E
	N	O	G	A	I	N		T	R	U	E	D
G	O	R	E		V	A	M	O	O	S	E	D
O	U	T	S	T	A	R	E		A	H	M	E
A	G	E		A	T	O	N		M	E	I	R
T	H	X		P	E	W	S		S	S	T	S

156

F	R	O	M		S	E	R	I	F		I	N	S	P
E	U	R	O		E	N	E	R	O		N	E	I	L
A	T	T	N		A	S	P	E	R		D	E	L	E
T		O	C	C	U	R		E	R	O	D	E	D	
	A	R	C	H	A	E	O	P	T	E	R	Y	X	
O	M	E	L	E	T		E	O	N	S				O
H	I	R	E	E		C	A	R	P		E	A	R	P
A	G	A		K	N	A	V	I	S	H		D	O	E
R	O	N	S		O	P	A	L		A	P	I	A	N
E		T	B	A	R		E	M	E	E	R	S		
	B	R	A	C	H	I	O	S	A	U	R	U	S	
G	O	U	R	D	S		L	I	S	P	S			C
I	S	N	T		A	F	I	R	E		O	L	G	A
G	O	A	L		R	E	V	E	L		N	E	A	R
A	N	T	E		K	E	E	N	S		A	I	D	E

Mystery Words: GALLIMIMUS
                VELOCIRAPTOR

157

S	A	M	U	R	A	I		P	R	O	B	A	L	L
O	B	I		E	M	T		H	E	X		D	Y	E
S	E	N		G	A	S	C	O	N	Y		M	R	T
A	L	T	A	I		O	H	N	O		L	A	I	C
		M	O	N	K	E	Y	W	R	E	N	C	H	
D	O	M	I	N	O		R		N	O	N			
I	P	O	D		S	I	T	S		G	A	S	P	S
M	E	R	E		A	N	Y	O	N	E		P	O	T
P	R	E	S	O	L	D		R	U	R	A	L	L	Y
L	O	N		R	E	U	S	E	D		M	E	A	L
E	N	O	L	A		S	A	R	I		B	E	N	E
			I	N	S		T		S	P	E	N	D	S
S	L	E	D	G	E	H	A	M	M	E	R			
H	I	P	S		D	A	N	A		A	S	K	I	N
I	B	E		B	A	N	G	K	O	K		I	G	O
L	Y	E		I	T	D		E	O	E		L	E	D
L	A	S	S	O	E	S		R	O	D	E	N	T	S

158

F	L	E	D		A	D	J	O	I	N	T
P	E	N	A	L	L	Y		P	R	O	W
S	A	C	L	I	K	E		T	I	N	A
	V	A	L	P	A	R	A	I	S	O	
D	E	G	A	S		L	O	E	S	S	
W	O	E	S		O	W	E	N	S		K
A	N	D		S	O	A	P	S			I
R		D	E	P	T	H		S	L	R	
F		G	U	E	S	T		T	A	I	L
S	M	I	R	K		T	O	W	N	S	
	E	V	I	S	C	E	R	A	T	E	
P	L	E	A		A	W	E	S	O	M	E
K	E	R	N		T	E	S	T	I	E	R
G	E	S	S	O	E	S		S	T	N	S

SOLUTIONS

159

```
A I L S   A H A S   P C S
C O O T   L O G O G R A M
D W A R F F O R T R E S S
C A M E L   P E S A C H
      T A H O E   F E M A
T E A T I M E   T   D E P
I N F I R M   C I C E R O
N S F   S   C H A R R E D
G U R U   P R I M A
  R O N N I E   A S T R A
H I N D U P A N T H E O N
I N T O N A T E   E R S T
P G S   S L E W   R A Y S
```

160

```
M I T O C H O N D R I O N   I B I D
I T E   R U F F   A T N O   N O N O
N S A   E M T S   T I E S   H U T U
C O R O N A E   S E N S E   A T O B
E   F E N N E C   H E E L   L
R A F F L E   R U S S O   G I M M E
  S E E S   M I L L E T   G N A S H
C E R N   S T E L A E   E N G A G E
H A N D S O N   P R O M O   L
R   M U S E D   S I G N O R I
O R C H I L   R E S E A T   I M A X
M O D A L   S T E A D Y   D E S K
O N C U E   L E D G E   M U C K E R
S   N Y S E   E N C A G E   A
O B I T   C E L L S   O L D S A L T
M A C E   O K A Y   A L A E   G O T
E W E R   T E R N   B O W E   R C A
S L R S   T R A N S C R I P T I O N
```

161

```
G A U C H O S   B E L D A M E
A L P H A   T H E A   O N Y X
G O T A T   A I N T   G E N T
S T O I C   I S N O   T W A S
    S H A R P E N E R
T U B E   U R I S   R O M P S
A P R   P R O D   A R T E R Y
G O A H E A D   F R E S H E N
U N Y O K E   C O E D   T E C
P E S T O   B O R N   B A N S
    D E C I M E T E R
O G L E   H A M S   L I M B S
D A Y S   I S I T   A G O R A
D I R K   M E T E   T H R E W
S T A S H E D   D I E T E R S
```

Mystery Words: RAYA AND THE LAST DRAGON

162

```
D O G S L E D D I N G
I L I E   E   D E U S
P E L T S   A H O R S E
L   I N T R O   F H A
O N S   O A S T S   M
M O T O W N   S P L A Y
A R E N A S   P E A L
  T E E N   C R A V E D
S H R U G   H I K A R U
C   P E C A N   S T N
A M C   L U I G I   G
D A L A S I   S W A M I
S T E P   N   O L I N
  T O B O G G A N I N G
```

SOLUTIONS

163

S	H	I	N		E	S	S	A	Y	E	R	S
C	O	N	E		N	I	T	S		L	O	L
A	L	D	O		T	R	O	T		I	M	A
R	E	I	N	T	E	R	P	R	E	T		B
E	Y	E	S	O	R	E	S		L	I	M	B
			U	A	E		E	L	S	I	E	
S	H	T	E	T	L		C	A	S	T	O	R
M	A	Y	A	S		B	O	G				
A	L	P	S		B	O	W	L	D	E	R	S
S		H	Y	P	O	T	H	E	R	M	I	A
H	O	O		D	O	R	A		D	A	N	G
U	S	O		A	T	E	N		R	I	G	A
P	U	N	I	S	H	E	D		E	L	O	N

164

	C	A	F	F	E	A	M	E	R	I	C	A	N	O
D	A	L	E		F	L	A	Y		A	L	A	N	
R	I	P	E		S	T	Y	E	S		S	O	F	T
I	N	O	I	L		O	O	R	T		T	E	T	
P		N	O	G	S		A	I	R	S	A	C		
P	O	P	G	U	N		S	T	R	I	A		A	
E	V	E		D	A	C	H	A		S	T	A	M	P
D	E	E	S		T	H	E	R	M		I	S	U	P
E	R	R	O	R		I	D	E	A	S		P	S	U
Y		L	O	I	N	S		I	N	A	S	E	C	
E	C	H	O	E	S		I	D	I	G		C		
	L	A	S		A	C	E	S		P	A	R	S	I
B	A	S	H		N	O	R	A	D		T	O	O	N
E	R	N	O		C	I	A	O		H	O	H	O	
L	A	T	T	E	M	A	C	C	H	I	A	T	O	

Mystery Words: SPANISH STEPS
TREVI FOUNTAIN

165

M	A	S	S	E		M	P	E	G		A	V	G	S
I	S	L	E	T		C	O	C	O		B	A	M	A
S	W	A	T	H		S	I	L	L		B	L	A	B
D	E	M	A	N	D		G	A	D	A	R	E	N	E
E			I	R	A	N	I	A	N					R
A	V	A	S	C	U	L	A	R		G	U	E	S	S
L	I	L	O		D	O	N	S		I	N	T	R	A
S	A	U	L		G	U	T		A	N	D	H	O	W
	M	O	P	E	D		F	L	A	R	E			
G	E	N	I	U	S		M	A	T		A	R	U	M
R	O	U	S	T		L	A	C	E		W	I	K	I
A	S	S	T	S		E	N	T	R	A	N	C	E	S
N			C	R	U	I	S	E	R					L
D	A	B	C	H	I	C	K		D	I	C	K	I	E
P	R	E	P		C	O	I	N		G	H	A	N	A
A	G	R	A		I	M	N	O		H	E	R	O	D
S	O	N	S		N	A	S	H		T	R	A	N	S

166

C	L	A	P	P	E	R	B	O	A	R	D
R	U	B	E		S	H	Y		W	O	O
I	N	C	R		S	E	A		R	A	S
B	A	S	I	N	E	T		P	Y	R	E
			S	A	X	O	N	S			
S	H	A	H	S		R	E	A	L	M	S
T	I	P		T	H	I	R	T	E	E	N
E	Y	E	P	I	E	C	E		T	M	I
W	A	X	I	E	R		I	N	S	E	T
			G	R	A	N	D	E			
F	A	D	S		L	U	S	T	R	U	M
O	U	R		A	D	D		T	A	R	O
O	T	E		E	E	G		L	I	N	T
T	O	W	E	R	D	E	F	E	N	S	E

SOLUTIONS

167

```
J E T B L A C K   S C A R
I Z E   A M O N   O H I O
F R A   M I N I   M O S T
F A L L I N G S T A R   E
      G N U   H O L D I N
S E N S A T E   P I A N O
A P E   E S C     T E N
M E C C A   L A B M A Z E
P E K A N S   N Y E
H   W I S H I N G W E L L
I T E R   A B O O   D O O
R O A N   P E N N   I R A
E R R S   E X S E R T E D
```

168

```
  I N T E R S T E L L A R D U S T
A M Y   L O W E   E I D E R   O H M
D O A   O W A R   A L I B I   F I E
A F L   I S B N   R I N S E   A N T
  F A Q S   S S N     S A R G E
C   B A S K   A S S O R T S     O
R A H S   P A R R   T B A   K N A R
E T E   M A N E T   R O Y   M O B S
S T A M E N   N O F E E   J O N A H
C I V I L   D E R A T   T O M A T O
E L E M   H E W   S C R A G   M O W
N A N O   M C A   C H I C   G E R E
T   S T O O L I E   S H O E     R
M A S A I     N S C   D E S C
O C T   C R A G S   A S A D   E O N
O R R   T O L E T   I T B E   T N N
N E O   A L O N E   R I B S   T A W
  S P A C E E X P L O R A T I O N
```

169

```
A D S   S T A N D S   P I E D
G E T   M I D W A Y   O R Z O
E M U L A T I O N S   T W I G
D O N A T E D   E T C H I N G
      S T R A P   H O N E Y
S P R E E   S E P T A L
P I E R R E   R O U T E M A N
A N G   S I D E S     A S I
M A S E R A T I   K I D N A P
      F A U V E S   L I E N S
S P I F F   M A P L E
L U N A T I C   M A N G E R S
O P E C   N A P O L E O N I C
T A P E   S T A S E S   I T A
S E T S   O S C A R S   D A D
```

Mystery Words: THE SECRET LIFE OF PETS

170

```
  F R O S T E D T I P S
  R A N I   N E I G H
D E N I M   T A N N I C
R E D O   A R F S     R
E     N O V A     O T O
A R G   C A P S C R E W
D E I S T S   H A G E N
L E V E E   B E D A U B
O V E R T I R E   N P R
C E N   N I N A     A
K   D I C E   B A L I
S C H E M A   J A P E D
  A U R A S   A C T S
F R E N C H T W I S T
```

SOLUTIONS

171

```
O N T V   B E V   P A V E
N O S I D E   I S A W A Y
A S P E R A   S E R E N E
S E S T E T   A N I S E S
T       A N G S T S
A L B U M I N     I M H O
G A R R Y K A S P A R O V
E B B S     R E U N I T E
    U V U L A S         R
G A L L O N   S H R E W D
A Q U I L A   T E A R E R
R U N N E R   A D M I R E
B A D E   M E R   S K E W
```

172

```
P E P P E R M I N T B A R K
A R E A   A H A B   J E E P
S O L I   S L A V S   O F N O
O S T R A C O D   A B I D E
    H A N   A S S   T O M
M I N C E M E A T P I E
A L A R M   A T O N A B L E
S I T U   F I R S T   S O I L
H A S S L I N G   D E L L S
    H O T C H O C O L A T E
O C R   I S A   K O I
B R A S S   T A R T L E T S
I O T A   T H E Y D   A V I A
E W O K   E I R E   P I N G
  S N I C K E R D O O D L E S
```

Mystery Words: SUGAR COOKIES
RED VELVET CAKE

173

```
  D E A T H O N T H E N I L E
C R A N   O N E A   N O R A S
R A V E   S A G O   G E L D S
I G E T I T   A S P E N
M       T A C T   E L D E S T
E M I T S   H E A L S   A A H
F O V E A   O R S O   C U R E
I D Y L L   P S S T   E X A M
C   C L I P   E A T S   O
T H E O   N I B S   H I N D U
I O N S   F E E S   R U E R S
O R D   L O R R E   A M U S E
N A S C A R   G E M S   T
    R U M B A   C H A D O R
O F F E R   A M E R   L I R A
A B A T E   H O L A   T A R P
F I V E L I T T L E P I G S
```

174

```
B L A S T   S T I R U P
R A N C H   N O M O R E
O N Y O U   I M P U G N
W E L L   I D E A T E S
    O D D N E S S
O W N S U P   S I L K
R I G   E U D A E M O N
B R E A S T E D   M A O
S E R B   A D R I F T
    E A R L Y O N
L I T T L E S   C E I L
A B A T I S   M O N T E
D E C O C T   A C C R A
S T O R E S   J O E Y S
```

SOLUTIONS

175

F	E	N	N	O	S	C	A	N	D	I	A	
O	R	C	S			P	A	O		E	P	I
S	L	A	Y		D	A	R	K	A	R	T	S
S	E	A	N	C	E		P	I	N			L
A			C	O	T	S		A	G	A	P	E
E	P	S		H	E	A	D		I	P	O	S
	I	N	D	O	C	H	I	N	E	S	E	
S	L	U	R		T	I	R	E		O	T	C
A	L	G	A	E		B	E	A	D			H
Y			P	D	A		C	L	O	A	C	A
S	O	M	E	W	H	A	T		L	U	R	K
O	O	N		I	S	R			O	D	O	R
	H	O	R	N	O	F	A	F	R	I	C	A

176

A	B	S	O	R	B		S	H	E	A		D	O	U	G	H	S
L	E	A	P		I	D	L	Y		D	V	R		S	M	U	G
M	A	K	E		T	I	E	D		D	I	E		V	E	N	T
S	U	E	D		T	R	U	E		T	E	S	T	I	N	G	S
		S	W	E	A	T		D	O	W	S	E	S			
C	P	U		A	R	C	H	I	E			R	A	G	A	S
R	A	N	K	I	N		M	E	D	L	A	R		A	S	P
O	R	B	I	T		C	A	P	P	E	L	L	A		S	P	A
C	L	O	T		D	I	S	S		B	A	L	S	A	M	I	C
K	A	S	H	M	I	R	I		G	A	M	Y		G	E	R	I
E	N	O		I	N	C	A	M	E	R	A		C	U	T	I	E
T	C	M		K	E	E	N	E	R		D	O	Y	E	N	S
T	E	S	L	A		D	M	I	T	R	I		R	S	T	
		A	D	M	I	T	S		G	O	U	L	D			
A	P	P	R	O	A	C	H		C	L	O	D		A	M	F	M
P	E	A	K		L	E	O		T	O	N	G		M	A	R	E
P	E	P	E		L	T	S		R	O	S	E		U	K	E	S
S	P	A	D	E	S		E	E	L	S		R	E	P	O	T	S

177

U	M	B	R	A	E		O	C	C	U	P	A	N	T
P	I	L	E		W	A	V	E		N	O	V	A	E
G	L	A	D		A	M	E	N		S	O	O	T	H
R	O	T	H		N	O	R	T	H	E	R	N	E	R
A	S	S	E	T		K	A	R	A	T				A
D			R	E	P		G	I	S		L	A	W	N
E	M	P	R	E	S	S	E	S		L	I	Z	A	
S	E	E	I	N	T	O		T	R	I	T	O	N	E
	T	O	N	Y		P	O	S	I	T	I	V	E	S
S	A	N	G		B	O	A		N	E	G			T
C			W	A	R	T	S		R	A	D	A	R	
H	A	R	M	O	N	I	C	A	S		T	O	N	O
U	S	U	A	L		F	A	V	E		O	R	I	G
S	H	E	L	F		I	K	E	A		R	I	M	E
S	E	S	T	E	R	C	E		N	I	S	S	A	N

Mystery Words: NEVER EAT MORE THAN YOU CAN LIFT

178

D	A	N	I	E	L		M	O	A	T	S
V	I	E	N	N	A		I	N	L	E	T
D	R	A	F	T	S		N	I	T	R	O
	C	R	O	E	S	U	S		A	R	N
L	O	B		R	E	N	T	F	R	E	E
I	V	E	S		S	I	R	E			
L	E	E	K	S		V	E	L	L	U	M
A	R	R	O	W	S		L	L	A	N	O
			A	A	H	S		A	U	E	L
H	I	L	L	T	O	P	S		R	N	D
A	N	I		C	O	A	C	H	E	D	
R	E	A	C	H		C	O	U	L	I	S
E	R	N	I	E		E	U	G	E	N	E
S	T	A	T	S		D	R	E	D	G	E

SOLUTIONS

179

S	A	G	A		L	A	N	D	F	O	R	M
A	X	I	S		I	S	A	W		V	E	E
G	O	G	H		C	H	I	E	F	E	S	T
O	N	S	A	L	E		F	L	I	R	T	S
P			M	I	N	G		L	A	C	Y	
A	S	S	E	S	S	E	D		T	O	L	D
L	E	M		P	E	N	A	L		M	E	I
M	A	A	M		S	O	F	A	B	E	D	S
	S	L	I	T		A	T	T	Y			P
H	O	L	D	U	P		N	E	E	D	L	E
E	N	F	I	L	A	D	E		L	E	O	N
E	E	R		S	I	B	S		A	M	O	S
D	R	Y	W	A	L	L	S		W	I	P	E

180

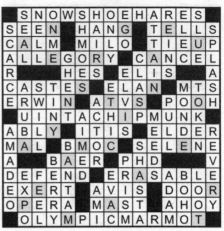

	S	N	O	W	S	H	O	E	H	A	R	E	S	
S	E	E	N		H	A	N	G		T	E	L	L	S
C	A	L	M		M	I	L	O		T	I	E	U	P
A	L	L	E	G	O	R	Y		C	A	N	C	E	L
R			H	E	S		E	L	I	S				A
C	A	S	T	E	S		E	L	A	N		M	T	S
E	R	W	I	N		A	T	V	S		P	O	O	H
	U	I	N	T	A	C	H	I	P	M	U	N	K	
A	B	L	Y		I	T	I	S		E	L	D	E	R
M	A	L		B	M	O	C		S	E	L	E	N	E
A		B	A	E	R		P	H	D					V
D	E	F	E	N	D		E	R	A	S	A	B	L	E
E	X	E	R	T		A	V	I	S		D	O	O	R
O	P	E	R	A		M	A	S	T		A	H	O	Y
	O	L	Y	M	P	I	C	M	A	R	M	O	T	

Mystery Words: ASSATEAGUE PONY
AMERICAN MARTEN

181

A	R	A	M	A	I	C		D	I	T	T	I	E	S
L	O	C	H		N	O	F	U	N		I	F	F	Y
A	N	T	Z		S	L	A	N	T		D	I	T	Z
I	D	I		L	E	T	I	N		B	E	T	S	Y
N	O	N	F	A	T		R	O	S	A				G
		R	U	S	K		A	N	E	R	G	Y
T	W	E	E	D		A	D	J	U	D	G	E	D	
B	A	L	E	S		B	A	I	N		G	L	A	M
S	L	A	B		M	A	N	N	A		W	I	N	O
P	E	T	E		A	L	E	X		C	H	E	S	T
	S	E	E	D	C	A	S	E		R	I	S	K	S
C	A	S	S	I	A		S	H	U	T			
U			D	U	A	D		A	D	E	P	T	S
S	H	A	K	O		M	A	D	R	E		R	A	H
T	O	T	O		J	E	W	E	L		G	O	B	I
O	L	A	F		A	N	G	L	O		R	U	L	E
M	E	D	I	U	M	S		A	W	A	R	D	E	D

182

E	C	O		S	L	A	M	B	A	N	G
P	H	S		H	I	B	E	R	N	I	A
I	A	T		I	M	A	G	I	N	E	S
T	R	I	M	M	E	R		B	U	C	S
A	G	N	E	S			M	I	L	E	Y
P	E	A	S		B	R	A	N			
H	U	T		B	R	A	G	G	A	R	T
S	P	O	T	L	E	S	S		G	E	O
			R	U	T	H		G	E	A	R
O	N	R	Y	E		F	A	L	L	S	
S	O	A	P		T	B	I	L	I	S	I
C	O	S	T	U	M	E	S		M	O	O
A	S	P	I	R	A	N	T		I	O	N
R	E	S	C	I	N	D	S		T	N	S

SOLUTIONS

183

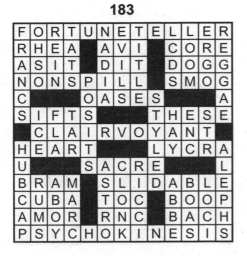

F	O	R	T	U	N	E	T	E	L	L	E	R
R	H	E	A		A	V	I		C	O	R	E
A	S	I	T		D	I	T		D	O	G	G
N	O	N	S	P	I	L	L		S	M	O	G
C			O	A	S	E	S					A
S	I	F	T	S			T	H	E	S	E	
	C	L	A	I	R	V	O	Y	A	N	T	
H	E	A	R	T			L	Y	C	R	A	
U		S	A	C	R	E						L
B	R	A	M		S	L	I	D	A	B	L	E
C	U	B	A		T	O	C		B	O	O	P
A	M	O	R		R	N	C		B	A	C	H
P	S	Y	C	H	O	K	I	N	E	S	I	S

184

D	E	B	I	T		S	L	I	C	E		A	B	S	U	R	D
A	L	O	H	A		A	I	D	E	S		S	E	A	M	E	R
V	E	N	O	M		M	E	A	N	T		U	L	L	A	G	E
E	V	A	P	E	R	O	N		T	O	R	S	O	S			
				S	H	A		P	I	P	E		W	A	R	P	S
I	N	S	I	T	U		S	A	M	P	L	E		B	A	I	O
W	O	O	D		M	O	N	R	O	E		L	A	A	G	E	R
A	R	M	Y		B	R	A	S		D	E	M	U	R	E	S	T
S	M	E	L	L		S	P	E	C		B	O	K				
			A	G	O		C	O	B	B			S	C	A	B	S
B	E	T	I	D	I	N	G		V	I	E	D		A	C	U	P
E	X	I	L	E	S		A	M	E	N	D	E		P	U	R	R
G	I	L	L		T	U	M	O	R	S		S	P	O	T	T	Y
S	T	E	I	N		L	E	N	S		J	K	L				
			N	A	T	A	N	T		R	E	S	E	A	R	C	H
K	O	S	O	V	O		E	A	T	A	T		A	I	O	L	I
E	A	S	I	E	R		S	N	O	U	T		C	R	O	A	T
G	R	A	S	S	Y		S	A	D	L	Y		H	Y	M	N	S

185

G	I	B	E		G	E	T	I	T		U	S	D	A
U	N	I	X		O	V	I	N	E		S	C	O	W
M	A	T	S		S	A	L	T	S		B	I	L	L
S	W	E	E	T	S			E	L	A	P	S	E	S
	A	R	C	H	I	P	E	L	A	G	O	S		
D	Y	S	T	O	P	I	A		S	T	R	I	K	E
U			R	E	N	T	S			S	T	O	O	D
C	A	P	T		D	U	S	T	S		S	N	A	G
T	R	U	E	S		P	O	E	T	S				E
S	C	R	E	E	N		U	P	R	U	S	H	E	S
	S	T	R	E	E	T	S	O	C	C	E	R		
B	A	L	E	F	U	L			P	H	A	G	E	S
A	J	A	R		R	E	C	A	P		M	I	M	I
B	A	N	E		A	N	O	D	E		P	R	I	M
A	X	E	D		L	A	S	E	D		S	A	C	S

Mystery Words: CROUCHING TIGER HIDDEN DRAGON

186

	H	A	R	D	P	R	E	S	S	E	D
S	E	M	P	R	E		D	O	H	A	
A	N	I	M	A	S		G	O	O	U	T
R	N	S		W	E	R	E	N	T		I
C	A	S	E		T	A	D		D	O	M
O			L	I	A	M		D	O	V	E
P	L	A	T	A		P	E	E	W	I	T
H	Y	S	O	N	S		K	I	N	D	A
A	R	U	N		P	U	G	S			B
G	E	N		W	A	N		M	E	W	L
U		C	O	A	T	E	D		T	A	I
S	W	I	G	S		A	U	B	U	R	N
	H	O	R	N		S	E	E	I	N	G
N	O	N	E	T	H	E	L	E	S	S	

SOLUTIONS

187

R	F	D		M	I	C	R	O	C	H	I	P
A	L	A	N	I	S			T	H	E	T	A
N	O	V	E	L	L	A		T	E	X	A	S
S	W	I	M		A	D	R	E	N	A	L	
O	N	S	E	T		V	E	R		P	I	S
M			S	A	R	A	H		B	O	C	K
E		P	I	X	I	L	A	T	E	D		I
R	I	O	S		M	O	B	I	L			N
S	N	L		D	E	R		A	L	V	I	N
	S	A	M	I	S	E	N		M	A	C	Y
T	U	R	I	N		M	E	D	A	L	E	D
E	R	I	K	A			B	O	N	S	A	I
D	E	S	E	R	T	E	R	S		E	X	P

188

S	O	F	T	S	O	A	P		P	I	E	R	C	E
A	W	A	Y		G	O	O	S	E		C	O	A	L
N	E	C	K		D	U	R	E	R		O	W	N	S
E	N	T	E	R	E	D		S	T	I	L	E	S	
S			U	N	A	P	T		F	I	R	T	H	
T	A	L	C	S		D	I	E	T	S				O
	M	O	U	T	H		O	T	I	O	S	I	T	Y
B	E	L	T		E	R	N	S	T		T	O	A	T
A	X	L	E	T	R	E	E		O	N	E	N	D	
R			H	O	S	E	S		O	N	E	A	L	
R	A	B	B	I		T	R	A	C	T				E
	M	E	A	S	L	Y		T	E	A	R	G	A	S
T	O	E	S		A	L	C	O	A		I	L	L	S
O	U	R	S		N	E	A	R	S		L	O	V	E
T	R	Y	I	N	G		L	I	E	G	E	M	A	N

Mystery Words: TURN YOUR WOUNDS INTO WISDOM

189

B	A	L	M	O	R	A	L	B	O	N	N	E	T	
A	N	I	O	N		C	Y	A	N		I	L	E	T
J	A	M	I	E		M	O	N	T		C	O	M	A
A	T	A	R	I		E	N	Z	O		A	P	P	T
		E	R	G	S		A	U	L	D	E	S	T	
F	O	S	S	I	L		K	I	R	I				O
E	N	T		C	E	D	E		L	E	T	G	O	
T	E	R	I		A	I	R	S		A	C	E	R	
A	D	I	R	O	N	D	A	C	K	C	H	A	I	R
	A	D	O	S		I	T	A	L		O	S	L	O
H	Y	E	N	A		I	B	I	S		E	S	T	
A			G	A	I	N		N	O	I	S	E	S	
R	E	D	D	E	E	R		H	E	R	B			
B	L	U	R		D	I	M	E		R	E	B	A	R
O	B	E	Y		I	D	O	S		E	R	A	S	E
R	O	T	E		L	E	O	S		L	I	K	E	N
	W	O	R	C	E	S	T	E	R	S	A	U	C	E

190

B	A	S	S	O	S		M	I	D	A	S	
E	L	T	O	R	O		A	M	I	S	H	
A	L	E	X	I	S		L	A	S	T	S	
D	I	R		S	U	B	T	Y	P	E		
S	E	N	S	O	R	I	A		O	R	S	
			K	N	E	E	S		S	O	U	
J	E	D	I		R	E	M	A	I	N		
U	N	O	P	E	N		B	L	D	G		
G	T	D		N	O	R	M	A				
S	I	D		G	R	U	E	S	O	M	E	
	R	E	S	I	D	E	D		B	A	A	
P	E	R	O	N		F	I	L	E	T	S	
S	T	E	L	E		U	N	I	A	T	E	
P	Y	R	E	S		L	A	S	H	E	S	